# Progress Assessment Support System
## with Answer Key

## HOLT

# Social Studies
## United States History

**HOLT, RINEHART AND WINSTON**

A Harcourt Education Company

Orlando • **Austin** • New York • San Diego • London

ISBN 0-03-043559-5

3 4 5 6 7 8 9   082   09 08 07

# Contents

Progress Assessment

# Contents

Progress Assessment

# Contents

Progress Assessment

# To the Teacher

The Progress Assessment Support System (PASS) consists of the following elements:

- Diagnostic Test
- Test-Taking Tips
- Section Quizzes
- Chapter Tests
- Unit Tests
- End-of-Year Test
- Answer Key

Each element is designed to help you assess your students' progress in mastering the concepts and information in the textbook. You will be able to determine which students need additional assistance and which ones are progressing satisfactorily.

The **Diagnostic Test** covers the major concepts and facts that you will cover during the year. This test assesses what students know about the subject on their first day.

The **Test-Taking Tips** are suggestions to students about how to be more successful on tests. You may want to photocopy these tips and give them to each student. Review the tips with students occasionally, especially before a major test. The tips may help relieve some of the anxiety that affects some students when they have to take a test.

Each **Section Quiz** assesses students' knowledge of the material in that section. These quizzes do not duplicate the questions asked in the textbook.

Similarly, the **Chapter Tests** assess students' knowledge of the material in an entire chapter. These tests are different from the assessment material in the textbook.

The **Unit Tests** take the assessment process to the next level: students are assessed on what they have learned in the chapters that make up a unit. Units are usually two, three, or four chapters long.

The **End-of-Year Test** repeats the questions in the Diagnostic Pre-Test. This repetition of content will allow you to compare a student's results on both tests and determine the progress that student has made over the course of the year.

The **Answer Key** provides answers to each test and section quiz.

Progress Assessment

# Smart Test: Test-Taking Tips for Students

## MASTER THE QUESTION

Be sure that you *know what a question is asking*. Read the question at least twice before reading the answer choices. Approach it as you would a mystery. Look for clues. Watch for words like *not* and *except*—they tell you to look for the choice that is different from the other choices.

## TRACK YOUR TIME

Use all the time you are given to take a test in order to avoid making errors. Here are some *checkpoints* to help you monitor your time:

- How many questions should be completed when one quarter of the time is gone? When half the time is gone?
- What should the clock read when you are halfway through?
- If you find yourself behind your checkpoints, you can speed up.
- If you are ahead, you can—and should—slow down.

## STUDY THE DIRECTIONS

In order to follow directions you have to know what the directions are! Read all the directions as if they contain the key to lifetime happiness. Then read the directions again. Study the answer sheet. How is it laid out? What about the answer choices? Are they arranged

A     B
C     D          or     A     B     C     D?

Be very sure you know what to do and how to do it before you begin.

## TAKE IT ALL IN

When you finally hear the words "You may begin," briefly preview the test to get a mental map of your tasks:

- Know how many questions you have to complete.
- Know where to stop.
- Set your time checkpoints.
- Do the easy sections first.

## NEGATIVES DO NOT FIT

Be sure to watch for negative words in the questions such as *never, unless, not,* and *except*. When a question contains one of these negative words, look for the answer that *does not fit* with the other answers.

## JOT IT DOWN QUICK

You might have made a special effort to memorize some information for the test. If you are worried you will forget as soon as the testing period begins, jot it down on the back of your test or on your scratch paper as soon as you start the test. Then work on the test itself.

## ANTICIPATE THE ANSWERS

Before you read the answer choices, *answer the question yourself. Then, read the choices.* If the answer you gave is among the choices listed, it is probably correct!

## HOW MUCH DO I WRITE?

If a writing question contains the following terms, you will need several sentences for a complete answer:

- describe
- write
- justify
- why
- explain

Remember, it is also possible to use pictures to enhance your words.

## SIGNIFICANT DETAILS

You will often be asked to recall details from a reading passage. Read the question before you read the passage. Underline the details as you read. But remember that the correct answers do not always match the wording of the passage precisely.

## IN YOUR OWN WORDS

Sometimes the wording of a question might be a bit different than the language you are used to using. Read the question and restate the question in your own words to make sure you know what is being asked.

## GO WITH YOUR GUT

Your first impulse is most often correct. Be careful about changing your answers on multiple choice or true/false questions. If you do decide to change your answer, be totally confident in making the change.

## MASTER THE QUESTION #2

If you are taking a reading comprehension test, read the selection, master all the questions, and then *re-read the selection.* The answers will be likely to pop out the second time around. Remember: *A test isn't trying to trick you;* it's trying to test your knowledge and your ability to think clearly.

## SPOT THOSE NUMBERS

Have you ever said, "I got off by one and spent all my time trying to fix my answer sheet"? Make it a habit to

- match the number of each question to the numbered space on the answer sheet every time.
- leave the answer space blank if you skip a question.
- keep a list of your blank spaces on scratch paper or somewhere else—but not on your answer sheet. The less you have to erase on your answer sheet, the better.

## RELY ON 50/50

"I . . . have . . . no . . . clue." It is time to *make an educated guess*—not a wild guess, but an *educated* guess. Always read every choice carefully.

- *Watch out for distracters*—choices that may be true, but are too broad, too narrow, or not relevant to the question.
- Eliminate the least likely choice.
- Eliminate the next least-likely choice until you find the best answer.
- If two choices seem equally correct, look to see if "All of the above" is an option.
- If it is, that might be your choice.
- If no choice seems correct, look for "None of the above."

## TRY. TRY. TRY.

Keep at it. Don't give up. This sounds obvious, so why say it? You might be surprised by how many students do give up. Remember: The last question may be worth just as much as the first question. If the question you just finished was difficult, an easier one is probably coming up soon. Take a deep breath and keep at it.

## FIND THE MAIN IDEA

The main goal of a reading comprehension section is to test your understanding of a reading passage. Be sure to keep these suggestions in mind when you read a selection on a test:

- Read the passage once to get a general overview of the topic.

- If you don't understand the passage at first, keep reading. Try to find the main idea.

- Then, read the questions so that you'll know what information to look for when you re-read the passage.

## SEARCH FOR SKIPS AND SMUDGES

To avoid losing points on a machine-graded test make sure you

- did not skip any answers.

- gave one answer for each question.

- made the marks heavy and dark and within the lines.

- got rid of smudges.

Make sure there are no stray pencil marks on your answer sheet. Cleanly erase those places where you changed your mind. Check for little stray marks from the pencil tapping. *Check everything.*

## I'M STUCK!

If you come across a question that stumps you, don't get frustrated or worried. First, master the question to make sure you understand what is being asked. Then work through many of the strategies you have previously learned. If you are still stuck, circle the question and go on to others. Come back to the problem question later. What if you still have no idea? Practice the 50/50 strategy and then take your best educated guess.

## MINUTES TO GO

If you become short on time, quickly scan the unanswered questions to see which might be easiest to answer. Go with your instinctive answers to those questions to complete as many questions as possible.

## I'M DONE!

Whoa! You aren't finished with your test until you check it. First, take a look at how much time you have left. Go back and review your answers for any careless mistakes you may have made such as leaving a question blank or putting two answers to one question. Be sure to erase any stray marks, review the hardest questions you answered, and turn the test in at the end of the time period. There is nothing to be gained from finishing first—or last, for that matter!

**MULTIPLE CHOICE** For each of the following, write the letter of the best choice in the space provided.

_____ **1.** The earliest known civilization in North America is the
    **a.** Aztec.
    **b.** Inca.
    **c.** Maya.
    **d.** Olmec.

_____ **2.** What does *Renaissance* mean?
    **a.** awakening
    **b.** enlightenment
    **c.** knowledge
    **d.** rebirth

_____ **3.** Finding a sea route to Asia was significant because it
    **a.** gave Europeans the opportunity to hold political positions in foreign lands.
    **b.** allowed Europeans to bypass merchants who monopolized trade.
    **c.** introduced Europeans to new investors who would support exploration.
    **d.** showed Europeans that interactions with Asians were nothing new.

_____ **4.** Searches for a Northwest Passage were significant because they
    **a.** caused France and Italy to claim land in North America.
    **b.** raised European interest in North America.
    **c.** led French and Italian sailors to sail for other nations.
    **d.** resulted in the peaceful division of North America among European powers.

_____ **5.** What was the Great Awakening?
    **a.** a movement of thinkers who believed in the idea that reason and logic could improve social and political life
    **b.** the migration of thousands of English people to the New England colonies and the Caribbean islands
    **c.** the series of witchcraft trials in which groups of young girls accused church ministers of casting spells
    **d.** a religious movement that swept through the colonies and changed colonial religion, society, and politics

**Progress Assessment**

**6.** The Boston Tea Party was significant because it showed how
   **a.** unhappy colonists were with new British laws.
   **b.** important tea was to colonists in relation to other imports.
   **c.** easily colonists could tell cheap tea from expensive tea.
   **d.** angry colonists were even before the Boston Massacre.

**7.** Why was the phrase "taxation without representation" so important to the revolutionary cause?
   **a.** Colonists did not wish to support a government in which they had no voice.
   **b.** Great Britain would have ended taxation if colonists had kept the peace.
   **c.** Colonists believed that Great Britain should only tax certain items.
   **d.** Great Britain only taxed the colonists to force them into war.

**8.** According to the Constitution, what is the role of the judicial branch?
   **a.** giving legal advice
   **b.** interpreting the law
   **c.** writing new laws
   **d.** setting legal precedents

**9.** The framers of the Constitution created a system of checks and balances to
   **a.** outline the powers held by each branch of government.
   **b.** keep any one branch of government from becoming too powerful.
   **c.** give the people an opportunity to control the government.
   **d.** strengthen the powers held by each branch of government.

**10.** The Bill of Rights was added to the Constitution to
   **a.** protect citizens' rights.
   **b.** limit the powers of state governments.
   **c.** outline the rights of the federal government.
   **d.** state the ways in which citizens can participate in government.

**11.** The new federal government in America took actions that would set an example for the future. In George Washington's words, these exemplary actions "will serve to establish a
   **a.** procedure."
   **b.** precursor."
   **c.** policy."
   **d.** precedent."

_____ **12.** What is required for a person to become a naturalized citizen?
  **a.** obtaining legal-immigrant status and serving five years in the armed forces
  **b.** moving to the United States permanently and applying for citizenship
  **c.** surrendering any foreign passports and renouncing foreign citizenship
  **d.** reciting the pledge of allegiance once before a judge and daily thereafter

_____ **13.** The national debt can best be defined as the amount of money owed
  **a.** to the nation by the nation's citizens and by foreign countries.
  **b.** by the nation to foreign countries and the nation's citizens.
  **c.** to the federal government by individual states.
  **d.** by the federal government to domestic debtors.

_____ **14.** What happened to California's population as a result of the Gold Rush?
  **a.** The population grew, but not as much as it had during the Spanish and Mexican periods of settlement.
  **b.** The population boomed during "gold fever," but declined just as quickly because of inflation.
  **c.** Immigrants and Americans flocked to California to "get rich quick" and stayed to build a stable frontier society.
  **d.** Californios and Native Americans still outnumbered immigrants after the Gold Rush.

_____ **15.** Which of the following statements about the War of 1812 is true?
  **a.** It worsened the conflict between the North and the South.
  **b.** It intensified American Indian resistance to Americans.
  **c.** It severely damaged American manufacturing.
  **d.** It strengthened patriotism among Americans.

_____ **16.** What was a consequence of the Missouri Compromise?
   **a.** Missouri entered the Union as an independent territory.
   **b.** The practice of slavery was pronounced unconstitutional.
   **c.** Free states won a majority in the House of Representatives.
   **d.** An equal balance between free and slave states was maintained.

_____ **17.** The Oregon Trail
   **a.** ran through the Sierra Nevada.
   **b.** required protection by U.S. troops.
   **c.** was a popular route for merchants.
   **d.** took six months to travel.

_____ **18.** The nullification crisis was a dispute over the
   **a.** states' power to secede from the Union.
   **b.** states' power to reject federal laws they deemed unconstitutional.
   **c.** federal government's power to end tariffs.
   **d.** federal government's power to favor one region over another.

_____ **19.** Which of the following best describes the Trail of Tears?
   **a.** streams of blood that flowed from the Sauk Indians in the Black Hawk War
   **b.** forced 800-mile march Cherokee Indians made in their removal from Georgia
   **c.** line connecting Seminole Indian settlements up and down Florida's east coast
   **d.** unpublished works on the Cherokee population written by Sequoya

_____ **20.** The Industrial Revolution can best be described as a
   **a.** period of rapid growth during which machines became essential to manufacturing.
   **b.** series of explosive encounters between workers and wealthy factory owners.
   **c.** time of great excitement about mechanical approaches to controlling Nature.
   **d.** period of turmoil and upheaval within the U.S. government.

_____ **21.** Which of the following best describes a trade union?

    **a.** organization of workers who tried to improve pay and working conditions for members

    **b.** collection of workers who appealed to the courts for assistance against employers

    **c.** group of workers who arrived from poor countries and were willing to work for low pay

    **d.** alliance of workers who wanted to prevent their employers from competing with other manufacturers

_____ **22.** In the first half of the 1800s, what portion of white southern families had slaves?

    **a.** one-third

    **b.** one-half

    **c.** two-thirds

    **d.** three-quarters

_____ **23.** What did most cities rely on to fight crime in the mid-1800s?

    **a.** police forces

    **b.** volunteer night watches

    **c.** state troopers

    **d.** salaried war veterans

_____ **24.** In late 18th century America, the Second Great Awakening was a period of

    **a.** rebirth that led to the development of a culture centered on education.

    **b.** Christian renewal that began in the northeastern United States.

    **c.** reform that focused on improving the quality of life of the poor.

    **d.** American revival that brought back pre-Revolutionary War traditions.

_____ **25.** Which statement expresses the reason why the southern states decided to secede from the Union after the election of 1860?

    **a.** The southern economy and way of life would be destroyed.

    **b.** Slaves would begin an uprising if the states did not secede.

    **c.** Seceding from the Union would end the possibility of war.

    **d.** Secession would end the conflicts between northern states over slavery.

Progress Assessment

Name _____ Class _____ Date _____

Diagnostic Test

_____ **26.** Life for African Americans in the South changed after the Civil War because many African Americans
**a.** were now free because of the Emancipation Proclamation.
**b.** received equal rights and opportunities under the law.
**c.** had gained the respect of the white population of the South.
**d.** won citizenship as a result of the Union victory in the war.

_____ **27.** The Reconstruction Acts, passed by Congress in March 1867, affected the makeup of the southern states by
**a.** creating new governments and appointing Republican governors to each state in the South.
**b.** dividing the South into new states controlled by leaders who had not been supporters of the Confederacy.
**c.** dividing the South into five military districts controlled by a military commander.
**d.** creating a new boundary that separated Northern states that had seceded from the Union.

_____ **28.** Which of these events marked the beginning of the Civil War?
**a.** the election of Abraham Lincoln to the presidency
**b.** the abolition of slavery in the South
**c.** the declaration of war by President Lincoln
**d.** the firing of Confederate guns on Fort Sumter

_____ **29.** What was the transcontinental railroad meant to connect?
**a.** the southern United States to the North
**b.** the eastern United States to the West
**c.** Canada to the southern United States
**d.** Canada to Mexico and Central America

_____ **30.** Which of the following is true about stockholders?
**a.** They must pay the corporation's debts.
**b.** They can sell their stock shares at any time.
**c.** They are responsible for the corporation's policies.
**d.** They vote directly for the corporation's president.

Progress Assessment

_____ **31.** The reason for the decline in working conditions in American industries in the late 1800s was the
- **a.** drive to regulate monopolies.
- **b.** weakening of labor unions.
- **c.** emphasis on high profits and efficiency.
- **d.** elimination of health benefits.

_____ **32.** When did the "new immigrants" pour into the United States?
- **a.** from 1800 to 1860
- **b.** from 1850 to 1870
- **c.** during the 1880s
- **d.** during the 1900s

_____ **33.** What does the term mass transit refer to?
- **a.** the problem of traffic in big cities in the late 1800s
- **b.** a system of public transportation created to move a large number of passengers
- **c.** migration of middle-class families from the suburbs into big cities
- **d.** construction of electric trolleys in the major American cities of the late 1800s

_____ **34.** Politics during the Gilded Age can best be characterized as
- **a.** corrupt.
- **b.** useless.
- **c.** honest.
- **d.** helpful.

_____ **35.** What is one of the fundamental differences between capitalism and socialism?
- **a.** Under socialism, the government owns the factories and raw materials.
- **b.** Under socialism, unions are organized by industry rather than skill level.
- **c.** Under capitalism, the government can interfere in the marketplace and set prices.
- **d.** Under capitalism, unions use collective bargaining rather than aggressive tactics.

_____ **36.** Imperialism can best be described as
- **a.** a system in which there is no private property.
- **b.** a government run by the people.
- **c.** an empire built by founding colonies or conquering other nations.
- **d.** a method of ruling similar to communism.

_____ **37.** What happens in the situation known as a "stalemate"?
  **a.** Two countries are forced to break their alliance.
  **b.** Neither side can win a decisive victory.
  **c.** A victor is declared.
  **d.** Neither side is allowed to launch an attack.

_____ **38.** What hardships did American soldiers face in World War I?
  **a.** insufficiently trained for battle against the Central Powers
  **b.** forced to live amongst rats, lice, and the bodies of dead soldiers
  **c.** malnourished and often contracted Lyme disease
  **d.** forced to fight alongside French troops, who often mistreated them

_____ **39.** "Buying on margin" means buying stocks
  **a.** during a bull market at an inflated price.
  **b.** during a bear market in hopes of selling at a higher price.
  **c.** with borrowed money.
  **d.** directly at the stock market, instead of through a stockbroker.

_____ **40.** The decade after World War I was characterized by a clash between the ideals and values of
  **a.** rich and poor Americans.
  **b.** native-born Americans and immigrants.
  **c.** traditional rural and modern urban Americans.
  **d.** American women and men.

_____ **41.** What did the most popular art forms of the Depression era do?
  **a.** offered an escape from reality
  **b.** focused on the sadness of the time
  **c.** reminded people of their folk roots
  **d.** portrayed ordinary people

_____ **42.** The policy of avoiding war with an aggressive nation by giving into its demands is called
  **a.** blitzkrieg.
  **b.** brinksmanship.
  **c.** Luftwaffe.
  **d.** appeasement.

_____ **43.** *Sputnik* was the world's first
   **a.** artificial satellite.
   **b.** computer.
   **c.** hydrogen bomb.
   **d.** spaceship.

_____ **44.** How did the Vietnam War highlight race and class differences in the United States?
   **a.** College students, most of whom were white and from wealthier families, were able to get deferments releasing them from the draft.
   **b.** Minority Americans protested the killing of Vietnamese civilians, while most white Americans ignored the situation overseas.
   **c.** Americans with skilled jobs, mostly white workers who received higher-than-average salaries, were not drafted.
   **d.** The government cracked-down most violently on antiwar protests led by minorities in poor neighborhoods.

_____ **45.** A sit-in is a
   **a.** protest in which striking workers leave the work site.
   **b.** demonstration in which protesters sit down and refuse to leave.
   **c.** voter registration drive coordinated to alter the outcome of an election.
   **d.** meeting held by rights activists to plan their next course of action.

_____ **46.** What does the War Powers Act state?
   **a.** The public must be granted access to any information about the country's progress in war.
   **b.** The president can stop aggressors by any means necessary.
   **c.** The president must get congressional approval before committing troops to an armed struggle.
   **d.** Military officials can decide whether the country enters a war.

_____ **47.** Which act banned segregation in public places and outlawed discrimination in the workplace?
  **a.** Civil Rights Act of 1964
  **b.** Freedom Summer Act
  **c.** Voting Rights Act of 1969
  **d.** Montgomery Bus Act

_____ **48.** What is stagflation?
  **a.** rising employment without a change in prices
  **b.** fixed prices with rising unemployment
  **c.** falling prices with rising unemployment
  **d.** rising prices without economic growth

_____ **49.** In a service economy many people
  **a.** work for the government.
  **b.** serve in the military.
  **c.** provide services rather than produce goods.
  **d.** have jobs requiring little training.

_____ **50.** The term "global warming" refers to the
  **a.** policy that bans chemicals that damage the ozone layer.
  **b.** warming of the earth's surface due to holes in the ozone layer.
  **c.** rise in air temperature caused by carbon dioxide in the atmosphere.
  **d.** rise in ocean temperatures due to a lack of carbon dioxide in the atmosphere.

# The World before the Opening of the Atlantic

Section Quiz

**Section 1**

**FILL IN THE BLANK** For each of the following statements, fill in the blank with the appropriate word, phrase, or name.

1. Many scientists believe that the first people arrived in North America during the

   last _____.

2. Large amounts of water froze into huge, moving sheets of ice called

   _____.

3. The _____ was a bridge between northeastern Asia and present-day Alaska.

4. The people who crossed the bridge into Alaska between 38,000 and 10,000 BC

   were called _____.

5. _____ is the movement of people or animals from one region to another.

6. People who hunted animals and gathered wild plants for food were

   _____.

7. _____ is a region that includes what is now Mexico and parts of Central America.

8. The _____ built the first pyramids in the Americas.

9. The _____ were fierce warriors whose superior military ability was key to their success.

10. The _____ began as a small tribe in the Andes Mountains of South America.

Progress Assessment

# The World before the Opening of the Atlantic

**TRUE/FALSE** Mark each statement **T** if it is true or **F** if it is false. If false explain why.

_____ **1.** The Anasazi lived in the Four Corners region, which is where present-day Arizona, Colorado, New Mexico, and Utah meet.

_____

_____

_____ **2.** Kivas were aboveground houses made of heavy clay called adobe.

_____

_____

_____ **3.** The Hopewell was a culture along the Mississippi, Ohio, and lower Missouri river valleys that still exists today.

_____

_____

_____ **4.** Most Great Plains peoples were nomadic hunters, and many of them hunted buffalo using bows and spears.

_____

_____

_____ **5.** The Iroquois League helped the Anasazi become one of the most powerful Native American peoples in North America.

_____

_____

Progress Assessment

# The World before the Opening of the Atlantic    Section Quiz

**Section 3**

**FILL IN THE BLANK** For each of the following statements, fill in the blank with the appropriate word, phrase, or name.

1. The Saharan trade routes were run by a group of people from northern Africa

   called the _____.

2. Historians believe the first people in _____ were farmers along the Niger River.

3. These farmers were the _____ and they banded together for protection from nomadic herders.

4. People needed _____ in their diets to survive.

5. _____ was founded in the 600s by an Arab named Muhammad.

6. _____ believe that God had spoken to Muhammad through an angel and had made him a prophet.

7. Mali reached the height of its wealth, power, and fame under

   _____, its most famous ruler.

8. Enslaved _____ were often bought to perform menial labor and domestic chores.

9. _____, Djenné, and Gao were important trade cities in the Kingdom of Mali.

10. Kings traded _____, who were sometimes captured in war, for valuable goods such as horses, textiles, and weapons.

Progress Assessment

## The World before the Opening of the Atlantic

### Section Quiz

**Section 4**

**MATCHING** In the space provided, write the letter of the term, person, or place that matches each description. Some answers will not be used.

_____ **1.** a great teacher who wanted to make people think and question their own beliefs

_____ **2.** a philosopher and teacher who wrote a work called *Republic*

_____ **3.** taught that people should live lives based on reason, or clear and ordered thinking

_____ **4.** a form of government in which people rule themselves

_____ **5.** warriors who fought on horseback and were given land in exchange for military service

_____ **6.** disease that spread across Europe, killing an estimated 25 million people

_____ **7.** means "rebirth" and refers to the period that followed the Middle Ages in Europe

_____ **8.** developed a printing press that used movable type

_____ **9.** an economic system that unifies and increases the power and wealth of a nation

_____ **10.** businesses in which a group of people invest together

**a.** Aristotle

**b.** crusades

**c.** democracy

**d.** Johannes Gutenberg

**e.** joint-stock companies

**f.** knights

**g.** mercantilism

**h.** nobles

**i.** plague

**j.** Plato

**k.** Renaissance

**l.** Socrates

**m.** trade

Progress Assessment

Name _____ Class _____ Date _____

# The World before the Opening of the Atlantic    Chapter Test

**Form A**

**MULTIPLE CHOICE** For each of the following, write the letter of the best choice in the space provided.

_____ **1.** The Crusades changed Europe by
  **a.** forcing the Turks to give up Palestine.
  **b.** leading to increased trade with Asia.
  **c.** again allowing pilgrimages to the Holy Land.
  **d.** introducing Europeans to military life.

_____ **2.** Which statement presents a belief Native Americans held about land rights?
  **a.** A portion of land was to be set aside for future generations.
  **b.** The present generation had the right to exploit the land.
  **c.** The crops one grew were to be shared by all.
  **d.** Individual rights to use land were temporary.

_____ **3.** The cliff dwellings built by the Anasazi gave them protection against
  **a.** drought.
  **b.** dust storms.
  **c.** enemies.
  **d.** disease.

_____ **4.** The Hopewell and Mississippian mound builders were skilled
  **a.** farmers and traders.
  **b.** warriors.
  **c.** fishermen.
  **d.** explorers.

_____ **5.** How did joint-stock companies benefit investors?
  **a.** They guaranteed investors a return on their money.
  **b.** They protected investors against corrupt governments.
  **c.** They allowed investors to take fewer risks.
  **d.** They allowed investors to make money more quickly.

_____ **6.** Why was Plato significant?
  **a.** taught that people should live lives based on reason
  **b.** wrote the *Republic*, which described an ideal society
  **c.** used geometry to calculate the size of Earth
  **d.** helped to found the Roman Republic

Progress Assessment

_____ **7.** Which of the following best describes the Olmec?
  **a.** They were nomadic farmers who lived in huts.
  **b.** They developed the earliest known civilization in Mesoamerica.
  **c.** They formed a strong central government.
  **d.** They built networks of canals.

_____ **8.** How do scientists think people first arrived in North America?
  **a.** After the Ice Age, glaciers melted and people came in small boats.
  **b.** During the Ice Age, the sea froze and people crossed the ice.
  **c.** After the Ice Age, glaciers melted and people crossed land.
  **d.** During the Ice Age, the sea level dropped and people crossed land.

_____ **9.** During the Renaissance, the new emphasis on people rather than religion was called
  **a.** intellectualism.
  **b.** humanism.
  **c.** theism.
  **d.** mercantilism.

_____ **10.** What made the slave trade important to the West African economy?
  **a.** The slave trade sustained the economy during a time of famine.
  **b.** Slaves could be freed if they performed menial labor.
  **c.** Europeans lost interest in slave trade.
  **d.** Slaves could be traded for valuable goods in the Middle East and Europe.

_____ **11.** Why was the kingdom of Ghana significant?
  **a.** Sundiata ruled it with a strong army.
  **b.** It gained wealth from taxes and by controlling trade in salt and gold.
  **c.** Mansa Musa taught its people to read the Qur'an.
  **d.** It gained great wealth from its agriculture and diamond mines.

_____ **12.** The goal of the Iroquois League was to
  **a.** create a strong fishing community.
  **b.** strengthen the alliance against invasion.
  **c.** develop a monetary system.
  **d.** develop one language.

Progress Asessment

**PRACTICING SOCIAL STUDIES SKILLS** Study the image below and answer the question that follows.

_____ **13.** What does the image above indicate about Roman government during the Classical Period?

    **a.** that it was a direct democracy

    **b.** that it was a republic

    **c.** that all citizens voted on every issue

    **d.** that it was ruled by one leader

**FILL IN THE BLANK** Read each sentence and fill in the blank with the word in the word pair that best completes the sentence.

**14.** Evidence suggests that a group of people called _____ crossed from northeastern Asia to present-day Alaska between 38,000 B.C. and 10,000 B.C. (**Paleo-Indians/Inuits**)

**15.** A group's set of common values and traditions is known as

_____. (**environment/culture**)

**16.** Mali's _____ and Songhai's Askia the Great were both

Muslims. (**Mansa Musa/Tenochtitlán**)

**17.** In the mid-1400s, _____ developed a printing press that used movable type. (**Johannes Gutenberg/Roger Bacon**)

**18.** In the Middle Ages, nobles exchanged land for military service with

_____, or warriors who fought on horseback.

    (**Franks/knights**)

Progress Assessment

**The World before the Opening of the Atlantic,** *continued*     Chapter Test Form A

**TRUE/FALSE** Indicate whether each statement below is true or false by writing **T** or **F** in the space provided.

_____ **19.** The Berbers helped construct mosques in the kingdom of Ghana.

_____ **20.** The Olmec and Maya civilizations grew maize and lived in small villages.

_____ **21.** The period of the Renaissance in Europe was more orderly and stable than the Middle Ages had been.

_____ **22.** The Aztec was the first civilization to use canals to direct water through their cities.

_____ **23.** A ruler named Sundiata founded the Songhai empire.

_____ **24.** The people who migrated across the Bering Land Bridge were hunter-gatherers.

_____ **25.** Mansa Musa had scholars set up schools in Mali for the study of the Qur'an.

Progress Assessment

# The World before the Opening of the Atlantic

## Chapter Test

### Form B

**SHORT ANSWER** On a separate sheet of paper, answer each of the following questions in complete sentences.

1. Evidence suggests that Paleo-Indians crossed into North America between 38,000 BC and 10,000 BC. How did they cross?

2. How does a joint-stock company work?

3. What was the significance of the invention of the printing press?

4. How did the practice of slavery change in the 600s?

5. The Cayuga, Mohawk, Oneida, Onondaga, and Seneca nations all belonged to which group? What was their goal?

6. What did American law borrow from Roman law?

**PRACTICING SOCIAL STUDIES SKILLS** Study the map below and, on a separate sheet of paper, answer the question that follows.

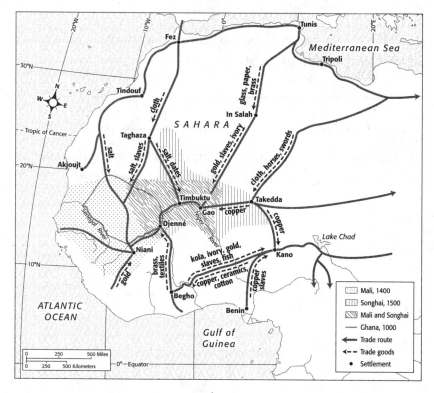

7. What do the large lines and the arrows represent in this map? What might these lines and arrows tell you about the Mali and Songhai empires?

**New Empires in the Americas**  Section Quiz

**Section 1**

**TRUE/FALSE** Mark each statement **T** if it is true or **F** if it is false. If false explain why.

_____ **1.** The Vikings were the first Europeans to make contact with North America.

_____

_____

_____ **2.** Vikings were skilled sailors who developed a new style of ship, called the longship.

_____

_____

_____ **3.** Prince Henry the Navigator was an explorer who set out on many voyages.

_____

_____

_____ **4.** A caravel is a device that enabled navigators to learn their ship's location by charting the position of the stars.

_____

_____

_____ **5.** The Portuguese sent many enslaved Africans to Europe and to the islands in the Atlantic, where they endured brutal living conditions.

_____

_____

Progress Assessment

Name _____ Class _____ Date _____

## New Empires in the Americas

### Section 2

**FILL IN THE BLANK** For each of the following statements, fill in the blank with the appropriate word, phrase, or name.

1. _____, a sailor from Genoa, Italy, was convinced he could reach Asia by sailing west across the Atlantic Ocean.

2. He asked King _____ and Queen _____ of Spain to pay for an expedition across the Atlantic.

3. The imaginary boundary that divided the Atlantic Ocean was the

   _____.

4. In 1501 explorer _____ led a Spanish fleet to the coast of present-day South America.

5. _____, a Portuguese navigator, set out with a fleet to reach the Philippine Islands and the Indian Ocean.

6. To go all the way around the globe is to _____ the globe.

7. The _____ was an exchange of plants and animals between the Americas, Europe, Asia, and Africa.

8. The _____ moved the Line of Demarcation 800 miles west.

9. Without intending to do so, the explorers introduced deadly new

   _____ to the Americas.

10. As part of triangular trade, Europeans shipped millions of enslaved

    _____ to work in the colonies in the New World.

Progress Assessment

## New Empires in the Americas

**MATCHING** In the space provided, write the letter of the term, person, or place that matches each description. Some answers will not be used.

_____ 1. soldiers who led military expeditions in the Americas

_____ 2. left Cuba to sail to present-day Mexico

_____ 3. ruler of the Aztec Empire

_____ 4. Aztec capital built on an island in the middle of the lake

_____ 5. Indian woman who helped Cortés win allies

_____ 6. military bases

_____ 7. discovered the coast of present-day Florida

_____ 8. system that gave settlers the right to tax local Native Americans or make them work

_____ 9. large farms that grew just one kind of crop

_____ 10. priest who tried to convert Native Americans to Christianity

**a.** Bartolomé de Las Casas

**b.** conquistadors

**c.** encomienda

**d.** Francisco Pizarro

**e.** Hernán Cortés

**f.** Inca

**g.** Malintzin

**h.** Moctezuma II

**i.** plantations

**j.** Ponce de León

**k.** presidios

**l.** Spain

**m.** Tenochtitlán

Progress Assessment

Name _____ Class _____ Date _____

# New Empires in the Americas

Section Quiz

**Section 4**

**FILL IN THE BLANK** For each of the following statements, fill in the blank with the appropriate word, phrase, or name.

1. In 1517 a German priest named _____ publicly criticized the Roman Catholic Church.

2. The _____ was a religious movement against the Catholic Church.

3. The _____ is a machine that produces printed copies using movable type.

4. French Protestants were known as _____.

5. _____ was the name given to English sailors who raided Spanish treasure ships.

6. The _____ was a huge fleet of warships meant to end the English plans.

7. Europeans wanted to find a _____, a water route through North America that would allow ships to sail from the Atlantic to the Pacific.

8. A French sailor named _____ led France's exploration of North America.

9. A _____ was a document giving permission to start a colony.

10. France built its first North American settlements in _____.

Progress Assessment

## New Empires in the Americas

Section Quiz

**Section 5**

**MULTIPLE CHOICE** For each of the following, write the letter of the best choice in the space provided.

_____ 1. What caused the European colonists to look for a new labor force?
   **a.** Native Americans refused to be enslaved.
   **b.** Enslaved Africans already spoke English and French.
   **c.** European diseases killed many Native Americans.
   **d.** The transportation costs were too great.

_____ 2. Who along with colonists suggested using enslaved Africans as workers?
   **a.** Hernán Cortés
   **b.** Bartolomé de Las Casas, a Spanish priest
   **c.** Fernandez de Oviedo
   **d.** King Alfonso

_____ 3. What was the Middle Passage?
   **a.** voyage of Africans across Atlantic to be sold as slaves
   **b.** pattern of trade involving the American colonies
   **c.** area of Africa where most slaves came from
   **d.** group of people that opposed slavery

_____ 4. Between the 1520s and 1860s how many Africans were shipped across the Atlantic as slaves?
   **a.** 4 million
   **b.** about 12 million
   **c.** 10 million
   **d.** none shipped between those times

_____ 5. The law considered enslaved Africans as
   **a.** equals.
   **b.** family.
   **c.** indentured servants.
   **d.** property.

Progress Assessment

Name _____ Class _____ Date _____

# New Empires in the Americas

**Chapter Test**

**Form A**

**MULTIPLE CHOICE** For each of the following, write the letter of the best choice in the space provided.

_____ **1.** What advantage did the Viking longship have over earlier vessels?
   **a.** size
   **b.** strength
   **c.** speed
   **d.** stability

_____ **2.** For which country did Jacques Cartier claim land during his two trips to Canada in 1534 and 1535?
   **a.** England
   **b.** France
   **c.** Italy
   **d.** the Netherlands

_____ **3.** How did enslaved Africans try to cope with life in the Americas?
   **a.** adopted the culture of the Native Americans
   **b.** sought refuge in their families, religion, art, and dance
   **c.** tried to start their own farming communities
   **d.** let their owners control their families and religion

_____ **4.** Which of the following best describes the Columbian Exchange?
   **a.** Plants and animals were transferred among Europe, Asia, Africa, and the Americas.
   **b.** Columbus discovered new animals in the Americas.
   **c.** New foods brought to Europe caused diseases.
   **d.** Explorers shipped Native Americans to Europe.

_____ **5.** Columbus's travels to the Americas created conflict between
   **a.** France and Spain.
   **b.** Africa and Spain.
   **c.** Spain and Portugal.
   **d.** France and Portugal.

_____ **6.** For which country did King Philip II lead the Catholic Reformation?
   **a.** Germany
   **b.** England
   **c.** France
   **d.** Spain

Progress Assessment

_____ **7.** What was the conquistadors' biggest advantage in defeating the Aztec and the Inca?
   **a.** strong leadership
   **b.** steel armor and weapons
   **c.** larger armies
   **d.** immunity to smallpox

_____ **8.** Who was Malintzin?
   **a.** Spanish conquistador who helped defeat the Inca
   **b.** Indian woman who helped defeat the Aztec
   **c.** Spanish conquistador who was captured at Tenochtitlán
   **d.** Indian woman who was killed by smallpox at Cuzco

_____ **9.** Pueblo settlements set up by the Spanish in New Spain served as
   **a.** military bases to protect towns and churches.
   **b.** trading posts for commerce and sometimes as centers of government.
   **c.** holy places for converting the native population to Catholicism.
   **d.** cultural sites for Spaniards to learn about Native American customs.

_____ **10.** Whose crew was the first to circumnavigate the globe?
   **a.** Amerigo Vespucci's
   **b.** Ferdinand Magellan's
   **c.** Vasco Núñez de Balboa's
   **d.** Giovanni da Verrazano's

_____ **11.** Why did colonists in need of cheap labor turn to slaves from West Africa?
   **a.** West African slaves had already built up immunity to European diseases.
   **b.** Plantation owners and farmers needed slaves familiar with agriculture.
   **c.** The pope had promoted the use of West African slaves in Catholic lands.
   **d.** The Portuguese government had legalized the sale of slaves in its colonies.

_____ **12.** Which of the following describes the Treaty of Tordesillas?
   **a.** It expanded Spain's lands east of the Line of Demarcation.
   **b.** It moved the Line of Demarcation 800 miles further west.
   **c.** It prevented war between Spain and Native American populations.
   **d.** It required people to have colonists' papers to collect gold on Hispaniola.

**PRACTICING SOCIAL STUDIES SKILLS** Study the graph below and answer the question that follows.

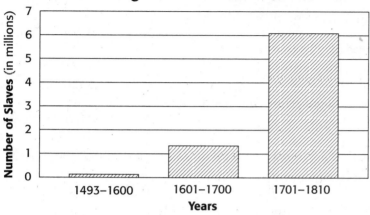

**Slaves Brought to the Americas, 1493–1810**

_____ **13.** Approximately how many slaves were brought to the Americas between 1493 and 1810?
   **a.** approximately 2.1 million
   **b.** approximately 5.1 million
   **c.** approximately 7.6 million
   **d.** approximately 5.6 million

**FILL IN THE BLANK** Read each sentence and fill in the blank with the word in the word pair that best completes the sentence.

**14.** A Spanish conquistador named _____ led the destruction of the Aztec Empire. (**Pedro de Alvarado/Hernán Cortés**)

**15.** Many _____ died as a result of exposure to new diseases brought by European explorers. (**enslaved Africans/Native Americans**)

**16.** The _____ aided explorers in finding new continents by allowing ship navigators to check location by charting the position of the stars. (**astrolabe/magnetic compass**)

**17.** _____ was the first European to discover a sea route to Asia. (**Ferdinand Magellan/Vasco da Gama**)

**MATCHING**  In the space provided, write the letter of the term, person, or place that matches each description. Some answers will not be used.

_____ **18.** voyage across the Atlantic Ocean that enslaved Africans were forced to endure

_____ **19.** a special type of ship that featured important advances in sailing technology

_____ **20.** New Netherland governor who conquered New Sweden in 1655

_____ **21.** large farms that grew just one kind of crop and made enormous profits for their owners

_____ **22.** publicly criticized the Roman Catholic Church with his ninety-five theses

_____ **23.** small colony on the Saint Lawrence River that opened trading routes for the French

_____ **24.** the scattering of millions of enslaved Africans across the New World

_____ **25.** helped Portugal become a leader in world exploration

**a.** Henry VIII

**b.** African Diaspora

**c.** the *encomienda* system

**d.** Martin Luther

**e.** Middle Passage

**f.** plantations

**g.** Peter Stuyvesant

**h.** Henry the Navigator

**i.** Quebec

**j.** Leif Eriksson

**k.** caravel

**New Empires in the Americas**                    Chapter Test

                                                              **Form B**

**SHORT ANSWER** On a separate sheet of paper, answer each of the following questions in complete sentences.

**1.** Who were the first Europeans to reach North America?

**2.** What role did the printing press play in the Protestant Reformation?

**3.** How were the failed attempts to find the Northwest Passage significant to exploration of North America?

**4.** What was the *encomienda* system? Why did the Spanish Crown establish it?

**5.** The Spanish conquered two great empires in the Americas. Which empire was the
second one to fall? Who led the conquest?

**6.** What was the significance of the Spanish Armada?

**PRACTICING SOCIAL STUDIES SKILLS** Study the map below and, on a
separate sheet of paper, answer the question that follows.

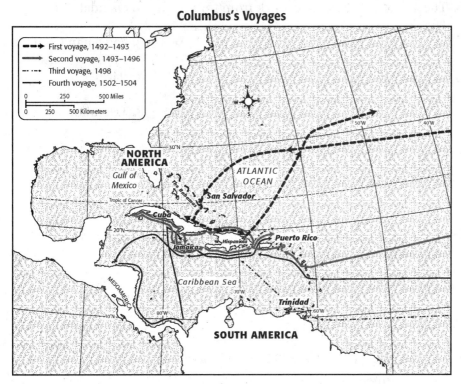

**Columbus's Voyages**

**7.** How many total years did Christopher Columbus spend on his four voyages?

**The English Colonies**

**MATCHING** In the space provided, write the letter of the term, place, or person that best matches each description. Some answers will not be used.

_____ 1. Founded on April 26, 1607, this Virginia colony was named after the English king.

_____ 2. He gained control of Jamestown in 1608 and pushed settlers to work hard and build better housing.

_____ 3. This was a powerful alliance of the Algonquian Indians.

_____ 4. This system of granting land gave colonists who paid their own way 50 acres of land, and an additional 50 acres for each person brought with them.

_____ 5. These colonists agreed to work from four to seven years on the farms of those who paid their journey to America.

_____ 6. This Maryland law was the first effort in the English colonies to support religious freedom.

_____ 7. He founded the colony of Georgia with the hope of attracting small farmers to settle there.

_____ 8. Many farms and plantations in the southern colonies grew these.

_____ 9. They were in large demand in the South due to the need for a large, agricultural workforce.

_____ 10. This former slave recorded his experiences in the southern colonies.

**a.** Bacon's Rebellion

**b.** cash crops

**c.** headright system

**d.** indentured servants

**e.** John Rolfe

**f.** John Smith

**g.** Jamestown

**h.** James Oglethorpe

**i.** Olaudah Equiano

**j.** Powhatan Confederacy

**k.** slaves

**l.** Toleration Act of 1649

## The English Colonies

**TRUE/FALSE** Mark each statement **T** if it is true or **F** if it is false. If false explain why.

_____ **1.** The Puritans' Mayflower Compact was an agreement to create fair laws to protect the general good.

_____

_____

_____ **2.** The Pilgrims settled with their families, who worked together to help survive in Plymouth.

_____

_____

_____ **3.** Anne Hutchinson disagreed with the Puritan leaders who believed that people needed the guidance of a minister and that women should not play an active role in the church.

_____

_____

_____ **4.** The New England economy was based on agriculture, trade, and fishing.

_____

_____

_____ **5.** Education in the New England colonies was important because parents wanted their children to be able to run their businesses successfully.

_____

_____

Name _____ Class _____ Date _____

# The English Colonies

**MULTIPLE CHOICE** For each of the following, write the letter of the best choice in the space provided.

_____ 1. What middle colony was originally founded by the Dutch, but later taken over by the English?
   **a.** Pennsylvania
   **b.** New Jersey
   **c.** Delaware
   **d.** New York

_____ 2. Why did William Penn create the colony of Pennsylvania?
   **a.** to provide a home for Quakers
   **b.** to practice nonviolence
   **c.** to escape Puritan control
   **d.** to break away from England

_____ 3. Thanks to Penn's work, Pennsylvania became an important example of what?
   **a.** free enterprise
   **b.** indentured servitude
   **c.** representative government
   **d.** public education

_____ 4. What is the term for crops that are always needed?
   **a.** staple crops
   **b.** natural crops
   **c.** plantation crops
   **d.** cash crops

_____ 5. What job did women in the middle colonies NOT hold?
   **a.** farmer
   **b.** lawyer
   **c.** indentured servant
   **d.** nurse

Progress Assessment

Name _____ Class _____ Date _____

## The English Colonies

**MATCHING** In the space provided, write the letter of the term or place that best matches each description. Some answers will not be used.

_____ 1. These were used in colonies to control local affairs and protect individual freedoms.

_____ 2. These organizations were created in some colonies to pass laws.

_____ 3. Passed in 1689, this legislation declared the supremacy of Parliament.

_____ 4. These meetings were the center of politics in New England.

_____ 5. This was the name of the journey in which Africans were transported across the Atlantic Ocean to be sold as slaves.

_____ 6. This raised ideas about spiritual and political equality among many colonists.

_____ 7. During this period thinkers used reason and logic to form ideas about how government should work.

_____ 8. Native Americans trusted these colonists more because they were less threatening than other colonists.

_____ 9. As a result of this, Great Britain gained Canada from the French.

_____ 10. This was an attempt by Native Americans to push white settlers out of the Ohio Valley.

**a.** assemblies

**b.** colonial courts

**c.** English Bill of Rights

**d.** Enlightenment

**e.** free enterprise

**f.** French

**g.** French and Indian War

**h.** Great Awakening

**i.** mercantilism

**j.** Middle Passage

**k.** Pontiac's Rebellion

**l.** town meetings

Progress Assessment

**The English Colonies**                    Section Quiz

**FILL IN THE BLANK** For each of the following statements, fill in the blank with the appropriate word, phrase, or name.

1. The British prime minister asked Parliament to tax the American colonists to help

    pay for _____.

2. In 1764 Parliament passed the _____ which set taxes on molasses and sugar imported by colonists.

3. Many colonists believed that Great Britain had no right to tax them without their

    _____.

4. _____ helped found the Committees of Correspondence to share ideas and information about challenging the British laws.

5. A popular method of protesting British laws was to _____, or refuse to buy British goods.

6. The _____ required colonists to pay for an official stamp, or seal, whenever they bought paper items.

7. Colonists formed a secret society known as the _____ that used violence to frighten tax collectors.

8. The "Bloody Massacre perpetrated in King Street" is also known as the

    _____.

9. In response to the Tea Act, the Sons of Liberty organized the

    _____ to protest the British law.

10. The _____ closed Boston Harbor, cancelled Massachusetts's charter, and forced colonists to house and supply British troops.

Name _____ Class _____ Date _____

## The English Colonies

**MULTIPLE CHOICE** For each of the following, write the letter of the best choice in the space provided.

_____ **1.** The Powhatan were significant because they
   **a.** brought food to help the colonists and taught them how to grow corn.
   **b.** took control of John Smith's colony.
   **c.** taught colonists how to grow tobacco.
   **d.** helped prevent the spread of disease.

_____ **2.** Why was the Stamp Act of 1765 particularly upsetting to the colonists?
   **a.** It was the first time Parliament had tried to tax colonists directly.
   **b.** It was the first attempt by Parliament to tax exports, not just imports.
   **c.** To enforce it, Britain's standing army used violence to frighten tax payers.
   **d.** To enforce it, Britain placed its own judges on the benches of colonial courts.

_____ **3.** What was the result of the French and Indian War?
   **a.** France lost land claims in North America and Britain gained Canada and most French lands east of the Mississippi.
   **b.** Spain gained Canada and Britain gained New Orleans.
   **c.** Land east of the Mississippi was divided equally between France and Britain.
   **d.** France began moving west to settle new lands.

_____ **4.** Why was the Toleration Act of 1649 significant to America's development?
   **a.** It stopped all conflicts between Catholics and Protestants.
   **b.** It was the first law supporting religious tolerance passed in the English colonies.
   **c.** It provided an example of how a representative democracy can pass laws in a fair and just manner.
   **d.** It was the first law to allow religious leaders to mandate one religion.

Progress Assessment

_____ **5.** How did women contribute to colonies' economies?
  **a.** ran farms, businesses, and practiced medicine
  **b.** managed slaves who worked as blacksmiths
  **c.** ran schools and hospitals
  **d.** worked in cities as skilled craftspeople

_____ **6.** Which quotation best expresses the point of view of a New England colonist on education?
  **a.** "All children need to learn to read, write, and do arithmetic."
  **b.** "Only a literate community can keep a record of its successes and failures for the benefit of future generations."
  **c.** "Trade is important to our community, which means people have to be able to make simple calculations."
  **d.** "All children need to be able to read the Bible."

_____ **7.** What was Anne Hutchinson's belief that angered Puritan church leaders?
  **a.** Women should not be religious leaders.
  **b.** Women who were accused of being witches should be sentenced to death.
  **c.** People could have a relationship with God without guidance from ministers.
  **d.** People could take land from American Indians without paying for it.

_____ **8.** The English Bill of Rights reduced the powers of the English monarch while
  **a.** Sir Edmund Andros ruled all of England.
  **b.** King James ruled all of England.
  **c.** Parliament gained power.
  **d.** Parliament lost power.

**TRUE/FALSE** Indicate whether each statement below is true or false by writing **T** or **F** in the space provided.

_____ **9.** During the Great Awakening, spiritual leaders such as John Locke argued that colonists would benefit from English rule.

_____ **10.** Part of the reason why Virginia colonists decided to use slave labor was that there were not enough indentured servants to meet the high demand.

_____ **11.** The colony of Pennsylvania was named after William Penn, a Quaker who believed in dealing fairly with local American Indians, welcoming immigrants, and tolerating other religions.

_____ **12.** Jamestown's population plummeted between 1609 and 1610 because of infertile soil, which caused many of Jamestown's original settlers to seek better farmland in the middle colonies.

_____ **13.** During the 1730s, sermons on spiritual equality led colonists to ask for political equality, a demand which set the stage for the American Revolution.

_____ **14.** To enforce the Stamp Act of 1765, Britain placed its own judges on the benches of colonial courts.

_____ **15.** Slaves contributed to the economy of the middle colonies by working in cities at skilled crafts such as blacksmithing and carpentry.

**PRACTICING SOCIAL STUDIES SKILLS** Study the pie charts below and answer the question that follows.

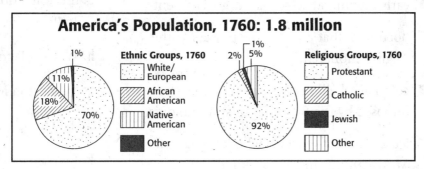

**America's Population, 1760: 1.8 million**

Ethnic Groups, 1760
1% — 11% — 18% — 70%
White/European
African American
Native American
Other

Religious Groups, 1760
1% — 2% — 5% — 92%
Protestant
Catholic
Jewish
Other

_____ **16.** Which of the following best describe America's population in 1760?
   **a.** White/European Catholics
   **b.** African American Protestants
   **c.** White/European Protestants
   **d.** White/European Jews

**The English Colonies,** *continued*

**MATCHING** In the space provided, write the letter of the term or person that matches each description. Some answers will not be used.

_____ **17.** closed the port of Boston, cancelled Massachusetts's charter, and increased colonists' anger at Britain

_____ **18.** proposed by Lord Baltimore to end restrictions on the religious rights of Christians in Maryland

_____ **19.** marked the first time Parliament had tried to tax colonists directly

_____ **20.** helped colonists by making an agreement with the Powhatan

_____ **21.** early attempt at colonial self-government

_____ **22.** document that reduced the powers of the English monarch

_____ **23.** colonial rebellion that led to strict acts imposed by the British against the colonists

_____ **24.** led a group of Puritans who left England for Massachusetts in 1630 seeking religious freedom

_____ **25.** After this event, the British Crown found two soldiers guilty of killing people by accident.

**a.** John Smith

**b.** the Boston Tea Party

**c.** the Intolerable Acts

**d.** the English Bill of Rights

**e.** John Winthrop

**f.** the Mayflower Compact

**g.** the Toleration Act of 1649

**h.** William Penn

**i.** the Boston Massacre

**j.** the Stamp Act

**k.** John Edwards

Progress Assessment

**The English Colonies**

Chapter Test

**Form B**

**SHORT ANSWER** On a separate sheet of paper, answer each of the following questions in complete sentences.

1. Why did two-thirds of Jamestown's colonists die by the time the first winter arrived?

2. Which of Anne Hutchinson's beliefs angered Puritan church leaders? Why?

3. What happened to Massachusetts in the aftermath of the Boston Tea Party?

4. Pontiac is one of the American Indian leaders who opposed what?

5. Who started a colony west of New Jersey to provide a safe home for Quakers?

6. What event caused tension between British soldiers and Bostonians to explode on March 5, 1770, directly sparking the Boston Massacre?

**PRACTICING SOCIAL STUDIES SKILLS** Study the charts below and, on a separate sheet of paper, answer the question that follows.

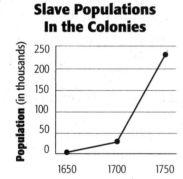

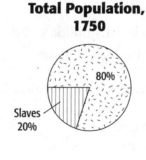

7. The population of slaves in the colonies grew by about how many times between 1700 and 1750?

Progress Assessment

**The American Revolution**                    Section Quiz

**Section 1**

**FILL IN THE BLANK**  For each of the following statements, fill in the
blank with the appropriate word, phrase, or name.

1. The First _____ was a gathering of colonial leaders who were
   deeply troubled about the relationship between Great Britain and the colonies in
   America.

2. _____ were colonists who chose to fight for independence
   from Great Britain.

3. A list of 10 resolutions to be presented to King George III was called the

   _____.

4. _____ got their name because they were ready to fight at a
   minute's notice.

5. _____ warned the colonists of the British advance toward
   Concord.

6. The British were called _____ because of the color of their
   uniforms.

7. The Massachusetts militia was declared the _____; it included soldiers from all colonies.

8. Congress named a Virginian, _____, to command the army.

9. Delegates signed the _____ Petition as a final attempt to
   restore harmony.

10. The _____ was an early battle that proved that the patriots
    could take on the British.

Progress Assessment

**The American Revolution**                    Section Quiz

**Section 2**

**MULTIPLE CHOICE** For each of the following, write the letter of the best choice in the space provided.

_____ **1.** Who was the author of a 47-page pamphlet called *Common Sense*?
   **a.** George Washington
   **b.** Patrick Henry
   **c.** Paul Revere
   **d.** Thomas Paine

_____ **2.** What document formally announced the colonies' break from Great Britain?
   **a.** Loyalists Papers
   **b.** Declaration of Independence
   **c.** Common Sense pamphlet
   **d.** Colonial Uprise

_____ **3.** Those who chose to side with the British were called
   **a.** Loyalists.
   **b.** colonists.
   **c.** minutemen.
   **d.** Patriots.

_____ **4.** Who tried to influence her husband to include women's rights in the Declaration?
   **a.** Betsy Ross
   **b.** Abigail Adams
   **c.** Dolley Madison
   **d.** Martha Washington

_____ **5.** By the 1780s, which colonies were taking steps to end slavery?
   **a.** Georgia colonies
   **b.** southern colonies
   **c.** New England colonies
   **d.** southwestern colonies

**The American Revolution**

**MATCHING** In the space provided, write the letter of the term, person, or place that matches each description. Some answers will not be used.

_____ **1.** Commander of the Continental Army

_____ **2.** Connecticut officer who went behind British lines to get secret information

_____ **3.** Foreign soldiers who fought for pay

_____ **4.** Author of *The American Crisis,* a series of pamphlets

_____ **5.** Dressed as a man and fought in several battles

_____ **6.** Important victory against the Hessians

_____ **7.** Young Frenchman who volunteered to serve in the Continental Army without pay

_____ **8.** Born in Scotland, naval hero for the Patriots

_____ **9.** Controlled the land west of the Appalachians

_____ **10.** A Surveyor along the Ohio and Kentucky Rivers, he volunteered to lead the western campaign

**a.** American Indians

**b.** Battle of Trenton

**c.** Deborah Sampson

**d.** Friedrich Von Steuben

**e.** George Rogers Clark

**f.** George Washington

**g.** John Paul Jones

**h.** Marquis de Lafayette

**i.** mercenaries

**j.** Molly Pitcher

**k.** Nathan Hale

**l.** Patriots

**m.** Thomas Paine

Progress Assessment

**The American Revolution**

**TRUE/FALSE** Mark each statement **T** if it is true or **F** if it is false. If false explain why.

_____ **1.** The colonists planned to free any enslaved Africans that agreed to fight for them.

_____

_____

_____ **2.** Marion's Brigade was a group of guerrilla soldiers that used surprise attacks to disrupt British communication and supply.

_____

_____

_____ **3.** The Battle of Yorktown was the last major battle of the American Revolution.

_____

_____

_____ **4.** Benedict Arnold was the general leading the British troops in the Battle of Yorktown.

_____

_____

_____ **5.** In the Treaty of Paris of 1783, Great Britain recognized the independence of the United States.

_____

_____

## The American Revolution

Chapter Test

**Form A**

**MULTIPLE CHOICE** For each of the following, write the letter of the best choice in the space provided.

_____ **1.** What delegate from Virginia encouraged colonists to fight for independence from Britain in support of the Patriot cause?
   **a.** Patrick Henry
   **b.** George Washington
   **c.** Thomas Jefferson
   **d.** Paul Revere

_____ **2.** Among the list of 10 resolutions included in the Declaration of Rights, one was to
   **a.** assure the colonists that "Britain sought a peaceful resolution."
   **b.** ensure the colonists' right to "life, liberty, and property."
   **c.** convince the colonists that they were "not ready to challenge Britain."
   **d.** remind the colonists that they were British citizens "entitled to rights."

_____ **3.** The Battle of Lexington is important because it
   **a.** forced colonists to comply with British rule.
   **b.** was the longest battle of the Revolutionary War.
   **c.** resulted in so many British casualties.
   **d.** was the first battle of the Revolutionary War.

_____ **4.** When voicing their opinions to the Second Continental Congress delegates were
   **a.** always in agreement and the meeting was unnecessary.
   **b.** somewhat divided on minor details of their plan.
   **c.** far from unified but were open to compromise.
   **d.** completely at odds and failed to come to a consensus.

Progress Assessment

_____ **5.** Colonists who chose to side with the British were known as
   **a.** Redcoats.
   **b.** Patriots.
   **c.** Loyalists.
   **d.** Whigs.

_____ **6.** What inspired colonists to draft the Declaration of Independence?
   **a.** Paul Revere's ride.
   **b.** Thomas Paine's *Common Sense*
   **c.** Washington's strong command of the Continental Army
   **d.** the Battle of Bunker Hill

_____ **7.** Why was the Battle of Saratoga a turning point for the Patriots?
   **a.** The Patriots gained the support of France and Spain.
   **b.** The Redcoat victory made Patriot soldiers more determined to win the war.
   **c.** The Patriots got a Prussian to train the Continental Army.
   **d.** The Patriots realized they did not need foreign allies.

_____ **8.** What is the significance of the Battle of Yorktown?
   **a.** It convinced colonists to comply with British rule.
   **b.** It allowed the French to gain colonial territory.
   **c.** It showed the British that they could reduce their number of troops to defeat the colonists.
   **d.** It was the last major battle of the American Revolution.

_____ **9.** As a result of the First Continental Congress
   **a.** the Declaration of Independence was drafted.
   **b.** the Declaration of Rights was drafted.
   **c.** colonists agreed to comply with the majority of British rules.
   **d.** King George agreed to comply with the majority of the colonists' demands.

**PRACTICING SOCIAL STUDIES SKILLS** Study the passage below and
answer the question that follows.

> "Remember the Ladies, and be more generous and favorable to them
> than your ancestors. Do not put such unlimited power into the hands
> of the Husbands… If particular care and attention is not paid to the
> Ladies we are and will not hold ourselves bound by Laws in which we
> have no voice, or Representation."
>
> —Abigail Adams, quoted in *Notable American Women*

_____ **10.** Which of the following facts from the text best supports Abigail Adams's
statement?
   **a.** "Although many women were Patriots, the Declaration did not address
   their rights."
   **b.** "The signing of the Declaration made the rebellion a full-scale revolt
   against Britain."
   **c.** "*Common Sense* changed the way many colonists viewed their king."
   **d.** "In 1776 the colonists declared independence."

**FILL IN THE BLANK** Read each sentence and fill in the blank with the
word in the word pair that best completes the sentence.

**11.** As _____ prepared to lead the colonists against the British,
Congress tried to make peace with King George III.
**(Paul Revere/George Washington)**

**12.** The Battle of _____ was a turning point for the Patriots
because they gained the support of France, Spain, and Holland.
**(Bunker Hill/Saratoga)**

**13.** The winter at _____ was a difficult time for the Continental
Army, which lacked protection and supplies. **(Valley Forge/Fort Schuyler)**

**14.** The Patriots' victory at Yorktown was made possible by a strategic error on the

part of _____, who moved his troops in the hope of main-

taining communication with the British Navy.

**(Marquis de Lafayette/Charles Cornwallis)**

**15.** British troops, also known as _____, made easy targets as they retreated from Boston. (**Loyalists/Redcoats**)

**16.** *Common Sense*, a pamphlet written by _____, inspired colonial leaders challenge British authority. (**Thomas Paine/Patrick Henry**)

**17.** Native Americans mostly sided with the _____ in supporting the war effort. (**British/Patriots**)

**TRUE/FALSE** Indicate whether each statement below is true or false by writing **T** or **F** in the space provided.

_____ **18.** As a result of the 1783 Treaty of Paris, land west of the thirteen colonies was given to France.

_____ **19.** The main issue debated during the Second Continental Congress was whether foreign allies would be beneficial.

_____ **20.** Thomas Jefferson felt the colonists had the right to break away from Great Britain because he did not believe in the idea of a social contract.

_____ **21.** The Battle of Trenton was different from previous battles because the Patriots went on the offensive.

_____ **22.** The Declaration of Independence did not address the rights of Native Americans.

_____ **23.** The rejection of the Olive Branch Petition led to the meeting of the First Continental Congress.

_____ **24.** Bernardo de Gálvez was one of many foreigners hired by the Patriots to fight as a mercenary during the American Revolution.

_____ **25.** Thousands of African American slaves signed on with the British Army because they were promised their freedom.

## The American Revolution

**SHORT ANSWER** On a separate sheet of paper, answer each of the following questions in complete sentences.

1. Who was nicknamed "the Swamp Fox," and why?

2. What was the main challenge the Patriots faced against the British at sea? How did they overcome it?

3. Who was Bernardo de Gálvez and how did he contribute to the American Revolution?

4. How did the Second Continental Congress decide to handle the British?

5. How did Thomas Paine's pamphlet *Common Sense* change the way many people viewed their king? What other significant effects did it have?

6. Who was the main author of the Declaration of Independence?

**PRACTICING SOCIAL STUDIES SKILLS** Study the diagram below and, on a separate sheet of paper, answer the question that follows.

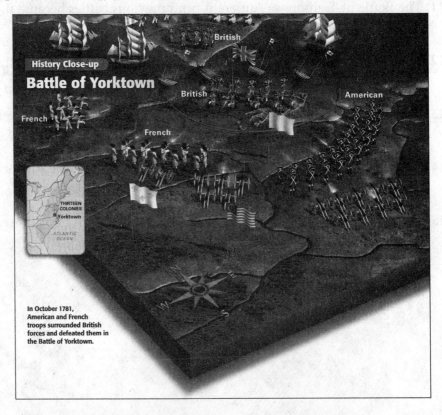

History Close-up
**Battle of Yorktown**

British

British

American

French

French

THIRTEEN COLONIES
Yorktown
ATLANTIC OCEAN

In October 1781, American and French troops surrounded British forces and defeated them in the Battle of Yorktown.

7. Based on the diagram, do you think it was a wise decision for the British to retreat to Yorktown? Why or why not?

Progress Assessment

# Our Colonial Heritage

Unit Test

Form A

**MULTIPLE CHOICE** For each of the following, write the letter of the best choice in the space provided.

_____ **1.** Which event directly sparked the Boston Massacre?
   **a.** A crowd of sailors dared colonists to fight with British troops.
   **b.** A lone British soldier standing guard hit a colonist during an argument.
   **c.** An African American sailor shot and wounded a British soldier.
   **d.** Colonists spread negative propaganda about British troops.

_____ **2.** Which of the following is true about most of the Native American groups that lived in southeastern North America?
   **a.** They lived in cone-shaped shelters called *teepees*.
   **b.** They lived in farming villages governed by village councils.
   **c.** They were nomadic hunters who followed deer and elk.
   **d.** They built shelters from heavy clay called adobe.

_____ **3.** What was the main issue debated during the Second Continental Congress?
   **a.** whether to seek war or peace
   **b.** how to plan a surprise attack against Britain
   **c.** how to convert more colonists to the Patriot cause
   **d.** whether foreign allies would be beneficial

_____ **4.** Among colonists, which group made the greatest contribution to the war effort?
   **a.** soldiers
   **b.** mercenaries
   **c.** spies
   **d.** militia men

_____ **5.** Direct democracy is best defined as a form of government in which
   **a.** all citizens participate.
   **b.** representatives vote on issues.
   **c.** laws are publicly displayed.
   **d.** monarchs rule colonies.

Progress Assessment

_____ **6.** In the year 1000, strong winds blew Leif Eriksson's ship off course to
   **a.** the Cape of Good Hope.
   **b.** Greenland.
   **c.** Portugal.
   **d.** the North American coast.

_____ **7.** The African slave who purchased his freedom and devoted himself to ending slavery was
   **a.** Olaudah Equiano.
   **b.** Metacomet.
   **c.** Pontiac.
   **d.** Squanto.

_____ **8.** The term African Diaspora refers to the
   **a.** harsh voyage taken by slaves across the Atlantic Ocean.
   **b.** forced labor of West Africans in mines and on farms and plantations.
   **c.** scattering of enslaved Africans all across the New World.
   **d.** regulation of slave treatment and behavior by colonial lawmakers.

_____ **9.** The Black Death affected the European economy by
   **a.** killing most of the crops.
   **b.** causing a shortage of workers.
   **c.** causing Europeans to move to Asia.
   **d.** slowing trade between cities.

_____ **10.** What was the social impact of the Great Awakening?
   **a.** It unified various groups of Americans who shared evangelical beliefs.
   **b.** It led ministers to sentence to death those accused of witchcraft.
   **c.** It deepened misunderstandings between American Indians, slaves, and white settlers.
   **d.** It strengthened the cultural authority of the upper-class colonists.

_____ **11.** What happened to the Roanoke colony after the summer of 1587?
   **a.** The colonists were brutally assaulted by French explorers.
   **b.** Dutch explorers invaded the colony and named it their own.
   **c.** Widespread disease killed off most of the colonists there.
   **d.** The colonists abandoned the site and the reason is still a mystery.

Progress Assessment

_____ **12.** How did Prince Henry the
Navigator help push exploration forward?
   **a.** He set out on a voyage to
   explore the west coast of
   Africa.
   **b.** He financed research by
   mapmakers and
   shipbuilders.
   **c.** He published Marco Polo's
   inspirational writings on
   the Silk Road.
   **d.** He led sailing expeditions
   to the New World.

_____ **13.** What early crop did both the
Olmec and the Maya grow?
   **a.** maize
   **b.** wheat
   **c.** barley
   **d.** tobacco

_____ **14.** Which of the following contributed to the success of the
Native American groups of
the far North?
   **a.** the development of
   advanced irrigation
   methods
   **b.** the use of sled dogs for
   transportation
   **c.** the favorable climate
   **d.** the rich and fertile farming
   soil

_____ **15.** In European nations, the
practice of carefully controlling trade to create and maintain wealth was called
   **a.** mercantilism.
   **b.** brokering.
   **c.** capitalism.
   **d.** profiteering.

**TRUE/FALSE** Indicate whether each statement below is true or false by
writing **T** or **F** in the space provided.

_____ **16.** The Protestant Reformation began in small French towns and quickly
spread to other European countries.

_____ **17.** Nearly 4 million enslaved Africans were sent to Brazil between the 1520s
and the 1860s.

_____ **18.** Mansa Musa had scholars set up schools in Mali for the study of the
Qur'an.

_____ **19.** The colonies with the strictest slave codes were the same ones that had
freed the most slaves.

_____ **20.** The ideas in Thomas Paine's *Common Sense* were considered bold at the
time, partly because most of the world was still ruled by monarchs.

_____ **21.** The Columbian Exchange affected Native American agriculture by getting American Indians to produce more tobacco, grow tomatoes, and use fertilizer.

_____ **22.** Louisiana was named by René-Robert La Salle in honor of King Louis XIV of France.

_____ **23.** Henry the Navigator helped publish Marco Polo's popular book about traveling through Asia.

_____ **24.** John Cabot's explorations became the basis for England's claim to land in North America.

_____ **25.** Sir Walter Raleigh received a charter from England that gave him permission to start a colony in the New World.

_____ **26.** Henry Hudson discovered the Northwest Passage in 1609.

**PRACTICING SOCIAL STUDIES SKILLS** Study the map below and answer the question that follows.

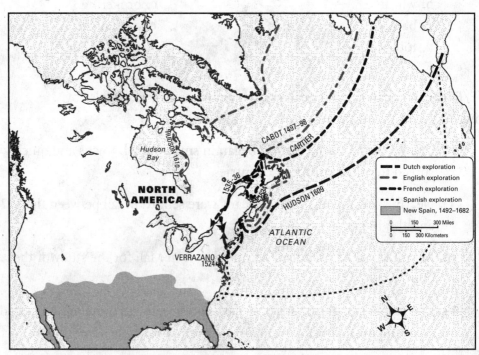

_____ **27.** Which of the following explorers traveled farthest west?
   **a.** Henry Hudson
   **b.** Giovanni da Verrazano
   **c.** John Cabot
   **d.** Jacques Cartier

**FILL IN THE BLANK** Read each sentence and fill in the blank with the word in the word pair that best completes the sentence.

**28.** _____ 's explorations were funded by King Ferdinand and Queen Isabella of Spain. (**Juan Ponce de León/Christopher Columbus**)

**29.** At dawn on April 19, 1775, British soldiers searched for a major storehouse

of colonial weapons rumored to be located in _____.

(**Concord/Lexington**)

**30.** In New England, political life centered on the _____, where people talked about and decided on local issues, such as paying for schools. (**church service/town meeting**)

**31.** The Greek philosopher _____ wrote the *Republic.*
(**Plato/Socrates**)

**32.** _____ was the capital of the Incan empire.
(**Tenochtitlán/Cuzco**)

**33.** According to commonly held Native American religious beliefs,

_____ and Sky were the sustainers of life. (**Sun/Earth**)

**34.** In 1630, _____ led the fleet of ships that carried Puritan colonists from England to Massachusetts, where they planned to build an ideal Christian community. (**Richard Mather/John Winthrop**)

**35.** The _____, signed by 41 of the male passengers of the ship, describes the principles of the Pilgrim colony's government.
(**Mayflower Compact/Jamestown Agreement**)

**36.** _____, a Patuxet Indian, taught the Pilgrims of the Plymouth colony to fertilize the soil on their farms with fish remains.
(**Squanto/Santos**)

**37.** Colonial families were sometimes divided over where to pledge their political sup-

port. Even the great Patriot Benjamin Franklin had a _____

son. (**Loyalist/Redcoat**)

**38.** An uprising in which colonists protested trade and land agreements with

American Indians was known as _____.

**(the Toleration Act of 1649/Bacon's Rebellion)**

**MATCHING** In the space provided, write the letter of the term that matches each description. Some answers will not be used.

_____ **39.** carried out guerrilla warfare in the South and became known as the Swamp Fox

_____ **40.** wealthy Florentine banking family

_____ **41.** thought citizens should make laws and people had a natural right to govern themselves

_____ **42.** "the lost colony"

_____ **43.** launched a surprise attack near the town of Vincennes, undermining British support in the West

_____ **44.** spirit of a Native American ancestor or animal

_____ **45.** Inca capital that was captured by Pizarro

_____ **46.** believed that people could have a relationship with God without guidance from ministers

_____ **47.** important trading city in Mali's empire

_____ **48.** founder of the Church of England

_____ **49.** system in which goods and slaves were traded among the Americas, Britain, and Africa

_____ **50.** movement in the 1700s based on the idea that reason and logic could improve society

**a.** George Rogers Clark

**b.** Thomas Paine

**c.** Roanoke

**d.** triangular trade

**e.** Djenné

**f.** Francis Marion

**g.** Minister Thomas Hooker

**h.** Cuzco

**i.** Anne Hutchinson

**j.** totem

**k.** Medici

**l.** Henry VIII

**m.** Soninke

**n.** Enlightenment

**o.** Great Awakening

**Our Colonial Heritage**

Unit Test

Form B

**SHORT ANSWER** On a separate sheet of paper, answer each of the following questions in complete sentences.

**1.** What disease killed about 25 million people in Europe during the Middle Ages?

**2.** The surviving members of Magellan's crew were the first sailors to do what?

**3.** Who took control of Jamestown in 1608? How did he change its conditions?

**4.** Why did the Pilgrims immigrate to America?

**5.** How did the Declaration of Independence raise questions about slavery?

**6.** Name two of the four military leaders at the Battle of Yorktown.

**PRACTICING SOCIAL STUDIES SKILLS** Study the map below and, on a separate sheet of paper, answer the question that follows.

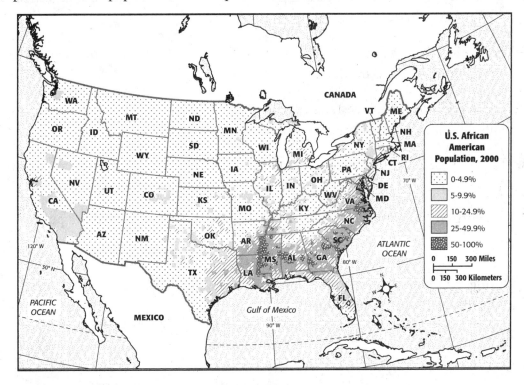

**7.** Which region of the country had the highest percentage of African Americans in 2000? Based on what you know about the African Diaspora, why might that be the case?

**Forming a Government**                    Section Quiz

**Section 1**

**FILL IN THE BLANK** For each of the following statements, fill in the blank with the appropriate word, phrase, or name.

1. _____, signed in 1215, required the king to follow the same laws as other English people.

2. The English Bill of Rights kept the king or queen from passing new taxes or changing laws without the approval of _____.

3. The first government of the United States did not have a president or a national _____.

4. The Confederation Congress passed the _____ to create a system for surveying and dividing public lands.

5. Colonial documents such as the _____ and the Connecticut constitution influenced American government.

6. The Virginia Statute for _____ established a precedent of religious tolerance and freedom.

7. The constitutions of many states expanded _____, or voting rights, by allowing any white man who paid taxes to vote.

8. The _____ was a document that created the first central government for the United States.

9. The Northwest Ordinance of 1787 established territorial representation, public education and prohibited _____ in the Northwest Territory.

10. During the American Revolution most colonies wrote _____ that supported limited, republican governments.

                                                                    Progress Assessment

**Forming a Government**

**MULTIPLE CHOICE** For each of the following, write the letter of the best choice in the space provided.

_____ **1.** What problem did the United States have with Britain following the Revolutionary War?

  **a.** Battles broke out between Americans and British merchants.

  **b.** The British army refused to leave many U.S. cities.

  **c.** Britain restricted trade with the United States.

  **d.** Britain refused to sign the Treaty of Paris.

_____ **2.** What led farmers in Massachusetts to rebel?

  **a.** high taxes

  **b.** the lack of a national government

  **c.** the closure of the port at New Orleans

  **d.** the ratification of the Articles of Confederation

_____ **3.** What are creditors?

  **a.** people who loan money

  **b.** people who owe money

  **c.** people who steal money

  **d.** people who save money

_____ **4.** Which of the following was to blame for economic and other problems in the United States after the Revolution?

  **a.** a weak military

  **b.** high inflation

  **c.** a weak central government

  **d.** disputes with American Indians

_____ **5.** What nation was the most important trade partner of the United States?

  **a.** China

  **b.** France

  **c.** the Netherlands

  **d.** Great Britain

Progress Assessment

# Forming a Government

**MATCHING** In the space provided, write the letter of the term or person that matches each description. Some answers will not be used.

_____ **1.** This was held in May 1787, to discuss ways to improve the Articles of Confederation.

_____ **2.** This plan proposed creating a national government with a two-house legislature with representation determined only by population.

_____ **3.** This delegate played an instrumental role in the drafting of the Constitution.

_____ **4.** He was the New Jersey delegate who presented the small-state plan.

_____ **5.** This agreement ended the debate between large and small states.

_____ **6.** Delegates looked to this system to establish the sharing of power between national and state governments.

_____ **7.** This branch of government is responsible for proposing and passing laws.

_____ **8.** This refers to the idea that political power rests in the hands of the people.

_____ **9.** This agreement determined how slaves would be counted for representation and placed a ban on asking for an end to the slave trade.

_____ **10.** This system was designed to keep any one branch of government from becoming too powerful.

**a.** checks and balances

**b.** Constitutional Convention

**c.** executive branch

**d.** federalism

**e.** Great Compromise

**f.** James Madison

**g.** legislative branch

**h.** nationalism

**i.** New Jersey Plan

**j.** popular sovereignty

**k.** Three-Fifths Compromise

**l.** Virginia Plan

**m.** William Paterson

Progress Assessment

# Forming a Government

**TRUE/FALSE** Mark each statement **T** if it is true or **F** if it is false. If false explain why.

_____ **1.** Many Antifederalists did not want the Constitution to include a bill of rights.

_____

_____

_____ **2.** Federalists were those who did not support the Constitution.

_____

_____

_____ **3.** The Bill of Rights protects the rights of individuals.

_____

_____

_____ **4.** The *Federalist Papers* were a series of essays that helped to persuade people to support the Constitution.

_____

_____

_____ **5.** Checks and balances are official changes that can be added to the Constitution.

_____

_____

**Forming a Government**                     Chapter Test

                                                 **Form A**

**MULTIPLE CHOICE** For each of the following, write the letter of the best choice in the space provided.

_____ **1.** Which factors indicate that there was an economic depression in the United States after the Revolutionary War?

   **a.** Trade laws differed across states and each state followed its own interests.

   **b.** The country went deeper into debt as it raised taxes.

   **c.** Both the price of goods and the value of money increased.

   **d.** Trade activity was minimal and inflation and unemployment were on the rise.

_____ **2.** Women, African Americans, and Native Americans did not take part in the Constitutional Convention because they

   **a.** did not have the rights of citizens.

   **b.** opposed expanding the central government.

   **c.** were protesting against the new constitution.

   **d.** could not find a delegate to represent them.

_____ **3.** The Annapolis Convention of 1786 failed to answer the needs of the nation because

   **a.** many delegates did not attend the convention.

   **b.** the delegates did not agree on the role of the Congress.

   **c.** most states changed their positions after the convention.

   **d.** the Congress limited citizens' liberties to prevent insurrection.

_____ **4.** Thomas Jefferson's Virginia Statute for Religious Freedom declared that

   **a.** governments must punish religious discrimination.

   **b.** governments were responsible for funding churches.

   **c.** no person who worked on behalf of a religious institution had to pay taxes.

   **d.** no person could be required to pay for a church with tax money.

Progress Assessment

_____ **5.** The *Federalist Papers* tried to reassure Americans about the new federal government created under the Constitution by stating that it would

    **a.** be more like Great Britain's.

    **b.** not overpower the states.

    **c.** one day abolish slavery in the nation.

    **d.** grant the states political independence.

_____ **6.** Why did Congress decide to pass the Land Ordinance of 1785, which divided western lands into townships?

    **a.** Congress wanted to create a region where slavery was banned.

    **b.** Native Americans were illegally exploiting territories in the western lands.

    **c.** Congress wanted to sell lots to the public to pay the nation's debts.

    **d.** Colonial governments had already expanded their borders into western lands.

_____ **7.** The New Jersey Plan, which was presented at the Constitutional Convention, stated that

    **a.** individual states would have to raise and fund their own armies.

    **b.** individual states would be responsible for regulating commerce.

    **c.** each state would have an equal voice in the federal government.

    **d.** each state would have a say in nominating judges to the Supreme Court.

_____ **8.** In 1784 officials from which country closed the lower Mississippi, which the United States had used to ship goods to eastern markets?

    **a.** France

    **b.** Spain

    **c.** Britain

    **d.** Canada

_____ **9.** What did Daniel Shays and his men protest in 1786?

    **a.** the death penalty

    **b.** the use of debtors' prisons

    **c.** federal control of the judicial system

    **d.** high taxes and heavy debts

**PRACTICING SOCIAL STUDIES SKILLS** Study the map below and
answer the question that follows.

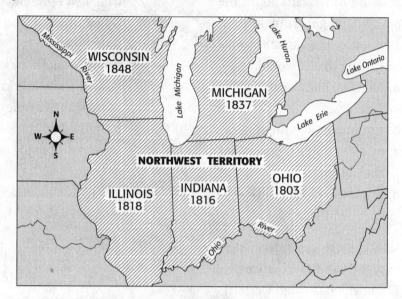

_____ **10.** According to the map, which of the following statements is true?

    **a.** Michigan was the last northwestern territory to become a state.

    **b.** Indiana was the first northwestern territory to be surveyed.

    **c.** The southern boundary of the Northwest Territory is the Ohio River.

    **d.** The Northwest Territory is divided in two by the Mississippi River.

**TRUE/FALSE** Indicate whether each statement below is true or false by
writing **T** or **F** in the space provided.

_____ **11.** Passed in 1689, the English Bill of Rights prevented the king and queen
from passing taxes or changing laws without Parliament's consent.

_____ **12.** Federalism was created to balance the power of the central government
with the power of the states.

_____ **13.** Under the Articles of Confederation, the executive branch was to lead the
national government.

_____ **14.** At the Constitutional Convention, the delegates ultimately decided that
slaves were not citizens and should not be counted when determining a
state's representation.

_____ **15.** Shays's Rebellion inspired most Americans to call for the establishment of
a national army.

**MATCHING**  In the space provided, write the letter of the term or person that matches each description. Some answers will not be used.

_____ **16.** branch of government responsible for interpreting the laws

_____ **17.** became known as the Father of the Constitution for his ideas about government

_____ **18.** agreement reached that created a two-house legislature

_____ **19.** opposed the Constitution because it did not have a section protecting individual rights

_____ **20.** official changes made to the Constitution

_____ **21.** agreement that only a portion of a state's slaves would count in determining its representation in Congress

_____ **22.** sharing of power between central and state governments

_____ **23.** branch of government that proposes and passes the laws

_____ **24.** document created to protect the rights of citizens

_____ **25.** idea that political power belongs to the people

**a.** Bill of Rights

**b.** federalism

**c.** George Mason

**d.** judicial branch

**e.** popular sovereignty

**f.** Great Compromise

**g.** James Madison

**h.** legislative branch

**i.** Three-Fifths Compromise

**j.** amendments

**k.** the New Jersey Plan

**l.** Antifederalists

**SHORT ANSWER** On a separate sheet of paper, answer each of the following questions in complete sentences.

1. After which two British documents did the Americans model their new government?

2. What was the main cause of Shays's Rebellion? What was its purpose?

3. What dispute did the Great Compromise resolve? How did it resolve it?

4. What did the Three-Fifths Compromise state?

5. What were the *Federalist Papers*? What was their position on the Constitution?

6. What is the idea of popular sovereignty?

**PRACTICING SOCIAL STUDIES SKILLS** Study the map below and, on a separate sheet of paper, answer the question that follows.

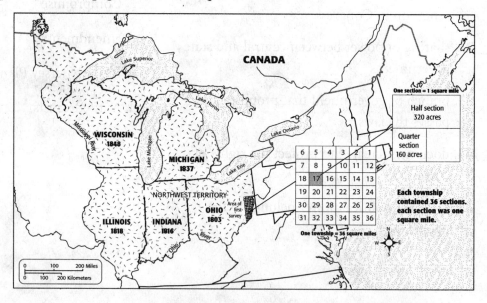

7. According to the map, how did the Land Ordinance of 1785 divide western land?

Progress Assessment

## Citizenship and the Constitution

**MATCHING** In the space provided, write the letter of the term or person that matches each description. Some answers will not be used.

_____ **1.** Article I of the Constitution establishes the structure and function of this branch.

_____ **2.** This grants Congress the right to create laws to address new or unexpected issues.

_____ **3.** This amendment limits presidents to only two terms.

_____ **4.** This house of Congress has 435 representatives.

_____ **5.** Powers shared by both state and federal governments are known as these.

_____ **6.** This power of the House of Representatives has been used twice—once against President Andrew Johnson, and once against President Bill Clinton.

_____ **7.** This power allows the president to cancel laws passed by Congress.

_____ **8.** He was the first African American Supreme Court justice.

_____ **9.** Thirteen of these make up part of the judicial branch.

_____ **10.** To serve in this office, a person must be at least 35 years old and be a native-born citizen of the United States.

**a.** appeals courts

**b.** concurrent powers

**c.** elastic clause

**d.** executive

**e.** House of Representatives

**f.** impeach

**g.** legislative

**h.** president

**i.** reserved powers

**j.** Senate

**k.** Thurgood Marshall

**l.** Twenty-second Amendment

**m.** veto

Progress Assessment

## Citizenship and the Constitution

**TRUE/FALSE** Mark each statement **T** if it is true or **F** if it is false. If false explain why.

_____ **1.** James Madison promised that a Bill of Rights would be added to the Constitution.

_____

_____

_____ **2.** The First Amendment includes freedom of religion, freedom of the press, freedom of speech, freedom of assembly, and the right to petition the government.

_____

_____

_____ **3.** The Fifth, Sixth, Seventh, and Eighth Amendments provide guidelines that protect the rights of crime victims.

_____

_____

_____ **4.** The Seventh Amendment grants those accused of a crime the right to an attorney.

_____

_____

_____ **5.** The Eighth Amendment states that any powers not given to the federal government or prohibited to the states thereby belongs to the states and the people.

_____

_____

Progress Assessment

Name _____ Class _____ Date _____

# Citizenship and the Constitution

Section Quiz

**Section 3**

**FILL IN THE BLANK** For each of the following statements, fill in the blank with the appropriate word, phrase, or name.

1. One way to become a citizen of the United States is to go through the process of

   _____.

2. _____ are people who permanently move to a new country.

3. People born in a foreign country are citizens of the United States if at least

   _____ parent is a U.S. citizen.

4. American citizens are expected to obey _____ and respect authority figures, like law enforcement officials.

5. Good citizenship means paying _____ for services like public roads, police, and public schools.

6. Young men are expected to register with the _____ at 18 years of age, pledging their willingness to be drafted by the military.

7. Many Americans _____ in their communities through community service groups like Citizens on Patrol.

8. Some Americans choose to give money to candidates through

   _____, which collect money for candidates who support certain issues.

9. American citizens can participate in government by learning about issues and

   candidates and by _____ in elections.

10. In order to become a U.S. citizen, immigrants must demonstrate knowledge of

    English and show basic knowledge of _____ and

    government.

Progress Assessment

## Citizenship and the Constitution

Chapter Test

### Form A

**MULTIPLE CHOICE** For each of the following, write the letter of the best choice in the space provided.

_____ 1. Which abuse inspired the inclusion in the Bill of Rights of the Fourth Amendment rule against "unreasonable searches and seizures"?

a. impressments of British naval officers discovered on U.S. ships during the Revolutionary War

b. colonists being forced to have their belongings inspected for illegal goods by British soldiers

c. court-ordered takeovers of property owned by farmers who were in debt due to high property taxes

d. confiscation of goods brought from the West Indies on the grounds that they were smuggled

_____ 2. The First Amendment protects

a. the right to a speedy and public trial.

b. the right to keep and bear arms.

c. freedom of religion, speech, the press, and assembly.

d. freedom from unreasonable searches and seizures.

_____ 3. The function of the Ninth and Tenth Amendments is to

a. protect rights not addressed by the first eight amendments.

b. summarize the rights listed in the first eight amendments.

c. preserve the balance of power among state governments.

d. delegate powers from the states to the federal government.

_____ 4. The president can check the power of the legislative branch by

a. vetoing a law.

b. issuing an executive order.

c. granting a pardon.

d. petitioning Congress.

_____ 5. A federal court can strike down a state or federal law if it finds that the law

a. is unconstitutional.

b. overlaps existing laws.

c. goes against existing laws.

d. repeats basic common sense.

Progress Assessment

_____ **6.** The federal government has separate branches to
   **a.** keep any one branch from growing too powerful.
   **b.** make the government run more efficiently.
   **c.** provide flexibility in the interpretation of laws.
   **d.** ensure one branch is in charge at all times.

_____ **7.** The government enforces the idea that it is a citizen's duty to know the law by
   **a.** testing naturalized citizens on the meaning of specific laws.
   **b.** punishing lawbreakers who claim ignorance of the law.
   **c.** requiring law to be taught in public schools and colleges.
   **d.** forcing citizens to learn about the law by serving on juries.

_____ **8.** American men 18 years or older have to register with the Selective Service so
   **a.** the local court system can call on them to sit for jury duty.
   **b.** they can qualify for financial aid programs in state colleges.
   **c.** the federal government can contact them in case of a draft.
   **d.** they can vote.

_____ **9.** What were the two main goals of the Constitution's framers?
   **a.** create local governments and elect a president
   **b.** establish a capital and define borders
   **c.** raise taxes to build the treasury and pay off war debts
   **d.** protect citizens' rights and defend the country

**FILL IN THE BLANK** Read each sentence and fill in the blank with the word in the word pair that best completes the sentence.

**10.** The doctrine of _____ divides government so that no one branch can become too powerful. (**separation of powers/balance of power**)

**11.** According to the principle of _____, the decisions of the greatest number of people in a society make policy for everyone. (**majority rule/democracy**)

**12.** In the United States, _____ have most of the same rights and responsibilities as native-born Americans. (**legal immigrants/naturalized citizens**)

**13.** The House of Representatives can _____, or vote to bring serious charges against, a president, vice president, and all civil officers of the United States. (**indict/impeach**)

**14.** Only _____ has the power to declare war. (**Congress/the Senate**)

**PRACTICING SOCIAL STUDIES SKILLS** Study the map below and answer the question that follows.

## The Electoral College

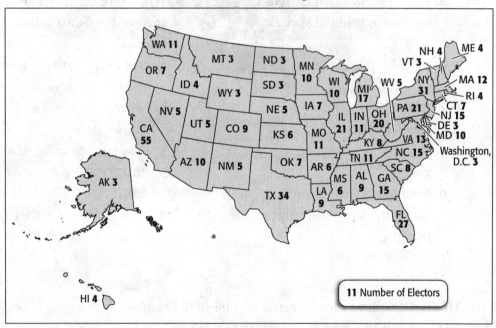

_____ **15.** Based on the map, what can you conclude about the electoral college?

    **a.** New Mexico has a greater number of electoral votes than Kansas.

    **b.** Massachusetts has twice as many electoral votes as Vermont.

    **c.** The number of electors per state is not based on the physical size of the state.

    **d.** The number of electors per state is based on the size of the state's population.

**MATCHING**  In the space provided, write the letter of the term or person that matches each description. Some answers will not be used.

_____ **16.** protects the rights of the accused by requiring that laws be applied fairly

_____ **17.** U.S. government penalty for an immigrant who breaks the law

_____ **18.** gives authorities permission to go through someone's property

_____ **19.** power to take personal property to benefit the public

_____ **20.** Its members fight for a common cause and organize speeches and rallies to support the cause.

_____ **21.** Its members raise money and give it to candidates who support certain issues.

_____ **22.** Supreme Court justice whose appointment to the Court in 1967 made it more diverse

_____ **23.** what a grand jury decides to do if there is enough evidence against a person

_____ **24.** Supreme Court justice who was appointed by President Ronald Reagan in 1981

_____ **25.** divides power between the states and the federal government

**a.** deport

**b.** double jeopardy

**c.** due process

**d.** eminent domain

**e.** federal system

**f.** impeach

**g.** indict

**h.** interest groups

**i.** political action committees (PACs)

**j.** Sandra Day O'Connor

**k.** search warrant

**l.** Thurgood Marshall

**Citizenship and the Constitution**      Chapter Test

**Form B**

**SHORT ANSWER** On a separate sheet of paper, answer each of the following questions in complete sentences.

1. What is the purpose of the doctrine of the separation of powers?

2. How are the rights of naturalized citizens different from the rights of native-born Americans?

3. Why was the Bill of Rights added to the Constitution?

4. A major American newspaper knowingly published a false report that a congressman had used taxpayer money to buy an expensive new car. What might happen to the newspaper?

5. What is the government's power of eminent domain?

**PRACTICING SOCIAL STUDIES SKILLS** Study the passage below and, on a separate sheet of paper, answer the question that follows.

> What political power could ever carry on the vast multitude [large number] of lesser undertakings which the American citizens perform every day, with the assistance of the principle of association [joining a group]? Nothing, in my opinion, is more deserving of our attention than the intellectual and moral associations of America.
>
> —Alexis de Tocqueville

6. In the opinion of Alexis de Tocqueville, why should citizens who are motivated to take political action join political groups?

## Launching the Nation

# Section Quiz

### Section 1

**FILL IN THE BLANK** For each of the following statements, fill in the blank with the appropriate word, phrase, or name.

1. In 1789 the electoral college unanimously selected _____ as the first president of the United States.

2. As president, George Washington established an important precedent by creating different _____ in the executive branch for the various areas of national policy.

3. _____ had to entertain guests and attend social events with her husband.

4. In 1790 most Americans lived in the _____, where they worked on farms.

5. An action or a decision that later serves as an example is a

   _____.

6. The _____ created three levels of federal courts within the judicial branch.

7. Most Americans wanted their new government to improve trade and to

   _____ them.

8. The first capital of the United States was in _____.

9. In the late 1700s, only two cities in the United States had populations greater than 25,000—New York and _____.

10. President Washington picked Alexander Hamilton as his secretary of the treasury

    and _____ as his secretary of state.

Progress Assessment

## Launching the Nation

**TRUE/FALSE** Mark each statement **T** if it is true or **F** if it is false. If false explain why.

_____ **1.** As secretary of the treasury, Alexander Hamilton's biggest challenge was paying off the national debt.

_____

_____

_____ **2.** Thomas Jefferson believed in a strong federal government.

_____

_____

_____ **3.** Alexander Hamilton promoted an economy based on manufacturing and economic growth, while Jefferson believed that agriculture was the key.

_____

_____

_____ **4.** Both Alexander Hamilton and Thomas Jefferson believed the nation needed a national bank and a national mint.

_____

_____

_____ **5.** According to Alexander Hamilton's strict construction of the Constitution, Congress could not create a national bank.

_____

_____

Progress Assessment

**Launching the Nation**                                      Section Quiz

Section 3

**FILL IN THE BLANK** For each of the following statements, fill in the blank with the appropriate term, phrase, or name.

**1.** In 1791 Congress passed a tax on American-made _____ as part of a plan to help pay the federal debt.

**2.** The _____ stated that the United States would not take sides with any European countries at war with one another.

**3.** Supreme Court Chief Justice _____ was sent to negotiate a treaty with Great Britain for damages to American ships.

**4.** Edmond Genet was disappointed when the United States refused to send

_____ to help France fight the British.

**5.** In his Farewell Address, George Washington warned against political divisions,

foreign alliances, and public _____.

**6.** Americans were satisfied with _____ because Spain agreed to change the Florida border and reopen the port at New Orleans.

**7.** In 1790 and 1791 a Native American group under the command of

_____ defeated U.S. forces in the Northwest Territory.

**8.** Many Americans supported the _____ because they believed the French were trying create a democracy.

**9.** The _____ ended the fighting between Native Americans and the U.S. and gave the government right of entry to Native American lands in the Northwest Territory.

**10.** Farmers in western Pennsylvania protested what they believed was an unfair tax

in the _____.

Progress Assessment

## Launching the Nation

**MATCHING** In the space provided, write the letter of the term, place, or person that matches each description. Some answers will not be used.

_____ **1.** He helped found the Federalist Party.

_____ **2.** This party favored a strong federal government and supported industry and trade.

_____ **3.** The election of 1796 saw the development of these groups that help elect people and shape policies.

_____ **4.** These laws allowed the president to remove foreign residents he thought were involved in treason or plots against the government.

_____ **5.** This political party promoted limits to the power of the federal government.

_____ **6.** He won the presidential election of 1796 and became the second president of the United States.

_____ **7.** He lost the election of 1796 and later tried to declare the Alien and Sedition Acts unconstitutional.

_____ **8.** Americans in this region tended to favor limits on the power of the federal government.

_____ **9.** Incident in which French agents asked American officials for a bribe to consider a treaty between the United States and France.

_____ **10.** Problems with this country led many Americans to call for war.

**a.** Alexander Hamilton

**b.** Alien and Sedition Acts

**c.** Democratic-Republican Party

**d.** Federalist Party

**e.** France

**f.** James Madison

**g.** John Adams

**h.** North

**i.** political parties

**j.** South

**k.** Talleyrand Affair

**l.** Thomas Jefferson

**m.** XYZ affair

Progress Assessment

**Launching the Nation**                    Chapter Test

                                             Form A

**MULTIPLE CHOICE** For each of the following, write the letter of the
best choice in the space provided.

_____ **1.** In 1790 how did Americans
feel about the future of their
new government?
**a.** Their expectations were
high because they trusted
their leaders to protect
their economic and secu-
rity interests.
**b.** They were uncertain about
whether the democratic
experiment would
succeed.
**c.** Their expectations were
low because they ques-
tioned the president's honesty and disliked the First
Lady.
**d.** They worried because
they knew the nation was
deeply in debt from the
Revolutionary War.

_____ **2.** Americans wanted George
Washington to be president
because
**a.** he was seen as an honest
leader.
**b.** he urged them to vote for
him.
**c.** he passed the Judiciary Act
of 1789.
**d.** his wife Martha was
popular.

_____ **3.** The Alien and Sedition Acts
were passed by the Federalists
to
**a.** eliminate opposition to
war.
**b.** decrease government
power.
**c.** imprison foreigners.
**d.** punish French speakers.

_____ **4.** Secretary of State Thomas
Jefferson criticized U.S. policy toward France because he
**a.** wanted to allow France to
use American privateers.
**b.** believed the United States
owed France support since
France backed it during
the Revolutionary War.
**c.** thought the United States
could benefit from trade
with France.
**d.** thought it would take
away power from
Alexander Hamilton.

Progress Assessment

_____ **5.** The rivalry between which two political parties dominated the election of 1796?
  **a.** Democrats and Republicans
  **b.** Liberals and Conservatives
  **c.** Democratic-Republicans and Federalists
  **d.** Federalists and Royalists

_____ **6.** The main threat faced by Americans in the Northwest Territories was
  **a.** tornadoes that destroyed much of the farmland.
  **b.** Native American tribes supplied with guns and ammunition by the British.
  **c.** Native American attacks on supply lines into the territories.
  **d.** harsh winter conditions and inadequate forts.

_____ **7.** In the XYZ affair, French agents would
  **a.** sign a treaty in exchange for weapons.
  **b.** accept no amount of money and insist on waging war.
  **c.** sign a treaty in exchange for U.S. territory in the Caribbean.
  **d.** discuss a treaty to protect U.S. shipping in exchange for a bribe.

_____ **8.** Which of these slogans might a Federalist have shouted at a party rally?
  **a.** Central Government over All!
  **b.** States Rule!
  **c.** Power to the People!
  **d.** Jefferson for President!

_____ **9.** President Washington personally led the army against the participants in the Whiskey Rebellion because he felt
  **a.** individual farmers must pay off the national debt through taxes.
  **b.** the federal government was owed taxes for providing settlers with protection and opportunities for trade.
  **c.** people needed to understand the constitutional right of Congress to institute tax laws.
  **d.** the rebellion might spark similar incidents of violence.

**PRACTICING SOCIAL STUDIES SKILLS** Study the quotation below and answer the question that follows.

> "The duty of holding a neutral conduct may be inferred . . . from the obligation which justice and humanity impose on every nation . . . to maintain inviolate [unchanging] the relations of peace and amity [friendship] towards other nations."
>
> —George Washington, from his Farewell Address

_____ **10.** Which statement accurately paraphrases George Washington's views?
   **a.** Washington believed education was key to a strong society.
   **b.** Washington believed that the United States would be torn apart by political parties.
   **c.** Washington felt any just and humane nation would practice neutrality.
   **d.** Washington felt the United States should fight other nations to preserve its freedom.

**TRUE/FALSE** Indicate whether each statement below is true or false by writing **T** or **F** in the space provided.

_____ **11.** George Washington urged the Senate to reject Jay's Treaty.

_____ **12.** In George Washington's farewell address, he warned against making foreign alliances and burdening future generations with debt.

_____ **13.** In 1790 American farmers were independent people who didn't want government interfering in their daily lives.

_____ **14.** Thomas Jefferson felt that the American economy would do best if it relied on agriculture.

_____ **15.** President John Adams wanted to go to war with France, but Congress would not give him approval.

_____ **16.** Repaying the full value of all bonds was part of Alexander Hamilton's economic plan.

_____ **17.** The Judiciary Act of 1789 created three levels of federal courts and defined their powers and relationship to the state courts.

_____ **18.** "Loose construction" is the idea that certain parts of the Constitution do not need to be upheld or enforced.

Progress Assessment

**FILL IN THE BLANK** Read each sentence and fill in the blank with the word in the word pair that best completes the sentence.

19. The _____ is a body of delegates from each state that represents the people's vote in choosing the president.
(**electoral college/democratic convention**)

20. The new federal government in America took actions intended to set an example for the future. In George Washington's words, these exemplary actions would "serve to establish a _____." (**precedent/mandate**)

21. The _____, which deemed the Alien and Sedition Acts unconstitutional, supported the idea that state governments could challenge the federal government.
(**Neutrality Proclamation/Kentucky and Virginia Resolutions**)

22. In 1790, before General Anthony Wayne took command of the American army in the West, Miami chief _____ successfully led an alliance of Native Americans against U.S. forces. (**Tecumseh/Little Turtle**)

23. A _____ adds tax to the price of imported goods to shield domestic products from foreign competition. (**protective tariff/value added tax**)

24. The reason the United States needed to found a _____ was to stabilize the national economy. (**national mint/national bank**)

25. The _____ can best be defined as the amount of money owed by the United States. (**gross domestic product/national debt**)

Progress Assessment

**Launching the Nation**                    Chapter Test

                                                            **Form B**

**SHORT ANSWER** On a separate sheet of paper, answer each of the following questions in complete sentences.

1. Which treaty angered Southerners because it did not repay them for slaves they had lost during the Revolutionary War?

2. The Whiskey Rebellion occurred because farmers in areas such as western Pennsylvania were angry. What was the most direct cause of their anger?

3. How did Alexander Hamilton limit the national bank's power? Why?

4. Why did James Madison criticize the Neutrality Proclamation?

5. "In a democracy, the people, not a group of electors chosen by the states, should choose their leader." A citizen in America's new democracy might have made such a complaint about what?

6. How and why did Alexander Hamilton propose to raise prices on foreign products?

**PRACTICING SOCIAL STUDIES SKILLS** Study the passage below and, on a separate sheet of paper, answer the question that follows.

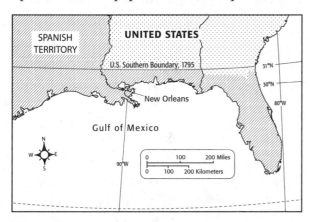

7. What defined the U.S. southern boundary?

Name _____ Class _____ Date _____

# A New Nation

**MULTIPLE CHOICE** For each of the following, write the letter of the best choice in the space provided.

_____ 1. The original purpose of the Constitutional Convention held in May 1787 in Philadelphia's Independence Hall was to
   a. grant citizenship to free African Americans.
   b. draft a Constitution of the United States.
   c. distribute power equally among the states.
   d. improve the Articles of Confederation.

_____ 2. According to George Washington's Farewell Address, what was the key to national success?
   a. political unity
   b. neutrality in foreign policy
   c. economic security
   d. checks and balances

_____ 3. After Shays's Rebellion, Americans admitted that the Articles of Confederation failed to
   a. create limited governments.
   b. uphold the ideals set forth in the Declaration of Independence.
   c. expand suffrage to include women.
   d. preserve the rights laid out in the Magna Carta.

_____ 4. Which statement best characterizes American farmers in 1790?
   a. They didn't want government interfering in their daily lives.
   b. They took every opportunity to organize and participate in community events.
   c. They wanted to have their tax money distributed to those less fortunate.
   d. They refused to accept any law designed to protect them from foreign rivals.

_____ 5. An amendment to the Constitution is
   a. a suggested addition.
   b. an official change.
   c. a legal clarification.
   d. a judicial opinion.

_____ 6. How was a vice president chosen in 1796?
   a. He ran alongside the presidential candidate.
   b. He was elected by popular vote.
   c. He was the presidential candidate who came in second.
   d. He was appointed by the president-elect.

Progress Assessment

_____ **7.** What is federalism?
  **a.** a government system in which the central government holds supreme power
  **b.** a system that keeps each branch of government from obtaining too much power
  **c.** the sharing of power between a central government and the states of a country
  **d.** the part of government responsible for making the laws of a country or nation

_____ **8.** How does a search warrant protect a person's individual rights?
  **a.** It allows law enforcement agents to preserve evidence in emergency situations.
  **b.** It permits the victim of a theft or burglary to make a citizen's arrest of the criminal at any time.
  **c.** It requires authorities to repay citizens whose property is taken for public use.
  **d.** It guards someone suspected of a crime from having officials go though their property for no reason.

_____ **9.** Which of these contributed to the Whiskey Rebellion?
  **a.** The federal government was overprotective of the settlers.
  **b.** Spain was blocking trade along the Mississippi River.
  **c.** Farmers could not afford the tax on whiskey.
  **d.** Farmers found whiskey difficult to transport.

_____ **10.** The Virginia Statute for Religious Freedom was one of the earliest expressions of which basic principle of American government?
  **a.** equality of opportunity
  **b.** freedom of speech
  **c.** separation of church and state
  **d.** due process of law

_____ **11.** Concurrent powers, or those shared by the states and the federal government, include the powers to
  **a.** coin money and regulate trade.
  **b.** tax, borrow money, and enforce laws.
  **c.** create local governments and hold elections.
  **d.** draft an army and conduct foreign policy.

_____ **12.** Citizens accept responsibility for protecting others' Sixth Amendment rights to a public trial by
- **a.** serving on juries.
- **b.** watching court cases on television.
- **c.** reading newspapers.
- **d.** discussing court cases with friends.

_____ **13.** People who buy items at low prices and hope to sell them for a profit are called
- **a.** delegates.
- **b.** representatives.
- **c.** bondholders.
- **d.** speculators.

_____ **14.** Which of these duties of a citizen is encouraged, but not required?
- **a.** serving on a jury
- **b.** paying taxes
- **c.** signing up for the draft
- **d.** voting in elections

_____ **15.** Interstate commerce is the act of
- **a.** states following their own trade interests.
- **b.** states having different trade laws.
- **c.** trade between two or more states.
- **d.** setting tariffs on trade between states.

_____ **16.** To which person or group did the framers of the Constitution grant legislative power?
- **a.** Congress
- **b.** the President
- **c.** the Supreme Court
- **d.** state governments

_____ **17.** What is an executive order?
- **a.** a presidential command that has the power of law
- **b.** a judicial ruling that frees those convicted of federal offenses
- **c.** a congressional override of a president's veto
- **d.** a declaration of war by any elected official in the president's cabinet

_____ **18.** What is the electoral college?
- **a.** a body of delegates from each state that represents the people's vote in choosing the president
- **b.** a school for the advanced study of voting practices and political campaigning
- **c.** a group of voters hand-picked for cabinet positions by the president-elect
- **d.** a name given to all voters who cast ballots in presidential elections

**PRACTICING SOCIAL STUDIES SKILLS** Study the quotation below and
answer the question that follows.

> What political power could ever carry on the vast multitude [large
> number] of lesser undertakings which the American citizens perform
> every day, with the assistance of the principle of association [joining
> a group]? Nothing, in my opinion, is more deserving of our attention
> than the intellectual and moral associations of America.
>
> —Alexis de Tocqueville

_____ **19.** In the opinion of the French diplomat Alexis de Tocqueville, why should
American citizens motivated to take political action become members of
interest groups?
  **a.** Interest groups have greater access to political candidates than any single individual.
  **b.** Political associations do important work that even the largest government could not accomplish on its own.
  **c.** The best answer to propaganda is intelligent material that expresses the
values of unified citizens.
  **d.** Money is essential to the functioning of democracy and groups can
raise more cash than any individual.

**FILL IN THE BLANK** Read each sentence and fill in the blank with the
word in the word pair that best completes the sentence.

**20.** Signed in 1215, the _____ made the king subject to law.
**(Magna Carta/Articles of Confederation)**

**21.** Great Britain forced American merchants to pay high _____
on imports and exports and closed many of its ports to American ships in the late
1700s. **(tariffs/insurance)**

**22.** The _____ led a forced shutdown of the Supreme Court
in Springfield, Massachusetts to protest the way the state had decided to pay its
debts. **(Daniel Shays/James Wilson)**

**23.** A series of anonymously written essays called the _____
tried to reassure Americans that a strong central government would not
overpower the states. **(Federalist Papers/Articles of Confederation)**

**24.** The Three-Fifths Compromise helped settle the debate over

_____ at the Constitutional Convention.

**(representation/taxation)**

**25.** The Second Continental Congress passed the Articles of Confederation, the new

national constitution on November 15, 1777. Then it sent the Articles to each

state legislature for _____, or official approval.

**(amendment/ratification)**

**26.** In the United States in the late 1700s, inflation and the loss of trade with Great

Britain led to a period of low economic activity and high unemployment called a

_____. **(depression/national debt)**

**27.** To stop larger states from gaining too much power in the federal govern-

ment, William Paterson proposed the _____ Plan at the

Constitutional Convention. **(Virginia/New Jersey)**

**28.** _____ opposed the Constitution because they thought it

gave too much power to the central government. **(Federalists/Antifederalists)**

**29.** Under the Articles of Confederation, Congress passed the

_____, which created a system for bringing new states into

the Union. **(Land Ordinance of 1785/Northwest Ordinance of 1787)**

**TRUE/FALSE** Indicate whether each statement below is true or false by writing **T** or **F** in the space provided.

_____ **30.** According to Thomas Jefferson and James Madison, the most serious flaw in Alexander Hamilton's plan for a national bank was that it would not help the economy grow.

_____ **31.** Supreme Court decisions can be vetoed by the president and overridden by Congress.

_____ **32.** Supporters of gun-control laws have generally argued that the Second Amendment was designed to protect the individual's right to self-defense.

_____ **33.** Once someone has become a naturalized U.S. citizen, it is impossible for his or her citizenship to be taken away.

_____ **34.** The framers of the Constitution set up a federal system to make the government more elastic, or flexible.

_____ **35.** James Madison's promise to add a bill of rights to the Constitution made it possible for the document to pass.

_____ **36.** Two-thirds of both houses of Congress must vote in favor of a bill in order to override a president's veto.

_____ **37.** Private citizens can only influence government if they act as members of interest groups.

_____ **38.** According to the Constitution, the vice president plays the role of president of the Senate.

_____ **39.** A person accused of a serious crime cannot be tried in a court of law unless he or she has been indicted by a grand jury.

_____ **40.** The right to a prompt and fair trial is protected by the Bill of Rights.

Progress Assessment

**MATCHING** In the space provided, write the letter of the term or person that matches each description. Some answers will not be used.

_____ **41.** signed in November 1794 to settle disputes between the United States and Britain that arose in the early 1790s

_____ **42.** signed in October 1795 to settle border and trade disputes between the United States and Spain

_____ **43.** supported the idea that states could challenge the federal government

_____ **44.** gave the United States claim to most Native American lands in the Northwest Territory

_____ **45.** rebellion of French people against their king in 1789

_____ **46.** set of laws passed by the Federalist-controlled Congress in 1798 to crush opposition to war

_____ **47.** Congress enacted its charter in February 1791 to make the economy more stable

_____ **48.** bribery scandal that caused Federalists in Congress to call for war with France

_____ **49.** set up the federal court system and the court's location

_____ **50.** fight between General Wayne's troops and Native Americans that ended the frontier war

**a.** Judiciary Act of 1789

**b.** Pinckney's Treaty

**c.** Alien and Sedition Acts

**d.** Kentucky and Virginia Resolutions

**e.** Jay's Treaty

**f.** French Revolution

**g.** Battle of Fallen Timbers

**h.** Treaty of Greenville

**i.** Bank of the United States

**j.** XYZ Affair

**k.** the U.S. Mint

**l.** Martha Washington

**SHORT ANSWER** On a separate sheet of paper, answer each of the following questions in complete sentences.

1. Why did the Antifederalists oppose the Constitution?

2. What did the Virginia Statute for Religious Freedom state?

3. How does the president keep the Congress in check?

4. What is majority rule and how can it interfere with the protection of people's individual rights? Give an example.

5. Alexander Hamilton argued against Thomas Jefferson's and James Madison's criticisms of his plans for a national bank on the basis of his belief in "loose construction." What is "loose construction" and how did Hamilton use it to his advantage?

6. Who issued the Neutrality Proclamation and what did it state?

**PRACTICING SOCIAL STUDIES SKILLS** Study the chart below and, on a separate sheet of paper, answer the question that follows.

**Urban vs. Rural
Population, 1790**

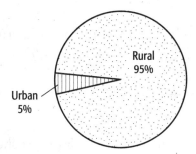

7. This chart depicts the urban and rural population of the United States in 1790. Where did five out of every 100 Americans live?

## The Jefferson Era

Section Quiz

### Section 1

**FILL IN THE BLANK** For each of the following statements, fill in the blank with the appropriate word, phrase, or name.

1. In the presidential election of 1800, Republicans Thomas Jefferson and

   _____ each received the same number of electoral votes.

2. The _____ broke the tie in the election of 1800 when Jefferson won on the thirty-sixth vote.

3. Jefferson wanted to limit the powers of the national _____.

4. The election of 1800 was important because it was the first time that one

   _____ had replaced another in power in the United States.

5. Under Jefferson, Congress allowed the _____ to expire.

6. Even though he had originally opposed it, Jefferson agreed to support the

   _____ which the Federalists had created.

7. Chief Justice _____ wrote the Supreme Court opinion that established the Court's power to check the power of the other branches of government.

8. _____ was an important Supreme Court ruling because it confirmed the Court's power to declare acts of Congress illegal.

9. The principle of _____ made the judiciary a much stronger part of the national government.

10. As president, Jefferson believed that the national government should be

    _____.

Progress Assessment

**The Jefferson Era**

**TRUE/FALSE** Mark each statement **T** if it is true or **F** if it is false. If false explain why.

_____ **1.** The Louisiana Purchase nearly tripled the size of the United States.

_____

_____

_____ **2.** King Louis XVI of France offered to sell the Louisiana Territory to the United States because he needed money for his war with Great Britain.

_____

_____

_____ **3.** Expeditions into western territories greatly increased American knowledge of the West.

_____

_____

_____ **4.** President Jefferson sent Meriwether Lewis and Zebulon Pike to explore the Louisiana Territory and to look for a river route to the Pacific Ocean.

_____

_____

_____ **5.** New Orleans was very important because many American goods passed through its port at the mouth of the Mississippi River.

_____

_____

Progress Assessment

# The Jefferson Era

Section Quiz

### Section 3

**MATCHING** In the space provided, write the letter of the term, place, or person that matches each description. Some answers will not be used.

_____ 1. Many Americans believed that this country was behind efforts to provide military aid to Native Americans in the western frontier.

_____ 2. Americans were angered by this British practice of forcing people to serve in their army or navy.

_____ 3. He asked Congress to declare war against Great Britain in 1812.

_____ 4. This law passed in 1807 greatly damaged Native Americans trade and hurt President Jefferson's popularity.

_____ 5. This Shawnee chief hoped to unite American Indians in the Northwest Territory against the United States.

_____ 6. He was the governor of Indiana Territory who defeated a union of Native Americans at the Battle of Tippecanoe.

_____ 7. Members of Congress who called for war against Britain were known as this.

_____ 8. This U.S. warship was built to protect American merchant ships from attack.

_____ 9. War between Great Britain and this country led to many problems for the United States.

_____ 10. This law, which replaced a previous ban on trade, outlawed trade with Britain, France, and their colonies.

**a.** Embargo Act

**b.** France

**c.** Geronimo

**d.** Great Britain

**e.** impressment

**f.** James Madison

**g.** Non-Intercourse Act

**h.** Spain

**i.** Tecumseh

**j.** Thomas Jefferson

**k.** USS *Constitution*

**l.** War Hawks

**m.** William Henry Harrison

Progress Assessment

**The Jefferson Era**

Section Quiz

**Section 4**

**FILL IN THE BLANK** For each of the following statements, fill in the blank with the appropriate word, phrase, or name.

**1.** In 1812, the United States and _____ went to war.

**2.** As a result of the decline in trade during the war, _____ in the United States was forced to grow.

**3.** Captain _____ was given the task of breaking Britain's control of Lake Erie.

**4.** The Battle of _____ was the last major conflict of the War of 1812.

**5.** As commander of the Tennessee militia, _____ defeated the Creek Indians at the Battle of Horseshoe Bend.

**6.** President Madison was forced to flee when the British attacked

_____ and set fire to many government buildings.

**7.** A disadvantage the United States faced in the war was that it's

_____ was not as large or as powerful as that of Great Britain.

**8.** The _____ was a gathering of New England Federalists who opposed the war.

**9.** Signed in Belgium on December 24, 1814, the _____ ended the War of 1812.

**10.** One of the positive effects of the war was that it increased a feeling of

_____ among Americans.

Progress Assessment

**The Jefferson Era**

Chapter Test

Form A

**MULTIPLE CHOICE** For each of the following, write the letter of the best choice in the space provided.

_____ 1. Which Federalist policy did President Jefferson keep when he took office?
  a. tax on whiskey
  b. Alien and Sedition Acts
  c. development of military forces
  d. Bank of the United States

_____ 2. Which of the following was a major theme of Thomas Jefferson's inaugural address?
  a. protecting civil liberties
  b. expanding the powers of government
  c. improving the capital's infrastructure
  d. repaying the national debt

_____ 3. What was one effect of the Battle of Tippecanoe in 1811?
  a. Tecumseh lost hope for a great Indian confederation.
  b. The British began to support the Native American rebels.
  c. Tecumseh was forced to sign the Treaty of Greenville.
  d. The United States began to pay more for Native American land.

_____ 4. Napoléon Bonaparte decided to sell the Louisiana Territory to the United States to
  a. gain U.S. support for France's war against Spain.
  b. ensure land would be set aside for Native Americans.
  c. reinforce military forces in the war against the British.
  d. extend the French empire into North America.

_____ 5. What was one reason that led New England Federalists to oppose the war against Britain?
  a. War would hurt southern planters and western farmers.
  b. Good relations with the British were essential to the health of New England's economy.
  c. The federal government should not increase the national debt caused by the Revolutionary War.
  d. The majority of the American people opposed the war.

Progress Assessment

_____ 6. Judicial review refers to the power of
  a. Congress to oversee decisions made by the Supreme Court.
  b. Congress to review the appointment of Supreme Court justices.
  c. the Supreme Court to declare an act of Congress unconstitutional.
  d. the judiciary to monitor the conduct of presidential elections.

_____ 7. Which of the following territories belonged to Spain until 1802?
  a. Indiana
  b. Mississippi
  c. Louisiana
  d. Michigan

_____ 8. Which of the following brought about the increase in trade in New Orleans in the early 1800s?
  a. an economic boom and commercial upswing in Spain
  b. France's threat of permanently shutting down the port
  c. an increase in settlers in states such as Kentucky, Tennessee, and Ohio
  d. Spain's potential sale of the port to the United States

_____ 9. Why was the Hartford Convention ineffective?
  a. The Federalists had increased their political power.
  b. Congress deemed the convention illegal.
  c. The war ended before the delegates could reach Washington.
  d. Their political rivals accused Federalists of supporting England.

_____ 10. What was one effect of the Embargo Act passed by Congress in 1807?
  a. More American ports were opened.
  b. American merchants lost money.
  c. British merchant ships were allowed to sail only into New Orleans.
  d. Foreign imports were allowed, but U.S. exports came to an end.

_____ 11. What did the Twelfth Amendment do after the Election of 1800?
  a. let the Supreme Court cast the deciding vote in deadlocked elections
  b. allowed Americans overseas to vote by mail
  c. abolished the practice of counting ballots by hand
  d. created a separate ballot for president and vice president

**MATCHING** In the space provided, write the letter of the term or person that matches each description. Some answers will not be used.

_____ **12.** led the way for an American invasion of Canada

_____ **13.** resulted in the end of British power in the Northwest

_____ **14.** ended the War of 1812

_____ **15.** last major conflict of the War of 1812

_____ **16.** Shawnee leader who worked to unite Native Americans against U.S. expansion

_____ **17.** led a naval fleet to victory against the British at the Battle of Lake Erie

_____ **18.** ended the Creek War and forced the Creek Indians to give up millions of acres of land

_____ **19.** commanded U.S. forces in the Battle of New Orleans

_____ **20.** Shoshone Indian who assisted the Lewis and Clark expedition

**a.** Battle of the Thames River

**b.** Battle of New Orleans

**c.** Battle of Lake Erie

**d.** Embargo Act

**e.** Andrew Jackson

**f.** Merriwether Lewis

**g.** Oliver Hazard Perry

**h.** Zebulon Pike

**i.** Sacagawea

**j.** Tecumseh

**k.** the Treaty of Fort Jackson

**l.** the Treaty of Ghent

**FILL IN THE BLANK** Read each sentence and fill in the blank with the word in the word pair that best completes the sentence.

**21.** In the hotly contested election of 1800, supporters of _____ claimed that a Thomas Jefferson presidency would bring to America the chaos of the French Revolution. (**John Marshall/John Adams**)

**22.** The first young members of Congress to call for a trade war against Britain were called _____. (**War Hawks/Warlords**)

**23.** _____ is the practice of forcing people to serve in the army or navy. (**Embargo/Impressment**)

**24.** In order to continue their control over the judiciary after the election of President

Jefferson, _____ legislators passed the Judiciary Act of 1801.

**(Democratic-Republican/Federalist)**

**PRACTICING SOCIAL STUDIES SKILLS**   Read the quotation below and
answer the question that follows.

> "The only way to stop this evil is for all the red men to unite in claim-
> ing a common and equal right to the land, as it was at first, and should
> be yet. Before, the land never was divided, but belonged to all, for
> the use of each person. No group had a right to sell, not even to each
> other, much less to strangers who want all and will not do with less."
>
> —Tecumseh

_____ **25.** Which of the following statements best describes Tecumseh's feelings
about western settlement?
   **a.** White settlers should sell land to Native Americans.
   **b.** Native Americans should unite to oppose white settlement.
   **c.** Native Americans and white settlers should be allowed to divide and
   sell land.
   **d.** White settlers should compromise by giving some land to Native
   Americans and selling more desirable land.

# The Jefferson Era

**SHORT ANSWER** On a separate sheet of paper, answer each of the following questions in complete sentences.

1. What was the significance of the case of *Marbury* v. *Madison*?

2. Which U.S. activity led the nation to get involved in the war between Britain and France when it broke out in 1803?

3. Why did the Embargo Act fail?

4. Why was the Louisiana Purchase significant to the United States?

5. Which battle destroyed Tecumseh's dream of a great Indian confederation?

6. What arguments did New England Federalists make against going to war with Britain in 1812?

**PRACTICING SOCIAL STUDIES SKILLS** Study the map below and, on a separate sheet of paper, answer the question that follows.

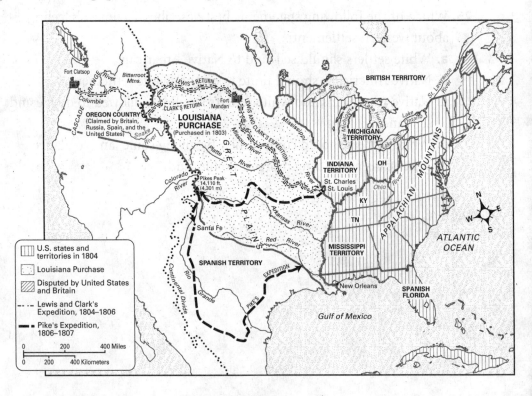

7. Along what river did Lewis and Clark travel for most of their expedition?

Progress Assessment

# A New National Identity

**TRUE/FALSE** Mark each statement **T** if it is true or **F** if it is false. If false explain why.

_____ **1.** The Rush-Bagot Agreement established the border between the United States and Canada.

_____

_____

_____ **2.** Thanks to the efforts of Secretary of State John Quincy Adams, the United States acquired Florida from Spain.

_____

_____

_____ **3.** The First Seminole War began when the United States tried to force the Seminole Indians to move to Spanish Florida.

_____

_____

_____ **4.** Most Americans did not support the revolutions for independence in Latin America.

_____

_____

_____ **5.** The Monroe Doctrine warned Latin American nations not to interfere with the politics of European nations.

_____

_____

Progress Assessment

**A New National Identity**

**MATCHING** In the space provided, write the letter of the term, place, or person that matches each description. Some answers will not be used.

_____ **1.** This state's application for statehood caused regional conflicts over the issue of slavery.

_____ **2.** He was a U.S. representative from Kentucky who supported nationalism and the American System.

_____ **3.** He became the sixth President of the United States after his victory in the election of 1824.

_____ **4.** This agreement prohibited slavery in any state or territory north of 36°30' latitude.

_____ **5.** This period was characterized by peace, pride, and progress.

_____ **6.** This transportation project ran from Albany to Buffalo, New York.

_____ **7.** This develops when people favor regional interests over those of a nation as a whole.

_____ **8.** This was the first road project built by the national government.

_____ **9.** This plan called for using tariff money to improve roads and canals.

_____ **10.** In the election of 1824, this candidate won the popular vote, but did not have enough electoral votes to win the election.

**a.** American System

**b.** Andrew Jackson

**c.** Cumberland Road

**d.** Era of Good Feelings

**e.** Erie Canal

**f.** Great Compromise

**g.** Henry Clay

**h.** John Quincy Adams

**i.** Maine

**j.** Missouri

**k.** Missouri Compromise

**l.** partisan politics

**m.** sectionalism

Progress Assessment

Name _____ Class _____ Date _____

**A New National Identity**                    Section Quiz

**MULTIPLE CHOICE** For each of the following, write the letter of the best choice in the space provided.

_____ **1.** Of the following, who was the first to gain international fame as a writer?
   **a.** George Washington
   **b.** Washington Irving
   **c.** Thomas Cole
   **d.** George Caleb Bingham

_____ **2.** James Fenimore Cooper popularized what type of writing?
   **a.** short story
   **b.** non-fiction
   **c.** autobiography
   **d.** historical fiction

_____ **3.** What type of songs were popular at religious revival meetings?
   **a.** ballads
   **b.** anthems
   **c.** spirituals
   **d.** battle hymns

_____ **4.** What art movement focused on national pride and appreciation of the American landscape?
   **a.** American school
   **b.** nationalism
   **c.** Hudson River school
   **d.** naturalism

_____ **5.** What type of schools began to gain support in the U.S. in the 1800s?
   **a.** state-funded schools
   **b.** private schools
   **c.** schools for women
   **d.** elementary schools

Progress Assessment

## A New National Identity

**MULTIPLE CHOICE** For each of the following, write the letter of the best choice in the space provided.

_____ **1.** Conflicts arose in the early 1800s between the United States and the Seminole Indian tribe in Florida because that tribe
  **a.** refused to leave Florida and attacked U.S. military posts.
  **b.** had refused to support U.S. efforts in the War of 1812.
  **c.** aided Spain in its conquest of Florida.
  **d.** raided U.S. settlements and aided runaway slaves.

_____ **2.** Which of the following statements best describes the election of 1824?
  **a.** Most people thought Andrew Jackson was a corrupt politician.
  **b.** Andrew Jackson won the popular vote but did not have enough electoral votes to win office.
  **c.** The legislature appealed to the Supreme Court to decide the election.
  **d.** Many people based their votes on their opinions about slavery.

_____ **3.** During the 1820s, sectionalism grew in the United States because
  **a.** citizens developed increased feelings of devotion to their nation.
  **b.** politicians disagreed over the interests of different regions.
  **c.** the federal government placed slaves on reservations to prevent conflict.
  **d.** many states separated from the nation and declared their independence.

_____ **4.** The primary goal of Henry Clay's American System was to
  **a.** prevent foreign wars from affecting the United States.
  **b.** industrialize the smaller towns in the United States.
  **c.** create a sense of nationalism in the United States.
  **d.** make the United States economically independent.

Progress Assessment

_____ **5.** What are spirituals?
  **a.** nationalistic anthems
  **b.** folk hymns
  **c.** medieval church songs
  **d.** Native American prayers

_____ **6.** In the early 1800s, education reforms resulted from the new American culture's views on education, which
  **a.** held the belief that education was mainly for the wealthy, so many boarding schools were founded.
  **b.** was a democracy that needed educated and informed citizens to survive, so public schools were supported.
  **c.** was interested in training people to enter the workforce, so value was placed on learning a trade.
  **d.** held the belief that people should be educated regardless of gender, so coeducational schools were founded.

_____ **7.** Which issue caused disagreement among educators in the 1830s?
  **a.** coeducation
  **b.** funding
  **c.** integration
  **d.** school prayer

_____ **8.** Which of the following best describes Thomas Cole?
  **a.** became famous for the short stories "Rip Van Winkle"
  **b.** American poet who wrote about frontier life
  **c.** landscape artist who founded the Hudson River school
  **d.** artist whose work depicted realistic images of everyday life

_____ **9.** What compromise did the United States and Spain reach in the Adams-Onís Treaty?
  **a.** The U.S. would receive the Missouri Territory from Spain in return for parts of the Oregon Country.
  **b.** The U.S. would receive control of East Florida from Spain in return for U.S. claims to what is now Texas.
  **c.** Spain would make Texas an independent territory.
  **d.** Spain would pay $5 million to the U.S.

Progress Assessment

**PRACTICING SOCIAL STUDIES SKILLS** Study the map below and
answer the question that follows.

### The Missouri Compromise

_____ **10.** As a result of the Missouri Compromise, Missouri entered the Union as a
- **a.** free state.
- **b.** free territory.
- **c.** slave state.
- **d.** slave territory.

**FILL IN THE BLANK** Read each sentence and fill in the blank with the
word in the word pair that best completes the sentence.

**11.** _____ was an American writer whose satirical writings
warned Americans to learn from the past and be cautious about the future.
(**James Fenimore Cooper/Washington Irving**)

**12.** The _____ was a compromise between Great Britain and
the United States that limited naval power on the Great Lakes for both countries.
(**Rush-Bagot Agreement/Adams-Onís Treaty**)

**13.** The _____ was a group of artists whose paintings showed
national pride and an appreciation for the American landscape.
(**Hudson River school/Audubon Society**)

**14.** The _____ was an official statement released by the president in 1822 that warned European powers not to interfere with the Americas. (**Missouri Compromise/Monroe Doctrine**)

**15.** The House of Representatives chose _____ as president in the election of 1842. (**John C. Calhoun/John Quincy Adams**)

**16.** The _____ was a period of peace, pride, and progress in the United States that lasted from 1815 to 1825. (**Era of Good Feelings/Second Enlightenment**)

**17.** The _____ ran from Albany to Buffalo, New York, and allowed people and goods to travel quickly by water between towns on the East Coast. (**Hudson River/Erie Canal**)

**18.** _____ strengthened ties between the United States and Latin America and led the country during its period of nationalism. (**James Monroe/John Quincy Adams**)

**TRUE/FALSE** Indicate whether each statement below is true or false by writing **T** or **F** in the space provided.

_____ **19.** The United States wanted sole control over Oregon Country to profit from the fertile farmland and good climate of the region.

_____ **20.** Following the American Revolution, Americans began to model architecture in the United States after the styles used in ancient Greece and Rome.

_____ **21.** General Andrew Jackson's presence in Florida angered Spanish leaders who refused to give up territory to the United States.

_____ **22.** During the early and mid-1800s, Americans went through a period of religious revivalism in which reawakening of religious faith was promoted.

_____ **23.** In the years following the American Revolution, songs called spirituals focused on everyday life.

_____ **24.** After the American Revolution, American writers began to create works that focused solely on European traditions and society.

_____ **25.** George Caleb Bingham's paintings depicted scenes from the American frontier.

Name _____ Class _____ Date _____

## A New National Identity

**SHORT ANSWER** On a separate sheet of paper, answer each of the following questions in complete sentences.

1. What did the Monroe Doctrine state?

2. Which American leader developed a plan known as the American System?

3. Why was maintaining a balance of slave and free states in the Union important to the authors of the Missouri Compromise?

4. What is a type of folk hymn that developed from the practice of calling out text from the Bible?

5. How did the writings of Washington Irving inspire painters in the United States?

6. During the early and mid-1800s, how did religion change in the United States?

**PRACTICING SOCIAL STUDIES SKILLS** Study the map below and, on a separate sheet of paper, answer the question that follows.

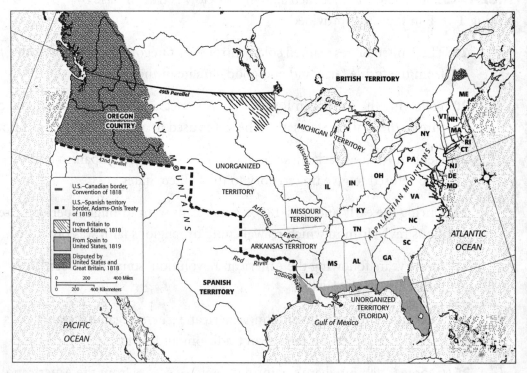

7. According to this map, what states or regions are included in the land disputed by the United States and Great Britain in 1818?

Progress Assessment

# The Age of Jackson

## Section Quiz

### Section 1

**FILL IN THE BLANK** For each of the following statements, fill in the blank with the appropriate word, phrase, or name.

1. Despite a loosening of voting requirements in the early 1800s,

   _____ and free blacks were still not given the right to vote.

2. As president, Andrew Jackson replaced less than one-fifth of federal

   _____ with his supporters.

3. Historians refer to the expansion of voting rights that took place in the early

   1800s as _____.

4. Andrew Jackson's informal group of advisors was known as the

   _____ because of the room in which they met.

5. In the presidential election of 1828, Adams ran as a National Republican while

   Jackson ran as a _____.

6. Andrew Jackson's campaign in the 1828 election relied on his image as a

   _____.

7. As secretary of state, _____ was one of Andrew Jackson's
   strongest supporters.

8. The supporters of _____ tended to be farmers, frontier settlers, and southern slaveholders.

9. Andrew Jackson defeated _____ in the election of 1828.

10. In the early 1800s state legislatures began making changes that broadened

    _____ by giving more people the right to vote.

# The Age of Jackson

**MATCHING** In the space provided, write the letter of the term, person, or place that matches each description. Some answers will not be used.

_____ 1. Although this man won the presidential election of 1836, he became unpopular as a result of the Panic of 1837.

_____ 2. Because this region relied on manufacturing, it supported high tariffs on imported goods.

_____ 3. This doctrine promotes the power of the states over the power of the federal government.

_____ 4. This Massachusetts senator stressed the need for the country to remain united.

_____ 5. President Jackson strongly opposed this institution and vetoed its renewal.

_____ 6. This region's economy was based on farming, especially of cash crops like tobacco and cotton.

_____ 7. John C. Calhoun resigned from the vice presidency as a result of this historical event.

_____ 8. Southerners opposed this act of Congress because it led to very high rates for imported manufactured goods.

_____ 9. A hero from the Battle of Tippecanoe, this man won the presidential election of 1840.

_____ 10. These differences are based on where people live and the economy in those areas. With nothing to overcome them they can give rise to sectionalism.

**a.** Daniel Webster

**b.** federalism

**c.** Martin Van Buren

**d.** North

**e.** Nullification Crisis

**f.** Panic of 1837

**g.** Second Bank of the United States

**h.** regional

**i.** South

**j.** states' rights

**k.** Tariff of Abominations

**l.** West

**m.** William Henry Harrison

Progress Assessment

Name _____ Class _____ Date _____

# The Age of Jackson

Section Quiz

**Section 3**

**MULTIPLE CHOICE** For each of the following, write the letter of the best choice in the space provided.

_____ 1. Why did the American government want to remove Native Americans?
   **a.** to open up more land for settlement by American farmers
   **b.** to protect the borders
   **c.** to end conflict with American settlers
   **d.** to force them to adopt American culture

_____ 2. What Native Americans were affected by the Indian Removal Act of 1830?
   **a.** those living in Indian Territory
   **b.** those living in New England
   **c.** those who could not speak English
   **d.** those living east of the Mississippi River

_____ 3. How did the Cherokee try to prevent conflict with Americans?
   **a.** by peacefully leaving their lands
   **b.** by filing a lawsuit against the government
   **c.** by adopting American culture
   **d.** by purchasing their lands

_____ 4. Which Native American group was led on the Trail of Tears?
   **a.** Chickasaw
   **b.** Sauk
   **c.** Cherokee
   **d.** Choctaw

_____ 5. How did President Jackson respond to the Supreme Court's ruling in *Worcester* v. *Georgia*?
   **a.** He ignored it.
   **b.** He sent the army to enforce it.
   **c.** He led an attack on Cherokee settlements.
   **d.** He vetoed it.

Progress Assessment

**The Age of Jackson**

**MULTIPLE CHOICE** For each of the following, write the letter of the best choice in the space provided.

_____ **1.** How did President Andrew Jackson react to Vice President John C. Calhoun's views on nullification?
   **a.** commended Calhoun because he supported nullification
   **b.** disagreed with Calhoun but refused to publicly oppose nullification
   **c.** openly disagreed with Calhoun and watched as Calhoun resigned
   **d.** fired Calhoun over the issue and forced duty collection on the South

_____ **2.** Though the economic policies adopted by President Jackson before the Panic of 1837 did not fix the country's economic problems, they did
   **a.** decrease inflation.
   **b.** privatize state banks.
   **c.** lower the national debt.
   **d.** help mend relations with banks.

_____ **3.** Which of the following statements describes the social situation of the United States before Jacksonian Democracy?
   **a.** Hundreds of craftspeople were opening shops in the cities.
   **b.** Small farmers were profiting from new technologies.
   **c.** Power was in the hands of a few wealthy individuals.
   **d.** Ordinary Americans were gaining a voice in government.

_____ **4.** Which of the following describes the frontier West in the early 1800s?
   **a.** relied heavily on trade with Britain
   **b.** suffered from low property values
   **c.** only limited types of crops farmed
   **d.** lacked services such as roads and water

_____ **5.** The Bureau of Indian Affairs was a

    **a.** congressionally-approved office established to protect Native Americans.

    **b.** federal government agency created to manage the removal of Native Americans to the West.

    **c.** federal government agency designed to negotiate with Creek and Chickasaw Indians.

    **d.** group established by the Mississippi legislature to track Native American deaths.

_____ **6.** Which group did Osceola lead against U.S. troops?

    **a.** Sauk

    **b.** Fox

    **c.** Cherokee

    **d.** Seminole

_____ **7.** Northerners supported tariffs in the early 1800s because tariffs helped them compete with

    **a.** British merchants.

    **b.** southern agriculturalists.

    **c.** British manufacturers.

    **d.** southern manufacturers.

_____ **8.** What did the Seminole Indians do after signing a treaty in 1832 in which they agreed to leave Florida within three years?

    **a.** immediately gave up their land

    **b.** respected the treaty and headed west

    **c.** ignored the treaty and resisted removal with force

    **d.** stayed in Florida and adopted white culture

_____ **9.** Martin Van Buren's success in the presidential election of 1837 can be attributed to the

    **a.** popularity of his stand against a domineering presidency.

    **b.** successful economic policies of his predecessor.

    **c.** inability of the opposing party to decide on one candidate.

    **d.** confidence inspired by his past as an army general.

**PRACTICING SOCIAL STUDIES SKILLS** Study the map below and answer the question that follows.

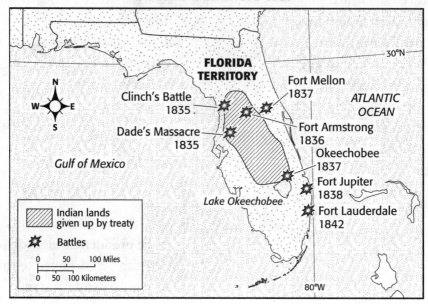

## Second Seminole War

_____ **10.** Which of the following battles of the Second Seminole War occurred first?
   **a.** Fort Jupiter
   **b.** Fort Mellon
   **c.** Okeechobee
   **d.** Clinch's Battle

**TRUE/FALSE** Indicate whether each statement below is true or false by writing **T** or **F** in the space provided.

_____ **11.** Andrew Jackson won many votes at the 1828 presidential election because he was Harvard-educated and his father had been the second U.S. president.

_____ **12.** The Kitchen Cabinet refers to a group of President Jackson's advisors who sometimes met in the White House kitchen.

_____ **13.** Sequoya was a Cherokee Chief who led hundreds of Native Americans during the Trail of Tears.

_____ **14.** The debate over the so-called Tariff of Abominations saw the North and South united against the federal government.

_____ **15.** The Whig Party favored a strong president and a weak Congress.

_____ **16.** The nullification crisis sparked a dispute over the right of the states to reject a federal law as unconstitutional.

**MATCHING**  In the space provided, write the letter of the term, person, or place that matches each description. Some answers will not be used.

_____ **17.** Native American leader who decided to fight U.S. officials rather than leave Illinois

_____ **18.** stated that only the federal government had authority over Native Americans

_____ **19.** forced march to Indian Territory taken by the Cherokee

_____ **20.** advanced the states' rights doctrine

_____ **21.** ruled that the national bank was constitutional

_____ **22.** practice of rewarding loyal supporters with government jobs

_____ **23.** argued that the United States was one nation, not a pact among independent states

_____ **24.** U.S. land in present-day Oklahoma

_____ **25.** one of Andrew Jackson's strongest allies in his official cabinet

**a.** Black Hawk

**b.** John C. Calhoun

**c.** William Henry Harrison

**d.** Indian Territory

**e.** Kitchen Cabinet

**f.** *McCulloch* v. *Maryland*

**g.** Osceola

**h.** spoils system

**i.** Trail of Tears

**j.** Martin Van Buren

**k.** *Worcester* v. *Georgia*

**l.** Daniel Webster

**The Age of Jackson**

**SHORT ANSWER** On a separate sheet of paper, answer each of the following questions in complete sentences.

1. What are historians referring to when they use the term "Jacksonian Democracy"?

2. What effect did the Tariff of Abominations have on sectional differences in Andrew Jackson's America?

3. What did the Supreme Court rule in *Worcester* v. *Georgia*?

4. What did the Indian Removal Act authorize?

5. Why did many northerners support tariffs?

6. What were John C. Calhoun's views on the Tariff of Abominations?

**PRACTICING SOCIAL STUDIES SKILLS** Study the map below and, on a separate sheet of paper, answer the question that follows.

**Second Seminole War**

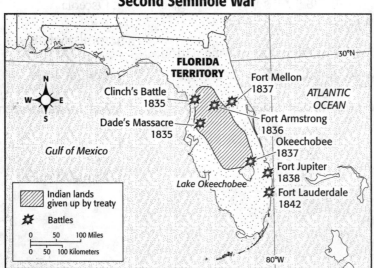

7. Which battle of the Second Seminole War occurred last?

Progress Assessment

**Expanding West**                                    Section Quiz

                                                      **Section 1**

**MATCHING** In the space provided, write the letter of the term, person, or place that matches each description. Some answers will not be used.

_____ **1.** Often fur traders and trappers, these people traveled west and lived dangerous lives, often adopting Native American customs and clothing.

_____ **2.** This route west led many settlers to Utah.

_____ **3.** This American merchant helped establish trade in the Pacific Northwest.

_____ **4.** This western territory was once claimed by the United States, Russia, Great Britain, and Spain.

_____ **5.** This route west stretched over 2,000 miles, from Missouri to Oregon and California.

_____ **6.** Americans traveled along this western trail to trade goods with Mexican merchants.

_____ **7.** This group of settlers traveled to the West to escape religious persecution.

_____ **8.** Demand for this item led traders further west.

_____ **9.** This trading post became an important American settlement in Oregon.

_____ **10.** Brigham Young established this Mormon settlement in Utah.

**a.** Astoria

**b.** fur

**c.** John Jacob Astor

**d.** Mormons

**e.** Mormon Trail

**f.** mountain men

**g.** Oregon Country

**h.** Oregon Trail

**i.** Joseph Smith

**j.** Salt Lake City

**k.** Santa Fe Trail

**l.** tobacco

**m.** Utah

                                                      Progress Assessment

## Expanding West

**TRUE/FALSE** Mark each statement **T** if it is true or **F** if it is false. If false explain why.

_____ **1.** Although greatly outnumbered, Texan forces defeated the Mexican Army at the Battle of the Alamo.

_____

_____

_____ **2.** Mexico hired empresarios to bring more settlers to Texas.

_____

_____

_____ **3.** In 1836, Texas declared its independence from Mexico.

_____

_____

_____ **4.** In return for free land, settlers in Texas had to agree to support Mexican independence from Spain.

_____

_____

_____ **5.** The Texas Revolution started when Mexico refused to allow settlers to own weapons.

_____

_____

Progress Assessment

**Expanding West**                                          Section Quiz

                                                                    **Section 3**

**FILL IN THE BLANK** For each of the following statements, fill in the
blank with the appropriate word, phrase, or name.

**1.** The land gained by the United States as a result of the Mexican War is known as

   the _____.

**2.** Seen as an expansionist candidate, _____ won the presidential election of 1844.

**3.** Mexico argued that the Texas border was the Nueces River, while the U.S. believed

   it was the _____ River.

**4.** In the Treaty of _____, the U.S. promised to protect the freedom of Mexicans living in lands gained from Mexico.

**5.** The Mexican War came to an end in 1847 when General Winfield Scott captured

   the Mexican cities of Veracruz and _____.

**6.** Southerners supported the annexation of Texas as a _____
   state.

**7.** Between 1845 and 1848, the Unites States annexed Texas and

   _____.

**8.** Because of their isolation, Spanish settlers in California, or

   _____, felt little connection to their government.

**9.** The view that nothing could stop the westward growth of the U.S. was known as

   _____.

**10.** The _____ was a rebellion by a group of American settlers in
   which they declared California an independent nation.

**Expanding West**

**TRUE/FALSE** Mark each statement **T** if it is true or **F** if it is false. If false explain why.

_____ 1. The gold rush transformed California's economy and population almost overnight.

_____

_____

_____ 2. Biddy Mason was a foreign immigrant who came during the gold rush and became one of the wealthiest landowners in California.

_____

_____

_____ 3. The only people who profited from the gold rush were miners.

_____

_____

_____ 4. Gold was discovered in California in 1848 at the Snake River.

_____

_____

_____ 5. The discovery of gold in California attracted only American settlers.

_____

_____

Progress Assessment

Name _____ Class _____ Date _____

## Expanding West

# Chapter Test

## Form A

**MULTIPLE CHOICE** For each of the following, write the letter of the best choice in the space provided.

_____ **1.** How did the U.S. government help traders traveling on the Santa Fe Trail?
  **a.** issued travel insurance to protect the traders' belongings
  **b.** granted an allowance to cover basic travel expenses
  **c.** lowered taxes on goods bought before the trip
  **d.** sent troops to protect against Native American attacks

_____ **2.** Which of the following shows how various cultures shaped one another in the Southwest after the Mexican Cession?
  **a.** American settlers taught Native Americans about mining in the mountains.
  **b.** American settlers introduced saddles to Mexican ranchers.
  **c.** Communities regularly celebrated both Mexican and American holidays.
  **d.** Communities printed laws in Native American languages.

_____ **3.** What role did the transcontinental railroad play in California's development?
  **a.** contributed to California's population explosion by bringing settlers to the West in the mid-1850s
  **b.** slowed down California's economy because it took two decades and many thousands of dollars to complete
  **c.** gave California's economy the means to grow by connecting the state to the rest of the country
  **d.** damaged California's environment by requiring the development of coal mining and timber industries

_____ **4.** What lesson might a western traveler have learned from the story of the Donner party?
  **a.** Don't look for shortcuts.
  **b.** Travel with a compass.
  **c.** Don't drink the water.
  **d.** Go west in the spring.

Progress Assessment

_____ **5.** Which practice caused Mormons to be persecuted in the 1850s?
   **a.** the ritualistic slaughter of animals
   **b.** marriage to more than one wife
   **c.** violence against non-Mormons
   **d.** prayer in public schools

_____ **6.** The American expansionists' slogan "Fifty-four forty or fight!" referred to the
   **a.** line to which they wanted their northern territory to extend.
   **b.** line that marked the northern border of what is now California.
   **c.** number of prisoners they wanted Santa Anna to release.
   **d.** number of Native Americans whose deaths they wanted to avenge.

_____ **7.** Which of the following best describes empresarios?
   **a.** Mexicans who opposed the revolution
   **b.** agents who brought settlers to Texas
   **c.** soldiers in the Texan army
   **d.** supporters of manifest destiny

_____ **8.** Which challenge did Mexican Americans face when American settlers poured into the Southwest after the Mexican War?
   **a.** Mexican land laws differed from U.S. land laws, which led to much confusion.
   **b.** Mexican holidays were not recognized by the American settlers.
   **c.** Mexican Americans were persecuted because they were mostly Roman Catholic.
   **d.** Mexican Americans had no rights over the land and were legally evicted.

_____ **9.** Which of the following was true about the U.S. army at the beginning of the Mexican-American War?
   **a.** greatly outnumbered the Mexican army
   **b.** more experienced and better organized
   **c.** better equipped than the Mexican army
   **d.** could not attract volunteers

## PRACTICING SOCIAL STUDIES SKILLS Study the map below and answer the question that follows.

**Trails Leading West**

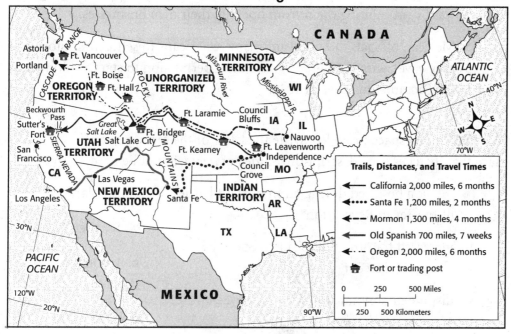

_____ **10.** Which trails were the same length and took the same amount of time to travel?

   **a.** the California and Oregon Trails

   **b.** the Santa Fe and Old Spanish Trails

   **c.** the Mormon and Santa Fe Trails

   **d.** the Oregon and Mormon Trails

**TRUE/FALSE** Indicate whether each statement below is true or false by writing **T** or **F** in the space provided.

_____ **11.** Americans moved westward in the early 1800s because French and British companies had depleted the lumber supply.

_____ **12.** A placer miner was employed to search for places that were most likely to contain gold.

_____ **13.** As a result of the population explosion of the "gold fever" years, California became eligible for statehood.

_____ **14.** One way in which Americans made life difficult for Chinese immigrants was by prohibiting them from opening their own businesses.

_____ **15.** Mexican officials did not want many Americans to settle in California, but they gave Swiss immigrant John Sutter permission to start a colony near the Sacramento River in 1839.

**MATCHING** In the space provided, write the letter of the term, person, or place that matches each description. Some answers will not be used.

_____ **16.** mission besieged during an important battle of the Texan Revolution

_____ **17.** increased the size of the United States by almost 25 percent

_____ **18.** dispute in Sonoma, California, between Mexicans and American settlers

_____ **19.** gave the United States much of Mexico's northern territory

_____ **20.** empresario who started a colony on the lower Colorado River in 1822

_____ **21.** Mexican general who was captured at the Battle of San Jacinto

_____ **22.** Mexican priest who led Native Americans and mestizos in a rebellion in 1810

_____ **23.** U.S. president who favored the annexation of Texas in 1844

_____ **24.** head of the Mormon Church after the murder of Joseph Smith

_____ **25.** idea that the United States was bound to expand to the Pacific Ocean and spread democracy

**a.** the Alamo

**b.** Stephen F. Austin

**c.** Antonio López de Santa Anna

**d.** Miguel Hidalgo y Costilla

**e.** John Tyler

**f.** the Mexican Cession

**g.** the Gadsden Purchase

**h.** the Treaty of Guadalupe Hidalgo

**i.** Brigham Young

**j.** manifest destiny

**k.** Bear Flag Revolt

**l.** Battle of Buena Vista

Name _____ Class _____ Date _____

# Expanding West

# Chapter Test

## Form B

**SHORT ANSWER** On a separate sheet of paper, answer each of the following questions in complete sentences.

**1.** What was "manifest destiny" and how did the slavery issue get tied up with it in the 1840s and 1850s?

**2.** What happened to California's population as a result of the Gold Rush? Why?

**3.** What was President Jackson's reason for refusing to annex Texas?

**4.** What was the significance of the Treaty of Guadalupe Hidalgo?

**5.** What were the terms of the Gadsden Purchase?

**6.** In 1822, an empresario started a colony on the lower Colorado River. What was his name?

**PRACTICING SOCIAL STUDIES SKILLS** Study the map below and, on a separate sheet of paper, answer the question that follows.

### Trails Leading West

**7.** Which trails were the same length and took the same amount of time to travel.

Progress Assessment

# The New Republic

**MULTIPLE CHOICE** For each of the following, write the letter of the best choice in the space provided.

_____ **1.** What happened during the Bear Flag Revolt?
   **a.** A union of Spanish settlers rose up against Californios in the Mission district of San Francisco.
   **b.** General Taylor led his troops across the Rio Grande to protect Texas against a Mexican uprising.
   **c.** John C. Frémont's mapping expedition fought off a black bear while crossing the Sierra Nevada.
   **d.** A small group of Americans seized the town of Sonoma and declared California's independence.

_____ **2.** The Embargo Act failed because
   **a.** the Non-Intercourse Act limited its scope.
   **b.** the Federalist Party rallied against it.
   **c.** it caused American merchants to lose money and had little effect on Britain and France.
   **d.** Spain replaced the loss of U.S. trade with increased trade in South America.

_____ **3.** In the early 1800s, American music focused on
   **a.** religion and national pride.
   **b.** the beauty of everyday life.
   **c.** political leaders and democratic values.
   **d.** cultural unity.

_____ **4.** Americans modeled much of their architecture after the architecture of ancient Athens and Rome because these civilizations
   **a.** created buildings that were inexpensive for Americans to reproduce.
   **b.** were founded on the same religious beliefs as the new American nation.
   **c.** created simple buildings that were a reflection of the "common man" in America.
   **d.** were based on some of the same political ideals as the new American nation.

_____ **5.** What was Daniel Webster's position on states' rights?
  **a.** The welfare of the nation should override the concerns of individual states.
  **b.** Federal authority should be upheld, but federal power should not be expanded.
  **c.** States needed a way to lawfully protest questionable federal legislation.
  **d.** Economic problems should dictate which regions executive orders favored.

_____ **6.** The Gadsden Purchase benefited the United States by
  **a.** promising to safeguard the property rights of long-time U.S. residents.
  **b.** giving the United States hunting rights in the area of Texas north of the Rio Grande.
  **c.** allowing the United States to purchase the northern part of present day Arizona.
  **d.** securing a southern route for a transcontinental railroad on American soil.

_____ **7.** Which description fits the group of people known as "forty-niners"?
  **a.** gold-seekers from America and abroad who migrated to California
  **b.** middle-aged married men with previous gold-mining experience
  **c.** individual prospectors of California gold-mining sites
  **d.** Mexicans and South Americans who immigrated to find gold

_____ **8.** What idea did the Whig Party favor when it formed to oppose Jackson in 1834?
  **a.** an expansion of the federal government
  **b.** the creation of a monarchic state
  **c.** a weak president and a strong Congress
  **d.** the broadening of the two-party system

_____ **9.** Young members of Congress who called for a trade war against Britain were called
  **a.** Battle Axes.
  **b.** Warlords.
  **c.** War Hawks.
  **d.** Red Coats.

                                                              Progress Assessment

_____ **10.** Who chose the winner of the election of 1824?
  **a.** majority of voters
  **b.** electoral college
  **c.** Supreme Court
  **d.** House of Representatives

_____ **11.** What was Cherokee Indian Sequoya's role in Native American history?
  **a.** led a Cherokee attack on Georgia troops
  **b.** created a writing system for the Cherokee language
  **c.** sued the state of Georgia for illegal occupation of Cherokee land
  **d.** modeled the first Cherokee government after the U.S. Constitution

_____ **12.** As a result of the population explosion of the "gold fever" years, California became
  **a.** eligible for statehood.
  **b.** richer than any other region in the country.
  **c.** more populous than any other region in the country.
  **d.** off limits to new immigrants.

_____ **13.** Which of the following reflects the significance of *Marbury* v. *Madison*?
  **a.** described the specific types of cases that could be brought before the Supreme Court
  **b.** established the Supreme Court's power to check the other branches of government
  **c.** limited the Supreme Court's effectiveness by requiring it to hear every case brought before it
  **d.** weakened the Supreme Court in relation to the White House and Congress

_____ **14.** The Louisiana Purchase was significant to the United States because it
  **a.** nearly doubled the size of the country.
  **b.** helped the United States challenge British power in North America.
  **c.** set a precedent regarding the purchase of territory without congressional approval.
  **d.** took New Orleans out of Spain's control.

_____ **15.** What did the Treaty of Ghent accomplish?
   **a.** It ended the War of 1812.
   **b.** It ended the Creek War.
   **c.** It banned tariffs on imports from Britain.
   **d.** It withdrew the unpopular Embargo Acts.

_____ **16.** The first thing the British did after their ranks were reinforced in April of 1814 was attack the city of
   **a.** New Orleans.
   **b.** Baltimore.
   **c.** Washington, D.C.
   **d.** New York.

_____ **17.** Who was Chief Black Hawk?
   **a.** leader of the Fox and Sauk Indians who decided to fight U.S. officials rather than leave Illinois
   **b.** Seminole leader who called upon his tribe to resist removal
   **c.** Cherokee leader who persuaded his tribe to appeal to the U.S. Courts instead of using violence
   **d.** Chickasaw leader who negotiated a treaty to get more supplies for the trip to Indian Territory

_____ **18.** Placer mining is the
   **a.** search for gold by washing gravel.
   **b.** excavation of underground tunnels for gold.
   **c.** search for places likely to have gold.
   **d.** examination of a mineral to see if it is gold.

_____ **19.** Which of the following is true about the battle at the Alamo in 1836?
   **a.** The battle lasted only one day.
   **b.** Mexico suffered a harsh defeat.
   **c.** All of the Alamo's defenders were killed.
   **d.** The Texan army captured General Santa Anna.

_____ **20.** What did the Supreme Court rule in *Worcester* v. *Georgia*?
   **a.** The Cherokee Indians had to move from their land in Georgia.
   **b.** The state of Georgia had no legal power over the Cherokee Indians.
   **c.** Only state governments had authority over American Indians.
   **d.** U.S. troops in any state had the right to remove American Indians.

Progress Assessment

**PRACTICING SOCIAL STUDIES SKILLS** Study the quotation below and answer the question that follows.

> [It is America's] manifest destiny to overspread and to possess the whole continent which Providence [God] has given us for the development of the great experiment of liberty. . ."

_____ **21.** Which of the following best supports these words by writer John O'Sullivan?
  **a.** America's need for freedom
  **b.** America's need for land
  **c.** improved relations between America and foreign nations
  **d.** religious freedom for all Americans

**TRUE/FALSE** Indicate whether each statement below is true or false by writing **T** or **F** in the space provided.

_____ **22.** Antonio López de Santa Anna started a colony on the lower Colorado River in 1822.

_____ **23.** The nullification crisis sparked a dispute over the right of the states to reject federal laws as unconstitutional.

_____ **24.** According to Thomas Jefferson, a primary task of the federal government includes delivery of the mail.

_____ **25.** Andrew Jackson led American forces to victory at the Battle of Tippecanoe.

_____ **26.** President Andrew Jackson annexed Texas after increased pressure from Texas voters.

_____ **27.** President Andrew Jackson opposed rewarding supporters with government jobs.

_____ **28.** The outcome of the Election of 1800 resulted in the peaceful change of power from the Federalists to the Democratic-Republicans.

_____ **29.** The transcontinental railroad hurt California's economy because it was so expensive to build.

_____ **30.** Seminole Indians signed but ignored a removal treaty in which they agreed to leave Florida.

_____ **31.** Spain decided to sell Louisiana to France because constant rebellions by American settlers were damaging trading activity.

**FILL IN THE BLANK** Read each sentence and fill in the blank with the word in the word pair that best completes the sentence.

**32.** The Lewis and Clark expedition was undertaken in order to explore

_____, learn about the plants and animals of the West, and

attempt to find a river route to the Pacific Ocean.

**(the Louisiana Purchase/New Spain)**

**33.** The _____ Indians were the first Native Americans removed to Indian Territory. **(Choctaw/Cherokee)**

**34.** After Joseph Smith founded the Church of Jesus Christ of Latter-day Saints,

members of the church became known as _____.

**(Mormons/Catholics)**

**35.** At public _____, political party members could select candidates for president and vice president, which led to the expansion of democracy in the 1820s. **(election rallies/nominating conventions)**

**36.** Part of the reason why the U.S. navy defeated the British navy in the War of 1812

was that the U.S. navy had powerful warships such as the

_____. **(USS *Constitution*/USS *Indianapolis*)**

**37.** In the early 1800s, Americans from the North supported

_____ because they helped them compete with British man-

ufacturers. **(manufacturing laws/tariffs)**

**38.** The American Fur Company bought skins from western fur traders and trappers

who came to be known as _____.

**(mountain men/empresarios)**

**39.** In 1832 Andrew Jackson vetoed the charter of the _____.
**(National Mint/Second Bank of the United States)**

**40.** American expansionists cried "Fifty-four forty or fight!" in reference to the line to

which they wanted _____ to extend.

**(their northern territory/the Gadsden Purchase)**

**MATCHING**  In the space provided, write the letter of the term or person that matches each description. Some answers will not be used.

_____ **41.** set the border between the United States and Canada at 49° N latitude as far west as the Rocky Mountains

_____ **42.** American writer whose work combined European influences with American settings and characters

_____ **43.** agreement made in 1820 that attempted to settle slavery conflicts

_____ **44.** American writer known for writing stories about the West and popularizing the historical fiction genre

_____ **45.** feeling of loyalty and pride to a nation

_____ **46.** founder of the Hudson River school

_____ **47.** treaty that settled border disputes between Spain and the United States

_____ **48.** U.S. Representative who hoped that internal improvements to the country would build national unity

_____ **49.** leader of the Latin American struggle for independence

_____ **50.** putting the interests of a region over the interests of the nation

**a.** Adams-Onís Treaty

**b.** George Caleb Bingham

**c.** Simon Bolívar

**d.** Henry Clay

**e.** Thomas Cole

**f.** Convention of 1818

**g.** James Fenimore Cooper

**h.** Washington Irving

**i.** Missouri Compromise

**j.** Monroe Doctrine

**k.** nationalism

**l.** sectionalism

Name _____ Class _____ Date _____

# The New Republic

## Unit Test

### Form B

**SHORT ANSWER** On a separate sheet of paper, answer each of the following questions in complete sentences.

1. What is impressment, and what role did it play in the War of 1812?

2. Why did many Americans admire ancient Greece and the Roman Republic?

3. What was the American System?

4. What ruling did the Supreme Court make in the case of *McCulloch* v. *Maryland*?

5. In what ways did democracy expand in the early 1800s?

6. What was the significance of the Gadsden Purchase?

**PRACTICING SOCIAL STUDIES SKILLS** Study the map below and, on a separate sheet of paper, answer the question that follows.

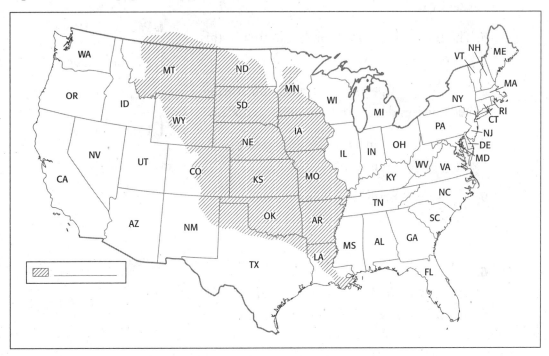

7. What information would complete the legend associated with the map above?

Progress Assessment

Name _____ Class _____ Date _____

# The North

**MATCHING** In the space provided, write the letter of the term, person, or place that matches each description. Some answers will not be used.

_____ **1.** Most mills were located in this region of the United States.

_____ **2.** The first breakthroughs of the Industrial Revolution took place in this industry.

_____ **3.** The efficient production of large numbers of identical goods is known as this.

_____ **4.** This period of rapid growth introduced machines in manufacturing and production.

_____ **5.** These parts are made from pieces that are exactly the same.

_____ **6.** The Industrial Revolution began first in this country.

_____ **7.** This event helped American manufacturing become less dependent on foreign goods.

_____ **8.** This American inventor promised to produce 10,000 muskets in two years.

_____ **9.** This skilled British mechanic brought his knowledge of cloth-producing machines to the United States.

_____ **10.** Because new machines were too large to fit in a person's home and needed a power source, these were built along streams.

**a.** Eli Whitney

**b.** Great Britain

**c.** Industrial Revolution

**d.** interchangeable

**e.** James Hargreaves

**f.** mass production

**g.** mills

**h.** Northeast

**i.** Pacific Northwest

**j.** Samuel Slater

**k.** textile

**l.** United States

**m.** War of 1812

Progress Assessment

Name _____ Class _____ Date _____

# The North

**TRUE/FALSE** Mark each statement **T** if it is true or **F** if it is false. If false explain why.

_____ 1. Workers created missions to improve pay and working conditions in the factories.

_____

_____

_____ 2. The Rhode Island system was a strategy of hiring families and dividing factory work into simple tasks.

_____

_____

_____ 3. Most mill owners in the United States had a difficult time finding workers.

_____

_____

_____ 4. The Lowell system was to hire young, unmarried men from cities to work in the factories.

_____

_____

_____ 5. Francis Cabot Lowell founded the Lowell Female Labor Reform Association and played a large role in the American labor movement.

_____

_____

**The North**

**MATCHING** In the space provided, write the letter of the term, person, or place that matches each description. Some answers will not be used.

_____ **1.** This was a period of rapid growth in the speed and convenience of travel.

_____ **2.** He invented the steamboat.

_____ **3.** Because of its location, this city became an important hub for transportation in the United States.

_____ **4.** This Supreme Court case regarding interstate commerce reinforced the federal government's power over the states.

_____ **5.** Companies in this industry soon became some of the most powerful businesses in the United States.

_____ **6.** This replaced wood as the main source of power for locomotives.

_____ **7.** This invention made river travel faster.

_____ **8.** In 1830, he built a small locomotive called the *Tom Thumb*.

_____ **9.** This is used to make the rails that trains ride on.

_____ **10.** The cutting down and removal of trees is the definition of this term.

**a.** Boston

**b.** Chicago

**c.** coal

**d.** deforestation

**e.** *Gibbons* v. *Ogden*

**f.** Industrial Revolution

**g.** iron

**h.** Peter Cooper

**i.** railroad

**j.** Robert Fulton

**k.** steamboat

**l.** steel

**m.** Transportation Revolution

Progress Assessment

Name _____ Class _____ Date _____

**The North**

**MULTIPLE CHOICE**   For each of the following, write the letter of the best choice in the space provided.

_____ **1.** Of the following, who invented the mechanical reaper?
   **a.** John Deere
   **b.** Samuel Morse
   **c.** Isaac Singer
   **d.** Cyrus McCormick

_____ **2.** How were prices of goods
affected by mass production?
   **a.** They rose.
   **b.** They went down.
   **c.** They stayed the same.
   **d.** They became unpredictable.

_____ **3.** Dots and dashes are used to
stand for each letter of the
alphabet in what system?
   **a.** Morse code
   **b.** Lowell system
   **c.** Cyrillic code
   **d.** factory system

_____ **4.** What device did Isaac Singer
help to improve?
   **a.** sewing machine
   **b.** cotton gin
   **c.** spinning jenny
   **d.** telegraph

_____ **5.** What device could send
information over wires across
great distances?
   **a.** steamboats
   **b.** telegraph
   **c.** mechanical reaper
   **d.** steel plow

**The North**

**MULTIPLE CHOICE** For each of the following, write the letter of the best choice in the space provided.

_____ **1.** Which statement best describes working conditions in the mills in the 1800s?
  **a.** Workers were fired after one absence, forcing untrained workers to replace them.
  **b.** Each worker was free to choose the time at which the workday began so long as 8 to 10 hours of work a day were completed.
  **c.** Some workers suffered from health problems such as chronic cough due to unsafe conditions.
  **d.** Workers were fed three times and their health was a top priority of caring managers and investors.

_____ **2.** The invention of the plow and the reaper helped the farming industry by
  **a.** allowing customers to buy on credit.
  **b.** causing cities to grow, creating a larger market.
  **c.** enabling farmers to plant and harvest huge crop fields.
  **d.** providing a product that, when sold, allowed many farmers to become rich.

_____ **3.** Companies built their factories closer to cities and transportation centers in the mid-1800s to
  **a.** increase wages.
  **b.** stabilize shipping costs.
  **c.** cause people to move from cities to rural areas.
  **d.** provide themselves with easier access to workers.

_____ **4.** In the mid-1800s, companies began to mass produce earlier inventions. What effect did this have on families?
  **a.** They could buy items they could not afford in the past.
  **b.** They could store fresh food safely for longer periods.
  **c.** Their everyday lives became more complicated.
  **d.** Families began creating their own inventions.

_____ **5.** Textile manufacturers kept the costs of running a mill low by
  **a.** cutting back on maintaining machinery.
  **b.** hiring children and paying them very little.
  **c.** training apprentices in exchange for years of labor.
  **d.** feeding workers instead of paying them wages in cash.

Progress Assessment

_____ **6.** The Transportation Revolution can best be described as a period of
  **a.** rebellion against foreign countries' use of American shipping lanes.
  **b.** economic depression brought on by inferior modes of travel.
  **c.** public disapproval of traditional modes of transit.
  **d.** rapid growth in the speed and convenience of travel.

_____ **7.** What challenges did engineers and mechanics face while building railroads?
  **a.** The American public was not interested in railroads.
  **b.** The railroads had to pass over mountains and rivers.
  **c.** Locomotives usually broke down before arriving at their destinations.
  **d.** Engineers did not have the necessary materials to build railroads.

_____ **8.** In the 1870s, the demand for coal increased as the demand for steel grew because
  **a.** coal was used to power most farming equipment.
  **b.** steel was noncombustible.
  **c.** railroads could only be powered by coal.
  **d.** coal was used in furnaces for steel production.

_____ **9.** How did technological developments during the Industrial Revolution enable people to build factories almost anywhere?
  **a.** Trains could bring raw materials to and ship finished goods from any location.
  **b.** The shift to steam power meant factories no longer had to be built near streams, rivers, or waterfalls.
  **c.** Trains and steamboats spread the population out so that any factory had a ready supply of workers.
  **d.** The invention of the telegraph put factory managers and their urban investors within easy reach.

_____ **10.** The water frame revolutionized production of cloth by
  **a.** increasing the number of workers needed to make cloth.
  **b.** washing cloth in water, which raised quality, but made cloth more costly.
  **c.** harnessing the power of flowing water, which sped up production.
  **d.** raising the quality level of home-spun cloth.

**PRACTICING SOCIAL STUDIES SKILLS** Study the quotation below and answer the question that follows.

> "I am persuaded that machinery moved by water [and] adapted to this business would greatly reduce the labor and facilitate [speed] the manufacture of this article."
>
> —Eli Whitney, quoted in *Technology in America,* edited by Carroll W. Pursell

_____ **11.** Eli Whitney's purpose for making this statement was to
   **a.** let his audience know about a new manufacturing facility.
   **b.** argue for the benefits of trying one of his ideas.
   **c.** describe in specific detail how a new invention of his works.
   **d.** convince manufacturers to add more workers to increase production.

**TRUE/FALSE** Indicate whether each statement below is true or false by writing **T** or **F** in the space provided.

_____ **12.** Isaac Singer is credited with the invention of the safety pin.

_____ **13.** During the War of 1812, Americans began to buy the items they needed from American manufacturers instead of foreign suppliers.

_____ **14.** Most early strikes by union members were unsuccessful because the courts and the police did not take their side.

_____ **15.** Changes to manufacturing were needed in the mid-1700s because demand was greater than the available supply of goods.

_____ **16.** Alfred Lewis Vail developed a system known as Morse code.

**MATCHING** In the space provided, write the letter of the person that matches each description. Some answers will not be used.

_____ **17.** developed mills featuring power looms that could spin thread and weave cloth in the same mill

_____ **18.** designer of the first full-sized commercial steamboat, the *Clermont*

_____ **19.** fought to obtain a 10-hour workday for employees of private businesses

_____ **20.** developed the mechanical reaper, a harvesting machine, in 1831

_____ **21.** developed the strategy of hiring families and dividing work into simple tasks, known as the Rhode Island system

_____ **22.** unsuccessfully sued to limit New York's waterway rights

_____ **23.** came up with the idea of interchangeable parts

_____ **24.** invented the telegraph

_____ **25.** built the small but powerful locomotive *Tom Thumb* in 1830

**a.** Aaron Ogden

**b.** Samuel Slater

**c.** Samuel F.B. Morse

**d.** Richard Arkwright

**e.** Peter Cooper

**f.** Eli Whitney

**g.** Francis Cabot Lowell

**h.** Robert Fulton

**i.** Cyrus McCormick

**j.** Sarah G. Bagley

**The North**

**SHORT ANSWER** On a separate sheet of paper, answer each of the following questions in complete sentences.

1. In what ways did the Transportation Revolution create a boom in business across the United States?

2. Who perfected the telegraph in 1832?

3. How can you tell that the water frame was one of the early technologies of the Industrial Revolution?

4. What was the Lowell system?

5. What did the Supreme Court decide in the case of *Gibbons v. Ogden*?

6. What British mechanic defied Parliament by memorizing designs for new textile machines and smuggling his knowledge into the United States?

**PRACTICING SOCIAL STUDIES SKILLS** Study the map below and, on a separate sheet of paper, answer the question that follows.

**Transportation Routes, 1850**

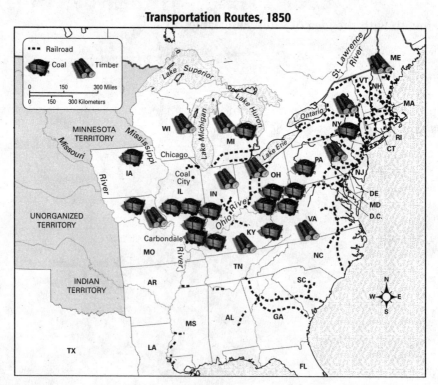

7. Name three states where timber could be found in the 1850s.

Name _____ Class _____ Date _____

# The South

**FILL IN THE BLANK** For each of the following statements, fill in the blank with the appropriate word, phrase, or name.

1. After the American Revolution, prices for major Southern crops

   _____.

2. Growing and processing _____ was very difficult.

3. _____ invented the cotton gin.

4. The _____ was the region that grew most of the country's cotton crop.

5. Farmers who owned more than 20 slaves were known as

   _____.

6. The growing demand for slaves led to an increase in the domestic

   _____.

7. One goal of _____ was to increase crop production.

8. The South's other successful food crops included rice, sweet potatoes, wheat, and

   _____.

9. The production of _____ was very time consuming because the leaves had to be cured and dried.

10. Joseph R. Anderson became the owner of the _____, one of the few examples of industrial growth in the South by 1848.

Progress Assessment

**The South**

**TRUE/FALSE** Mark each statement **T** if it is true or **F** if it is false. If false explain why.

_____ **1.** Southern society was centered around agriculture.

_____

_____

_____ **2.** In the early 1800s, all white southern families owned slaves.

_____

_____

_____ **3.** Yeomen were owners of large plantations and lots of slaves.

_____

_____

_____ **4.** Wealthy white southerners used religion to justify the institution of slavery.

_____

_____

_____ **5.** By 1860 more than half of all free African Americans lived in the South.

_____

_____

Progress Assessment

**The South**

**FILL IN THE BLANK** For each of the following statements, fill in the blank with the appropriate word, phrase, or name.

1. The _____ system in the South produced harsh living conditions.

2. The majority of slaves worked in the _____.

3. Supervisors, known as _____, sometimes slaves themselves, made sure slaves followed orders.

4. Slaves working inside the planter's _____ had better food and clothing than those in the fields.

5. On larger _____, slaves sometimes worked as skilled laborers, such as blacksmiths or carpenters.

6. Slaveholders viewed slaves as _____, not as people.

7. Slave _____ determined whether families would be kept together or separated.

8. The most important aspect of slave communities was the

_____.

9. By passing down family histories, and African customs, enslaved parents ensured that their children would never forget their _____.

10. Led by a slave from Virginia, the most violent slave revolt in the United States occurred in 1831 and is known as _____.

**The South**                                                          Chapter Test

                                                                          Form A

**MULTIPLE CHOICE** For each of the following, write the letter of the best choice in the space provided.

_____ **1.** Which of the following statements best describes free African Americans in the 1860s?
   **a.** Some of them were descendants of refugees from the Haitian Revolution.
   **b.** All of them moved to free states in the North after gaining their freedom.
   **c.** Many of them joined labor unions to help them bargain for higher wages.
   **d.** None of them had been willingly set free by their slaveholders.

_____ **2.** Many planters used the gang-labor system, in which all field hands
   **a.** were trained to do different tasks.
   **b.** focused on the same task at the same time.
   **c.** worked in shifts throughout the day.
   **d.** decided how to organize the day's work.

_____ **3.** Long-staple cotton differed from short-staple cotton in that it was
   **a.** much cheaper.
   **b.** easier to grow.
   **c.** easier to process.
   **d.** sold to Great Britain.

_____ **4.** Enslaved parents passed down their culture to their children by
   **a.** reading biblical tales of the exodus from slavery.
   **b.** sharing their family histories and telling folktales.
   **c.** singing Christian songs about freedom.
   **d.** demonstrating kindness to their slaveholders.

_____ **5.** Life in southern cities was similar to plantation life in the 1800s because
   **a.** public education was widely available.
   **b.** local governments funded water systems.
   **c.** slaves did most of the work.
   **d.** business owners maintained streets.

_____ **6.** While some slaves tried to escape permanently, most left for short periods, often to
   **a.** attend church.
   **b.** get medical attention.
   **c.** visit relatives.
   **d.** study in secret.

_____ **7.** Nat Turner led a rebellion of slaves against slaveholders because he
  **a.** had watched his father die as a result of a beating by his slaveholder.
  **b.** believed that God had told him to end slavery.
  **c.** was inspired by the success of other violent slave revolts.
  **d.** had tried and failed at non-violent methods of resistance.

_____ **8.** Unlike slaves who worked the fields, slaves working in planters' houses usually
  **a.** received payment.
  **b.** had better food, clothing, and shelter.
  **c.** worked shorter hours.
  **d.** did not work when they were sick.

_____ **9.** Tredegar Iron Works can best be described as a
  **a.** northern company that specialized in turning iron into steel by heating it.
  **b.** northern mine that provided coal to manufacturers of iron products.
  **c.** southern factory that turned iron into useful products like cannons and steam engines.
  **d.** southern manufacturing plant that produced locomotives for privately-owned companies.

_____ **10.** Skilled slaves had an advantage over unskilled slaves because they were sometimes allowed to
  **a.** work shorter hours.
  **b.** move from plantation to plantation.
  **c.** live in their owner's house.
  **d.** earn money and eventually buy their freedom.

**TRUE/FALSE** Indicate whether each statement below is true or false by writing **T** or **F** in the space provided.

_____ **11.** To encourage obedience, slave owners were likely to whip, shackle, or chain slaves, or place them in the stocks.

_____ **12.** Many of the first factories in the South produced iron products.

_____ **13.** Eli Whitney tried to keep the design of the cotton gin secret, but the invention was so revolutionary that other manufacturers often ignored the patent and produced their own machines.

_____ **14.** The increasing demand for slave labor and the banning of slave importation by Congress in 1808 led to an increase in the domestic slave trade.

_____ **15.** Though many slave women were separated from their own children, many of them were required to care for the children of their owners.

_____ **16.** Southern cotton planters relied on the region's rivers to ship goods because traffic from heavy corn and hemp shipments slowed road travel.

_____ **17.** Planters' wives were not allowed any contact with slaves.

**FILL IN THE BLANK** Read each sentence and fill in the blank with the word in the word pair that best completes the sentence.

**18.** Some slaves sang _____, which were Christian songs that blended African and European music. (**spirituals/folktales**)

**19.** Eli Whitney's cotton gin used a hand-cranked cylinder with wire teeth to remove seeds from _____ cotton. (**long-staple/short-staple**)

**20.** Crop brokers called _____ made deals with merchants, arranged passage for crops aboard trading ships, and provided financial advice. (**planters/factors**)

**21.** _____ owned small farms and often worked alongside their slaves. (**Planters/Yeomen**)

**22.** Slaves were most commonly sold at _____, which represented the greatest threat to their family bonds. (**auctions/marketplaces**)

**23.** The South's first major cash crop was _____. (**cotton/tobacco**)

**24.** Wealthy white southerners used _____ to justify the institution of slavery, arguing that some people were created to rule over others. (**the U.S. Constitution/religion**)

**PRACTICING SOCIAL STUDIES SKILLS** Study the map below and
answer the question that follows.

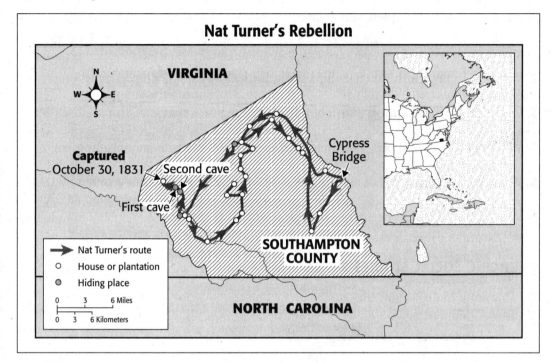

_____ **25.** About how many miles separate the second cave from the site of Turner's
capture?

    **a.** one

    **b.** three

    **c.** five

    **d.** seven

# The South

**SHORT ANSWER** On a separate sheet of paper, answer each of the following questions in complete sentences.

1. What does crop rotation involve and what is its purpose? Why was it introduced?

2. Why did many southern cities and states limit the rights of freed slaves?

3. Why did southern cotton planters rely on the region's rivers to ship goods?

4. What belief inspired Nat Turner to lead a group of slaves to kill slaveholders?

5. What was a yeoman? What percentage of all southern farmers were yeomen by 1860?

6. What job did drivers perform on large southern plantations?

**PRACTICING SOCIAL STUDIES SKILLS** Study the image below and, on a separate sheet of paper, answer the question that follows.

**Cotton Gin**

1. The operator turned the crank.

2. The crank turned a roller with teeth that stripped the seeds away from the cotton fiber.

3. Brushes on a second roller lifted the seed-less cotton off the teeth of the first cylinder and dropped it out of the machine.

4. A belt connected the rollers so that they would both turn when the crank was turned.

7. Which part of the cotton gin lifted the cotton fibers off the teeth of the first roller and dropped the cotton out of the machine? Write down the number.

Progress Assessment

Name _____ Class _____ Date _____

# New Movements in America

**MULTIPLE CHOICE** For each of the following, write the letter of the best choice in the space provided.

_____ **1.** Where did the millions of immigrants that settled in the U.S. in the 19th century come from?
   **a.** Asia
   **b.** Europe
   **c.** South America
   **d.** Australia

_____ **2.** Where did most of the Irish immigrants settle?
   **a.** the Northeast
   **b.** the mid-Atlantic
   **c.** the South
   **d.** the Midwest

_____ **3.** What were the Americans who opposed immigration called?
   **a.** politicians
   **b.** citizens
   **c.** migrants
   **d.** nativists

_____ **4.** The new social class that arose in the mid-1800s that was neither poor nor wealthy was known as which of the following?
   **a.** Know-Nothings
   **b.** nativists
   **c.** middle class
   **d.** lower class

_____ **5.** Many immigrants lived in dirty, overcrowded, and unsafe buildings known by which of the following terms?
   **a.** tenements
   **b.** condos
   **c.** duplexes
   **d.** townhomes

Progress Assessment

## New Movements in America

**MATCHING** In the space provided, write the letter of the term or person that matches that description. Some answers will not be used.

_____ **1.** characterized by the belief that people can rise above material things in life

_____ **2.** wrote the essay "Self-Reliance" in 1841

_____ **3.** edited the famous transcendentalist publication *The Dial*

_____ **4.** attempted to form a perfect society

_____ **5.** wrote the novel *The Scarlet Letter* in the 1800s

_____ **6.** Authored by Herman Melville, it is one of the finest American novels ever written.

_____ **7.** author of the haunting poem, "The Raven"

_____ **8.** Most of her short stories were published after her death.

_____ **9.** His story-poems became favorites in many American households.

_____ **10.** praised both American individualism and democracy in his simple unrhymed poetry

**a.** *Billy Budd*

**b.** Edgar Allan Poe

**c.** Emily Dickinson

**d.** Henry Wadsworth Longfellow

**e.** John Whittier

**f.** Margaret Fuller

**g.** *Moby-Dick*

**h.** Nathaniel Hawthorne

**i.** Ralph Waldo Emerson

**j.** traditions

**k.** transcendentalism

**l.** utopian communities

**m.** Walt Whitman

Progress Assessment

**New Movements in America**

**FILL IN THE BLANK** For each of the following statements, fill in the blank with the appropriate word, phrase, or name.

**1.** The _____ was a movement of Christian renewal in the 1790s and early 1800s.

**2.** After experiencing a dramatic conversion in 1821, _____ left his career as a lawyer and began preaching.

**3.** _____ sought to prevent religious revival meetings from being held in the city of Boston.

**4.** The effort to get people to exercise self-discipline to stop drinking hard liquor is referred to historically as the _____.

**5.** _____ was a middle-class reformer who helped to improve the living conditions of mentally ill patients nationwide.

**6.** _____ offered prisoners an education so that they could lead more productive lives upon their release.

**7.** People in the _____ movement wanted all children taught in a common place, regardless of background.

**8.** _____ opened the Perkins School for the Blind in 1831.

**9.** _____ started an all-female academy in Hartford, Connecticut.

**10.** In 1835 _____ became the first college to accept African Americans.

Progress Assessment

# New Movements in America

**TRUE/FALSE** Mark each statement **T** if it is true or **F** if it is false. If false explain why.

_____ **1.** "Abolitionist," as a term used in the debate over slavery in America, refers to an individual who was in favor of ending the practice.

_____

_____

_____ **2.** Antislavery reformers agreed on how much equality African Americans should have.

_____

_____

_____ **3.** Abolitionists found many ways to further their cause.

_____

_____

_____ **4.** Free African Americans, former slaves, and a few white abolitionists created what became known as the Underground Railroad.

_____

_____

_____ **5.** Because the North was the center of the abolitionist movement, all northerners were abolitionists.

_____

_____

Progress Assessment

**New Movements in America**

Section Quiz

**Section 5**

**MULTIPLE CHOICE** For each of the following, write the letter of the best choice in the space provided.

_____ **1.** She published *Letters on the Equality of the Sexes and the Condition of Women.*
  **a.** Elizabeth Cady Stanton
  **b.** Lucy Stone
  **c.** Sarah Grimké
  **d.** Susan B. Anthony

_____ **2.** Born Isabella Baumfree, she later took a name that reflected her mission in life.
  **a.** Lucretia Mott
  **b.** Susan B. Anthony
  **c.** Lucy Stone
  **d.** Sojourner Truth

_____ **3.** This was the first public meeting about women's rights held in the United States.
  **a.** World's Anti-Slavery Convention
  **b.** Seneca Falls Convention
  **c.** American Women's Rights Convention
  **d.** Declaration of Sentiments Union

_____ **4.** As a well-known spokes-person for the Anti-Slavery Society, she was once referred to as "the first who really stirred the nation's heart on the subject of women's wrongs."
  **a.** Lucy Stone
  **b.** Sojourner Truth
  **c.** Susan B. Anthony
  **d.** Elizabeth Cady Stanton

_____ **5.** New York finally gave married women ownership of their wages and property due largely to the efforts of this woman.
  **a.** Sarah Grimké
  **b.** Susan B. Anthony
  **c.** Elizabeth Cady Stanton
  **d.** Lucy Stone

Progress Assessment

Name _____ Class _____ Date _____

## New Movements in America

Chapter Test

Form A

**MULTIPLE CHOICE** For each of the following, write the letter of the best choice in the space provided.

_____ 1. What led to the flood of Irish immigrants entering the United States in the mid-1840s?
   a. potato blight
   b. unsafe working conditions
   c. religious persecution
   d. violent revolution

_____ 2. Which of the following is true about women's rights in the 1800s?
   a. Large cities allowed women to vote in local elections.
   b. Women could not serve on juries.
   c. Women asking for equality were punished under the law.
   d. Only married women could manage their own property.

_____ 3. Nathaniel Hawthorne, Edgar Allan Poe, and Emily Dickinson were
   a. founders of the common-school movement.
   b. writers during the Romantic period.
   c. creators of transcendentalism.
   d. leaders of the Second Great Awakening.

_____ 4. Why were many African American schools established in Philadelphia in the mid-1800s?
   a. Of all northern U.S. cities, Philadelphia had the largest African American population.
   b. As a center of Quaker influence, Philadelphia strongly supported the education of African American children.
   c. Laws in other northern cities barred freed African Americans from receiving any kind of education.
   d. Philadelphia's citizens believed that establishing African American schools would help the abolitionist cause.

_____ 5. What effect did Nat Turner's Rebellion of 1831 have on southern society?
   a. Many slaveholders freed their slaves.
   b. People stopped discussing slavery openly.
   c. Mob violence over the slavery issue increased dramatically.
   d. More whites began hiding fugitive slaves.

Progress Assessment

_____ **6.** The majority of German immigrants who entered the United States in the late 1840s were attracted by
   **a.** the supply of high-paying skilled jobs.
   **b.** economic opportunity and freedom from government control.
   **c.** protection of freedom of religion.
   **d.** political refuge and support for revolutionaries at home.

_____ **7.** Which of these ideas did religious leader Charles Grandison Finney express?
   **a.** Doing good deeds is not proof of faith.
   **b.** Religious leaders alone can be free from sin.
   **c.** Men are closer to God than women.
   **d.** Salvation is in the hands of the individual.

_____ **8.** One of the benefits of women's reform work was that
   **a.** some men became involved in the women's movement.
   **b.** most people began raising money for the women's movement.
   **c.** more women began educating their children at home.
   **d.** women began controlling their fathers' property.

_____ **9.** Which of the following was common in American cities in the mid-1800s?
   **a.** criminal activity
   **b.** public fire departments
   **c.** crowded subways
   **d.** sanitation services

**FILL IN THE BLANK** Read each sentence and fill in the blank with the word in the word pair that best completes the sentence.

**10.** The growth of industry and cities in the United States led to the development of a

new social class called the _____.

**(middle class/working class)**

**11.** The _____ was a movement of Christian renewal that swept through the United States during the 1790s and early 1800s.
**(Great Awakening/Second Great Awakening)**

**12.** The _____ was a document written by women's rights activists that described their beliefs about social injustice toward women. **(Declaration of the Rights of Women/Declaration of Sentiments)**

**13.** Reformer _____ spoke to the state legislature of Massachusetts about the fact that the mentally ill were housed with criminals in the state's prison system. **(Dorothea Dix/Margaret Fuller)**

**14.** The _____ was an organization that fought for the immediate emancipation of slaves and for racial equality for African Americans living in the United States. **(American Anti-Slavery Society/Know-Nothing Party)**

**PRACTICING SOCIAL STUDIES SKILLS** Study the quotation below and answer the question that follows.

> "That man over here says that women need to be helped into carriages and lifted over ditches, and to have the best place everywhere. Nobody ever helps me into carriages or over mud puddles, or gives me any best place . . . Look at me! I have ploughed and planted and . . . no man could head [outwork] me. And ain't I a woman?"
>
> —Sojourner Truth, quoted in *A History of Women in America* by Carol Hymowitz and Michaele Weissman

_____ **15.** Which of these statements best expresses the main idea of Sojourner Truth's speech given at a women's rights convention in 1851?
  **a.** Women should not be thought of as weaker than men and they deserve equality.
  **b.** African American women and white women should be considered equals.
  **c.** Women should use any means necessary to obtain equal rights in America.
  **d.** African American rights should be addressed by the government before women's rights.

New Movements in America, *continued*                    Chapter Test Form A

**MATCHING**  In the space provided, write the letter of the term or person that matches each description. Some answers will not be used.

_____ **16.** poorly designed apartment buildings that were home to large numbers of people

_____ **17.** escaped slave who succeeded in leading over 300 slaves to freedom on the Underground Railroad

_____ **18.** first public meeting about women's rights held in the United States

_____ **19.** started an all-female academy in Hartford, Connecticut

_____ **20.** escaped slave whose autobiographies were intended to expose the injustices of slavery

_____ **21.** organization designed to help fugitive slaves escape to the North

_____ **22.** philosophical movement that stressed the belief that people could rise above material things in life

_____ **23.** groups of people who joined together to try to form a perfect society

_____ **24.** women's rights activist who was one of the organizers of the Seneca Falls Convention

_____ **25.** Romantic poet who praised American individualism and democracy

**a.** utopian communities

**b.** Walt Whitman

**c.** Frederick Douglass

**d.** Elizabeth Cady Stanton

**e.** Seneca Falls Convention

**f.** Catharine Beecher

**g.** Underground Railroad

**h.** tenements

**i.** Harriet Tubman

**j.** transcendentalism

**k.** Horace Mann

**l.** Romanticism

**New Movements in America**

Chapter Test

**Form B**

**SHORT ANSWER** On a separate sheet of paper, answer each of the following questions in complete sentences.

1. Which factors increased immigration from Ireland to the United States in the mid-1840s?

2. Give the name of at least one important transcendentalist writer.

3. What was the significance of the Seneca Falls Convention?

4. How did Dorothea Dix contribute to the prison reform movement?

5. How did the federal government attempt to hinder the efforts of abolitionists?

6. How did William Lloyd Garrison attempt to spread the antislavery message in the United States?

**PRACTICING SOCIAL STUDIES SKILLS** Study the map below and, on a separate sheet of paper, answer the question that follows.

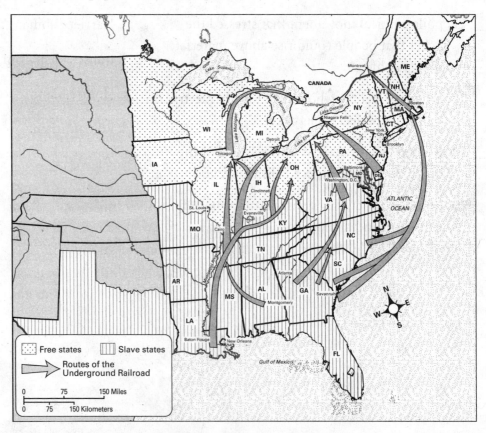

7. In which direction did the Underground Railroad go?

Progress Assessment

# A Divided Nation

Section Quiz

### Section 1

**FILL IN THE BLANK** For each of the following statements, fill in the blank with the appropriate word, phrase, or name.

1. The _____ of 1820 prohibited slavery north of latitude 36°30'.

2. Referring to the Mexican Cession, the _____ stated that "neither slavery nor involuntary servitude shall ever exist in any part of [the] territory."

3. Differences between Northerners and Southerners over the issue of slavery is an example of _____.

4. Proposed by Henry Clay, the _____ called for the admission of California as a free state, among other provisions.

5. Senator _____ of South Carolina asked that the slave states be allowed "to separate and part in peace."

6. On March 7, 1850, Senator _____ of Massachusetts spoke in front of the Senate in favor of the Compromise of 1850.

7. Fugitive slave _____ from Virginia was arrested in Boston in 1854.

8. The _____ made it a crime to help runaway slaves and allowed officials to arrest those slaves in free areas.

9. Within a decade of its publication in 1862, _____, an anti-slavery novel that electrified the nation, had sold 2 million copies.

10. Abraham Lincoln is said to have once referred to _____ as "the little lady who made this big war."

Progress Assessment

**A Divided Nation**

Section Quiz

**Section 2**

**MATCHING** In the space provided, write the letter of the term, place, or person that matches that description. Some answers will not be used.

_____ 1. Democratic presidential nominee in 1852

_____ 2. party whose candidate won the presidency in 1852

_____ 3. wanted to run a railroad to the Pacific from Chicago

_____ 4. act that divided the remainder of the Louisiana Purchase in two

_____ 5. territory with two governments in 1856

_____ 6. abolitionist who led an attack along the Pottawatomie Creek

_____ 7. Senator from Massachusetts who criticized the pro-slavery population of Kansas

_____ 8. beat a Senator unconscious with a cane

_____ 9. Debate over the expansion of this practice influenced the election of 1852.

_____ 10. May 1856 eruption of violence that engulfed a Kansas town

**a.** Charles Sumner

**b.** Democrats

**c.** Franklin Pierce

**d.** John Brown

**e.** Kansas

**f.** Kansas-Nebraska Act

**g.** Nebraska

**h.** Preston Brooks

**i.** slavery

**j.** Stephen Douglas

**k.** The Sack of Lawrence

**l.** Whigs

**m.** Winfield Scott

Progress Assessment

**A Divided Nation**

**MATCHING** In the space provided, write the letter of the term or person that matches that description. Some answers will not be used.

_____ **1.** formed in 1854 by groups united against the spread of slavery in the West

_____ **2.** won the presidential election of 1856

_____ **3.** slave that sparked controversy by suing for his freedom in 1846

_____ **4.** Chief Justice of the Supreme Court in 1857

_____ **5.** Republican nominee for the U.S. Senate from Illinois in 1858

_____ **6.** put the slavery question back in the hands of American citizens

_____ **7.** debates held in Illinois in 1858 regarding the spread of slavery in the West

_____ **8.** Republican nominee for president in 1856

_____ **9.** handed the abolitionist cause a setback with its decision in the *Dred Scott* case

_____ **10.** issue that made the Republican Party a "single-issue party"

**a.** Abraham Lincoln

**b.** Congress

**c.** Dred Scott

**d.** Freeport Doctrine

**e.** James Buchanan

**f.** John Emerson

**g.** John Frémont

**h.** Know-Nothings

**i.** Lincoln-Douglas

**j.** Republican Party

**k.** Roger B. Taney

**l.** slavery

**m.** Supreme Court

Progress Assessment

**A Divided Nation**                                    Section Quiz

**TRUE/FALSE** Mark each statement **T** if it is true or **F** if it is false. If false explain why.

_____ **1.** John C. Breckinridge led the raid on Harpers Ferry.

_____

_____

_____ **2.** African Americans came to Harpers Ferry to take part in the uprising.

_____

_____

_____ **3.** South Carolina was the first state to secede from the Union.

_____

_____

_____ **4.** The Confederate States of America formed its own constitution that guaranteed the right to own slaves.

_____

_____

_____ **5.** In the election of 1860, Abraham Lincoln did not carry any southern states.

_____

_____

Progress Assessment

Name _____ Class _____ Date _____

## A Divided Nation

**MULTIPLE CHOICE** For each of the following, write the letter of the best choice in the space provided.

_____ **1.** Which of the following best explains why the Democratic Party was not a strong force in the election of 1860?
   **a.** Many members of the Democratic Party decided to vote for a Republican candidate.
   **b.** The Democrats were a relatively new political party and had not yet gained enough support.
   **c.** Many southerners in the Democratic Party became abolitionists and supported other parties.
   **d.** The Democrats could not agree on a single candidate so their votes were divided between two candidates.

_____ **2.** In order to influence the debate over slavery, Harriet Beecher Stowe
   **a.** pushed for the start of the Civil War.
   **b.** exposed the harsh reality of slave life.
   **c.** accused the federal government of obeying the southern states.
   **d.** attacked political figures who supported slavery in the South.

_____ **3.** What was the position of South Carolina Senator John C. Calhoun in the debate for the Compromise of 1850?
   **a.** Slave states should separate peacefully from the Union.
   **b.** Slavery should end in the nation's capital.
   **c.** The federal government should ban the slave trade.
   **d.** California should enter the Union as a free state.

_____ **4.** The purpose of the Lincoln-Douglas debates was for Abraham Lincoln and Stephen Douglas to
   **a.** promote their candidacies for the U.S. Senate.
   **b.** spread the antislavery movement to the state of Illinois.
   **c.** gain supporters for the newly formed Republican Party.
   **d.** fight for the rights of African American slaves.

Progress Assessment

_____ **5.** The case of Anthony Burns was significant because it

    **a.** marked the end of the Fugitive Slave Act.

    **b.** was the first case of a fugitive being declared free.

    **c.** led to a harsher version of the Fugitive Slave Act.

    **d.** persuaded many to join the abolitionist cause.

_____ **6.** Chief Justice Roger B. Taney argued in 1857 that Congress could not prohibit someone from taking slaves into a federal territory because

    **a.** slaves were not citizens of the United States.

    **b.** federal territories could not rule against slavery.

    **c.** the slave trade was still allowed in every state.

    **d.** slaves were property defended by law.

_____ **7.** Democrats nominated James Buchanan to run in the 1856 presidential election because he was

    **a.** well liked by abolitionists.

    **b.** Stephen Douglas's vice president.

    **c.** politically inexperienced, but stood for slavery.

    **d.** absent from the debate over the Kansas-Nebraska Act.

_____ **8.** On the night of May 24, 1856, five pro-slavery men were killed in Kansas in an event called

    **a.** the Pottawatomie Massacre.

    **b.** John Brown's Raid.

    **c.** the Sack of Lawrence.

    **d.** Shays's Rebellion.

_____ **9.** What was Abraham Lincoln's opinion of John Brown's raid in Virginia?

    **a.** The antislavery movement should not be one of violence and bloodshed.

    **b.** Brown was justified in his methods of leading a violent attack in Virginia.

    **c.** Slaves in the South should have given stronger support to Brown's raid.

    **d.** The attack in Virginia needed to be better organized to effect change.

**PRACTICING SOCIAL STUDIES SKILLS** Study the maps below and
answer the question that follows.

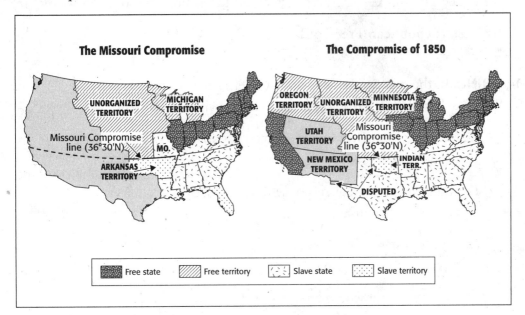

The Missouri Compromise     The Compromise of 1850

Free state     Free territory     Slave state     Slave territory

_____ **10.** According to the maps, which of the following is true?

  **a.** The number of slave states diminished between 1820 and 1850.

  **b.** There were many new slave territories after the Compromise of 1850.

  **c.** After 1850 the northwestern part of the nation was all free territories.

  **d.** By 1850 all unorganized territories had been divided among free states.

**FILL IN THE BLANK** Read each sentence and fill in the blank with the
word in the word pair that best completes the sentence.

**11.** After the election of 1860, many southern states seceded from the Union to form

  the _____ States of America. (**Confederate/Constitutional**)

**12.** The _____ settled most of the disputes between slave and
  free states over the issue of admitting California to the Union.
  (**Compromise of 1850/Wilmot Proviso**)

**13.** _____ was a slave who sued for freedom in federal court
  after living in free territory in Illinois. (**Anthony Burns/Dred Scott**)

**14.** The _____ proposed to divide the remainder of the
  Louisiana Purchase into two territories where the question of slavery would be
  decided by popular sovereignty. (**Compromise of 1850/Kansas-Nebraska Act**)

**15.** In 1854, members of various political parties joined to form the

_____ Party, which united against the spread of slavery in

the West. (**Republican/Free-Soil**)

**MATCHING** In the space provided, write the letter of the term or person that matches each description. Some answers will not be used.

_____ **16.** Mississippi native who was elected president of the Confederacy

_____ **17.** abolitionists' violent response to the Sack of Lawrence in Kansas

_____ **18.** rebellion staged by a group of abolitionists at Harpers Ferry, Virginia

_____ **19.** document that would have prohibited slavery in any part of the Mexican Cession

_____ **20.** U.S. senator from Illinois who proposed the Kansas-Nebraska Act

_____ **21.** act of formally withdrawing from the Union

_____ **22.** idea that police would enforce the voters' decision if it contradicted the Supreme Court's decision in the *Dred Scott* case

_____ **23.** political group formed by antislavery northerners who supported the Wilmot Proviso

_____ **24.** Democratic candidate in the election of 1852 who promised to honor the Compromise of 1850

_____ **25.** law that made it a crime to assist runaway slaves

**a.** secession

**b.** Freeport Doctrine

**c.** Stephen Douglas

**d.** Wilmot Proviso

**e.** Jefferson Davis

**f.** Fugitive Slave Act

**g.** John Brown's raid

**h.** Free-Soil Party

**i.** Abraham Lincoln

**j.** Franklin Pierce

**k.** Pottawatomie Massacre

**l.** John C. Calhoun

**A Divided Nation**

Chapter Test

Form B

**SHORT ANSWER** On a separate sheet of paper, answer each of the following questions in complete sentences.

**1.** Who led the Pottawatomie Massacre?

**2.** What were the main points of Abraham Lincoln's inaugural address in 1861?

**3.** Why was Abraham Lincoln successful in the election of 1860?

**4.** What was the significance of the Freeport Doctrine?

**5.** Who was Dred Scott?

**6.** After its victory in the Mexican War, the United States gained a large amount of land known as the Mexican Cession. How did political leaders in the 1840s propose to answer the question of whether or not to ban slavery in this territory?

**PRACTICING SOCIAL STUDIES SKILLS** Study the political cartoon below and, on a separate sheet of paper, answer the question that follows.

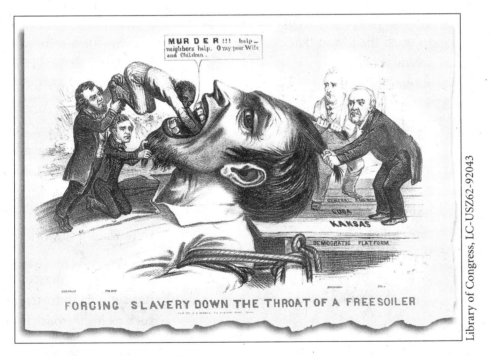

**7.** This political cartoon features an image of a Kansas Free-Soiler. What does this cartoon convey about the issue of slavery in this country?

**The Nation Expands**

Unit Test

Form A

**MULTIPLE CHOICE** For each of the following, write the letter of the best choice in the space provided.

_____ **1.** One issue the Republican Party rallied around in 1854 was the
   **a.** enforcement of the Fugitive Slave Act.
   **b.** fight against the spread of slavery in the West.
   **c.** idea of popular sovereignty in U.S. territories.
   **d.** support of the Kansas-Nebraska Act.

_____ **2.** Which of the following statements best describes how many white southerners justified slavery?
   **a.** State governments wanted to teach the lesson that freedom brings responsibility.
   **b.** Southern citizens felt that freed slaves could not take care of themselves.
   **c.** White churches were losing members to the independent church movement.
   **d.** Freed slaves could be self-sufficient, but should not mix with white society.

_____ **3.** What argument did some women make against the movement for equal rights?
   **a.** Men would view powerful women as unattractive.
   **b.** Public speaking and political activism were unladylike.
   **c.** Women should speak in public, but focus on their families while at home.
   **d.** Women and men were different rather than unequal.

_____ **4.** What was one argument given by Secretary of the Treasury Albert Gallatin about why there were so few factories in the United States?
   **a.** Urban areas were too messy to attract American workers from rural areas.
   **b.** There was a high availability of farmland in the United States.
   **c.** American factory workers were willing to work for low pay.
   **d.** The United States could not support industries such as iron production.

Progress Assessment

_____ **5.** What was a consequence of the Compromise of 1850?
  **a.** The federal government lost power over the states.
  **b.** Divisions between North and South became more distinct.
  **c.** Economic benefits of the slave trade were destroyed in all parts of the nation.
  **d.** The balance between free and slave states ended in the Union.

_____ **6.** The emergence of a middle class during the 1800s was brought about by the
  **a.** success of the nativist movement.
  **b.** decline in manufacturing.
  **c.** growth of industry and cities.
  **d.** improvement of factory conditions.

_____ **7.** Slave codes were
  **a.** strict state laws that controlled slaves' actions.
  **b.** a secret language slaves used to communicate.
  **c.** a set of rules for slave behavior set by a council of planters.
  **d.** the policy of slaves to always help one another.

_____ **8.** By 1860 Isaac Singer's company was the world's largest maker of
  **a.** clocks.
  **b.** iceboxes.
  **c.** safety pins.
  **d.** sewing machines.

_____ **9.** The election of 1860 was significant because it
  **a.** brought to light the divisions that existed in the United States over slavery.
  **b.** exposed the corruption of the electoral college in the election process.
  **c.** showed that the South was losing its political power in the nation.
  **d.** illustrated that a candidate did not have to carry a state to win.

_____ **10.** Horace Mann contributed to the education reform movement in the 19th century by
  **a.** developing new ways of instructing students with handicaps.
  **b.** fighting for improvements in the education of women.
  **c.** extending the length of the school year.
  **d.** sending children of all races to the same schools.

_____ **11.** The Supreme Court's ruling in *Dred Scott* v. *Sandford* established that
   **a.** slaves were not allowed to bring accusations against slaveholders.
   **b.** the Missouri Compromise's restriction on slavery was unconstitutional.
   **c.** establishing a residence on free soil makes a slave free.
   **d.** Congress had the legal power to ban slavery in federal territories.

_____ **12.** The man responsible for bringing new textile machines to the United States was
   **a.** Samuel Slater.
   **b.** Moses Brown.
   **c.** Richard Arkwright.
   **d.** James Hargreaves.

_____ **13.** By leading an armed resistance in Virginia in 1859, John Brown hoped to
   **a.** steal weapons and bring them to local slaves.
   **b.** fight the work of antislavery supporters in Virginia.
   **c.** control the slaves that had escaped in Virginia.
   **d.** show his anger about the *Dred Scott* decision.

_____ **14.** What contribution did Harriet Tubman make to the antislavery movement?
   **a.** As a conductor on the Underground Railroad, she led many fugitive slaves to freedom.
   **b.** She lectured members of the American Anti-Slavery Society about the evils of slavery.
   **c.** As the founder of a southern antislavery group, she helped stage many peaceful slave strikes.
   **d.** She persuaded many southern slaveholders to join the abolitionist movement.

_____ **15.** In the mid-1800s, leaders of free African American communities in the North were often influenced by
   **a.** utopian communities and their focus on cooperation.
   **b.** Romantic writers and their questioning of Puritanism.
   **c.** the Second Great Awakening and its spirit of reform.
   **d.** the temperance movement and its emphasis on self-discipline.

Progress Assessment

**TRUE/FALSE** Indicate whether each statement below is true or false by writing **T** or **F** in the space provided.

_____ **16.** Reformers wanted to limit alcohol consumption because they believed that alcohol abuse was the cause of many social problems.

_____ **17.** Angelina and Sarah Grimké were antislavery activists of the 1830s who tried to convince southern women to join the abolitionist movement.

_____ **18.** Transcendentalist thinkers believed that people should depend on outside authorities for guidance about how to conduct their lives.

_____ **19.** Americans Nathaniel Hawthorne, Edgar Allan Poe, and Henry Wadsworth Longfellow were all writers of the Romantic period.

_____ **20.** The antislavery movement inspired many women to join together to begin the women's rights movement.

_____ **21.** The period of Christian renewal in the United States during the 1790s and early 1800s took place only in the North.

_____ **22.** Elizabeth Cady Stanton began her fight for women's rights by speaking at the World Anti-Slavery Convention in 1840.

_____ **23.** Many of the Irish who immigrated to the United States in the mid-1840s were escaping a violent revolution in their country.

_____ **24.** The nonviolent rescue of Anthony Burns from a Boston jail in 1854 showed that abolitionists practiced peaceful resistance.

_____ **25.** Democrat Franklin Pierce won the election of 1852 because he strongly supported the Fugitive Slave Act and the Compromise of 1850.

_____ **26.** The Kansas-Nebraska Act upheld the conditions for permitting slavery in the territories established by the Missouri Compromise.

_____ **27.** After the Sack of Lawrence, abolitionist representative Charles Sumner was beaten unconscious with a cane by Senator Preston Brooks in the Senate chambers.

_____ **28.** In his "House Divided" speech, Abraham Lincoln declared that the United States would one day resolve its divisions over slavery.

_____ **29.** After the election of 1860, southerners decided to secede from the Union because they feared their economy would be destroyed without slave labor.

**PRACTICING SOCIAL STUDIES SKILLS** Study the graph below and answer the question that follows.

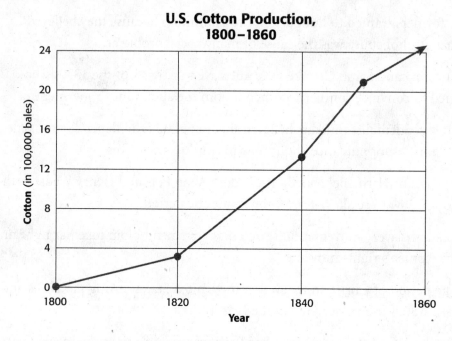

**U.S. Cotton Production, 1800–1860**

_____ **30.** According to the graph, the rate of U.S. cotton production increased most rapidly between
  **a.** 1780 and 1800.
  **b.** 1800 and 1820.
  **c.** 1820 and 1840.
  **d.** 1840 and 1850.

**FILL IN THE BLANK** Read each sentence and fill in the blank with the word in the word pair that best completes the sentence.

**31.** French writer Alexis de Tocqueville remarked that the contributions to daily

life made by the _____ made life more "convenient."

**(Transportation Revolution/Industrial Revolution)**

**32.** The _____ was responsible for shifting the location of many textile mills. **(assembly line/water frame)**

**33.** In the 1760s, the first breakthrough of the Industrial Revolution changed how

_____ were made. **(automobiles/textiles)**

**34.** A _____ was an organization of workers with a specific skill or from a single factory who tried to improve pay and working conditions for members. (**trade union/strike**)

**35.** _____ was a Supreme Court case about interstate trade. (*Gibbons* v. *Ogden/Dred Scott* v. *Sandford*)

**36.** On August 9, 1807, Robert Fulton's full-sized commercial steamboat called the

_____ traveled up the Hudson River against the current

without trouble. (*Clermont/Tom Thumb*)

**37.** Samuel Morse's invention, the _____, enabled people to send news quickly from coast to coast. (**telephone/telegraph**)

**38.** The _____ was a locomotive credited with bringing "railroad fever" to the United States. (*Clermont/Tom Thumb*)

**39.** The Wilmot Proviso created feelings of _____ throughout the country as people began to favor the interests of their regions over those of the nation as a whole. (**sectionalism/popular sovereignty**)

**40.** _____ was the author of *Uncle Tom's Cabin*—the novel that brought the injustices of slavery to the nation's attention. (**Harriet Beecher Stowe/Frederick Douglass**)

**MATCHING** In the space provided, write the letter of the term, person, or place that matches each description. Some answers will not be used.

_____ **41.** large-scale southern farmers who owned more than 20 slaves

_____ **42.** one of the most productive industrial factories of the South in the 1800s

_____ **43.** emotional Christian songs sung by slaves

_____ **44.** southern owners of small farms with few slaves

_____ **45.** patented the cotton gin in 1793

_____ **46.** the planting of a different crop on the same plot every few years

_____ **47.** slave whose violent rebellion led many states to strengthen their slave codes

_____ **48.** area of high cotton production in the South

_____ **49.** crop brokers who managed the trading of cotton

_____ **50.** used the labor of all field hands on the same task at the same time

**a.** Nat Turner

**b.** Eli Whitney

**c.** gang-labor system

**d.** slave codes

**e.** yeomen

**f.** planters

**g.** spirituals

**h.** cotton belt

**i.** folktales

**j.** Tredegar Iron Works

**k.** factors

**l.** crop rotation

**The Nation Expands**

Unit Test

Form B

**SHORT ANSWER** On a separate sheet of paper, answer each of the following questions in complete sentences.

1. What did Sarah G. Bagley do to improve working conditions for employees of private businesses?

2. What event prompted many states to strengthen their slave codes?

3. What did John Brown hope to accomplish by launching an attack on Harpers Ferry, Virginia?

4. Why did planters feel cotton would be a profitable "cash crop"? What advantage did cotton have over other staple crops?

5. Who proposed the Kansas-Nebraska Act? Why?

6. Secretary of the Treasury Albert Gallatin gave many reasons for the trouble American manufacturers had competing with the British. What were two of those reasons?

**PRACTICING SOCIAL STUDIES SKILLS** Study the image below and, on a separate sheet of paper, answer the question that follows.

Asher Durand's *The First Harvest in the Wilderness*

Brooklyn Museum of Art, Gift of the Brooklyn Institute of Arts and Science/Bridgeman Art Library

7. What features of this painting show that it is a good example of the Romantic movement?

**The Civil War**

Section Quiz

### Section 1

**TRUE/FALSE** Mark each statement **T** if it is true or **F** if it is false. If false explain why.

_____ **1.** In 1860, Abraham Lincoln became president of the United States.

_____

_____

_____ **2.** In his inaugural address, Lincoln promised to end slavery all over the South.

_____

_____

_____ **3.** Fort Sumter, a federal outpost in Charleston, South Carolina, was attacked by Confederate troops, beginning the Civil War.

_____

_____

_____ **4.** Wedged between the North and the South were the key border states of Delaware, Kentucky, Maryland, and Missouri.

_____

_____

_____ **5.** Cotton diplomacy was the idea that France would support the Confederacy because it needed the South's raw cotton supply.

_____

_____

**The Civil War**                              Section Quiz

### Section 2

**FILL IN THE BLANK** For each of the following statements, fill in the blank with the appropriate word, phrase, or name.

1. Confederate General _____ earned his nickname by "standing like a stone wall."

2. The first major battle of the Civil War was the _____.

3. _____ assembled a highly disciplined force of 100,000 soldiers called the Army of the Potomac.

4. The commander of the Confederate army was _____, a graduate of the Military Academy at West Point.

5. The Confederate troops forced the Union army to retreat from near Richmond in _____.

6. The _____ was the bloodiest single-day battle of the Civil War and of U.S. history.

7. While the two armies fought for control of the land, the Union _____ controlled the sea.

8. _____ were ships heavily armored with iron.

9. The *Monitor* was designed by Swedish born engineer _____.

10. The Union ship, the *Monitor*, engaged the Confederate ship, the _____, in battle to ensure the continuation of the Union's blockade.

Name _____ Class _____ Date _____

## The Civil War

**MULTIPLE CHOICE** For each of the following, write the letter of the best choice in the space provided.

_____ **1.** The Union strategy in the West centered on control of what river?
- **a.** Cumberland River
- **b.** Mississippi River
- **c.** Tennessee River
- **d.** Carolina River

_____ **2.** Who was the commander of the forces in the Union's western campaign?
- **a.** Ulysses S. Grant
- **b.** Robert E. Lee
- **c.** Stonewall Jackson
- **d.** George McClellan

_____ **3.** On April 6, 1862, although initially caught by surprise, Union troops forced the Confederates to retreat in what battle?
- **a.** Battle of Antietam
- **b.** Battle of Shiloh
- **c.** Seven Day's Battles
- **d.** Second Battle of Bull Run

_____ **4.** What city did the Union army lay siege to and after about six weeks finally capture?
- **a.** New Orleans
- **b.** Natchez
- **c.** Richmond
- **d.** Vicksburg

_____ **5.** In March 1862, what group of Native Americans aided the Confederates?
- **a.** Iroquois
- **b.** Cheyenne
- **c.** Cherokee
- **d.** Apache

Progress Assessment

Name _____ Class _____ Date _____

# The Civil War

**MATCHING** In the space provided, write the letter of the term or person that matches each description. Some answers will not be used.

_____ **1.** the freeing of slaves

_____ **2.** President of the United States during the Civil War

_____ **3.** the order to free the Confederate slaves

_____ **4.** escaped slaves

_____ **5.** consisted mostly of free African Americans

_____ **6.** established a small hospital in Virginia that became a major army hospital

_____ **7.** a constitutional protection against unlawful imprisonment

_____ **8.** forced military service

_____ **9.** founded the American Red Cross

_____ **10.** Democrats who spoke out against the war

**a.** Abraham Lincoln

**b.** Clara Barton

**c.** contrabands

**d.** Copperheads

**e.** draft

**f.** emancipation

**g.** Emancipation Proclamation

**h.** George McClellan

**i.** habeas corpus

**j.** Port Hudson

**k.** Republicans

**l.** Sally Louisa Tompkins

**m.** 54th Massachusetts Infantry

Progress Assessment

Section Quiz

## Section 5

**MATCHING** In the space provided, write the letter of the term, person, or place that matches each description. Some answers will not be used.

_____ **1.** Confederate general accidentally shot by his own troops

_____ **2.** key battle that finally turned the tide against the Confederates

_____ **3.** one of the most famous speeches in American history

_____ **4.** series of battles designed to capture the Confederate capital at Richmond, Virginia

_____ **5.** carried out the Union plan to destroy southern railroads and industries

_____ **6.** practice of destroying civilian and economic resources

_____ **7.** President of the Confederacy

_____ **8.** fell to Union soldiers, costing the South an important rail link and its center of industry

_____ **9.** where Lee surrendered to Grant, thus ending the Civil War

_____ **10.** how long the Civil War lasted

**a.** Atlanta

**b.** Appomattox Courthouse

**c.** Battle of Gettysburg

**d.** four years

**e.** George Pickett

**f.** Gettysburg Address

**g.** Jefferson Davis

**h.** Petersburg

**i.** six years

**j.** Stonewall Jackson

**k.** total war

**l.** Wilderness Campaign

**m.** William Tecumseh Sherman

Progress Assessment

Name _____ Class _____ Date _____

# The Civil War

## Chapter Test

### Form A

**MULTIPLE CHOICE** For each of the following, write the letter of the best choice in the space provided.

_____ 1. The Union and the Confederate armies built up their troops at the beginning of the war by
   a. relying on help from volunteers.
   b. allowing women and children to serve in the army.
   c. issuing a draft, which forced civilians to serve in the army.
   d. giving monetary rewards to people willing to serve in the army.

_____ 2. The Union's capture of Atlanta contributed to Lincoln's reelection because it showed Union voters that
   a. there would be few casualties in the war.
   b. the North was making progress in defeating the South.
   c. the South was willing to give in to Lincoln's demands.
   d. Lincoln's decision to emancipate slaves was justified.

_____ 3. In the Gettysburg Address, Lincoln referenced the Declaration of Independence when he emphasized
   a. preventing war.
   b. limited freedom for slaves.
   c. limited democracy.
   d. liberty, equality, and democracy.

_____ 4. The Battle of Antietam was a bloody battle that
   a. allowed Lee's army to advance northward.
   b. gave the North a slight advantage.
   c. marked the last battle of the Civil War.
   d. convinced Europe to support the Confederacy.

_____ 5. The border states Delaware, Kentucky, Maryland, and Missouri were all
   a. free states that sided with the Union.
   b. completely unified in their feelings about the war.
   c. against President Lincoln's war policies.
   d. slave states that did not join the Confederacy.

Progress Assessment

_____ **6.** Why did the Union find it difficult to maintain the blockade it set up to control southern ports?

    **a.** Its navy was not as strong as the Confederate forces.

    **b.** Its naval officers were inexperienced.

    **c.** The South had large ships to push through the blockade.

    **d.** Its navy had to patrol thousands of miles of coastline.

_____ **7.** How did many northern Democrats feel about Lincoln's Emancipation Proclamation?

    **a.** They were upset that slaves were not emancipated in the border states.

    **b.** They feared that freed slaves would come north and take their jobs at lower wages.

    **c.** They were in total agreement with Lincoln's decision to emancipate the slaves.

    **d.** They feared it would prolong the war.

_____ **8.** Clara Barton is famous for

    **a.** secretly housing Union army soldiers.

    **b.** being the first woman to serve in the military.

    **c.** organizing peace protests.

    **d.** delivering medicine to battlefields and founding the Red Cross.

_____ **9.** Which of the following describes the right of habeas corpus?

    **a.** a constitutional protection against unlawful imprisonment

    **b.** an order to free Confederate slaves

    **c.** an order to free all slaves

    **d.** a revolt by Copperheads demanding freedom

**PRACTICING SOCIAL STUDIES SKILLS** Study the chart below and answer the question that follows.

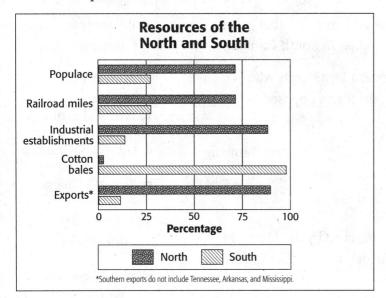

**Resources of the North and South**

Populace
Railroad miles
Industrial establishments
Cotton bales
Exports*

Percentage

North        South

*Southern exports do not include Tennessee, Arkansas, and Mississippi.

_____ **10.** According to the chart, which of the following statements is true?
   **a.** The North was more industrialized and more populated than the South.
   **b.** Southern cities could rely on a larger system of roads.
   **c.** The North produced 30% less cotton than the South.
   **d.** The South was more advanced in agriculture and industry.

**TRUE/FALSE** Indicate whether each statement below is true or false by writing **T** or **F** in the space provided.

_____ **11.** The Union victory in the Second Battle of Bull Run allowed the North to gain full control of the Mississippi River.

_____ **12.** Lincoln faced northern opposition to the Civil War after Congress approved a draft, or forced military service, in 1863.

_____ **13.** In the war in the West, Confederate and Union troops fought many battles for control of the Mississippi River.

_____ **14.** The Civil War began at Fort Sumter, a federal outpost in Charleston, South Carolina.

_____ **15.** While General George McClellan was slow and careful in training his men and planning attacks, General Robert E. Lee took risks and made unpredictable moves to throw off his enemies.

**MATCHING** In the space provided, write the letter of the term, person, or place that matches each description. Some answers will not be used.

_____ **16.** African American military unit that led the charge on Fort Wagner in South Carolina

_____ **17.** group of midwestern Democrats who sympathized with the South and opposed abolition

_____ **18.** Union General who led the western campaign during the Civil War

_____ **19.** escaped slaves

_____ **20.** series of battles launched by the Union to capture the Confederate capital at Richmond, Virginia

_____ **21.** Civil War battle in which the Union gained greater control of the Mississippi River

_____ **22.** type of warfare in which civilian and economic resources are destroyed

_____ **23.** unsuccessful attack made by the Confederacy on Union troops during the Battle of Gettysburg

_____ **24.** scene of the meeting between Union and Confederate leaders in which the Confederacy surrendered

_____ **25.** Union General whose two-part strategy was to destroy the South's economy and divide the South by gaining control of the Mississippi River

**a.** Wilderness Campaign

**b.** contrabands

**c.** Winfield Scott

**d.** Ulysses S. Grant

**e.** Pickett's Charge

**f.** Appomattox Courthouse

**g.** 54th Massachusetts Infantry

**h.** total war

**i.** Battle of Shiloh

**j.** Copperheads

**k.** ironclads

**l.** Robert E. Lee

# The Civil War

Chapter Test

**Form B**

**SHORT ANSWER** On a separate sheet of paper, answer each of the following questions in complete sentences.

1. How were civilians able to participate in the war effort? How did Clara Barton participate?

2. What did the North learn from the First Battle of Bull Run?

3. What was the name of the bloody Civil War battle that stopped the Confederacy's northward advances?

4. Why was the Siege of Vicksburg important to the Union's western campaign?

5. What ideals from the Declaration of Independence did Abraham Lincoln refer to in his famous Gettysburg Address? Why?

6. Why did the Union want control of the border states?

**PRACTICING SOCIAL STUDIES SKILLS** Study the political cartoon below and, on a separate sheet of paper, answer the question that follows.

Library of Congress/PRC Archive

7. Which part of General Winfield Scott's two-part strategy does this political cartoon illustrate? What does the snake represent?

Progress Assessment

**Reconstruction**

Section Quiz

**Section 1**

**TRUE/FALSE** Mark each statement **T** if it is true or **F** if it is false. If false explain why.

_____ **1.** Tired southern soldiers returned home to find that although the economy was badly damaged, cities and farms were in good condition.

_____

_____

_____ **2.** Reconstruction was the process of readmitting the former Confederate states to the Union.

_____

_____

_____ **3.** Established in 1865, the Freedmen's Bureau was an agency that provided relief for poor whites only.

_____

_____

_____ **4.** The Thirteenth Amendment declared the Emancipation Proclamation unconstitutional.

_____

_____

_____ **5.** Abraham Lincoln was assassinated by John Wilkes Booth on April 14, 1865.

_____

_____

_____ **6.** The Ten Percent Plan was Andrew Johnson's plan for readmitting southern states to the union.

_____

_____

Progress Assessment

# Reconstruction

**MATCHING** In the space provided, write the letter of the term or person that matches that description. Some answers will not be used.

_____ 1. laws that greatly limited the freedom of African Americans

_____ 2. group that wanted the Federal government to force change in the South

_____ 3. laws that divided the South into five military districts

_____ 4. leader of the Radical Republicans

_____ 5. process used by a legislative body to bring charges of wrongdoings against a public official

_____ 6. gave African American men the right to vote

_____ 7. president of the United States in 1866

_____ 8. banned slavery throughout the United States

_____ 9. presidential candidate that ran under the slogan "Let Us Have Peace"

_____ 10. firmly in Republican hands following the election of 1866

**a.** Andrew Johnson

**b.** Black Codes

**c.** Congress

**d.** Democrats

**e.** Fifteenth Amendment

**f.** impeachment

**g.** polls

**h.** Radical Republicans

**i.** Reconstruction Acts

**j.** Thaddeus Stevens

**k.** Thirteenth Amendment

**l.** Ulysses S. Grant

**m.** veto

Progress Assessment

Name _____ Class _____ Date _____

## Reconstruction

**FILL IN THE BLANK** For each of the following statements, fill in the blank with the appropriate word, phrase, or name.

1. African Americans were the largest group of southern _____ voters.

2. The son of a former slave, _____ was the first African American to serve in the United States Senate.

3. As more _____ took office, resistance to Reconstruction increased among the majority of white southerners.

4. The _____ was a group of white southerners from Tennessee who opposed civil rights for African Americans.

5. Democrats who brought their party back to power in the South were called

    _____.

6. _____ is the forced separation of whites and African Americans in pubic places.

7. By the 1880s, laws that enforced segregation in southern states, or

    _____ laws, were common in the southern states.

8. In an effort to deny the vote to African Americans, a _____ was instituted, requiring people to pay a tax before they could vote.

9. The landowners provided the land, tools, and supplies, while

    _____ provided the labor.

10. The _____ of 1875 guaranteed African Americans equal rights in public places such as theaters.

Progress Assessment

**Reconstruction**

Chapter Test

**Form A**

**MULTIPLE CHOICE** For each of the following, write the letter of the best choice in the space provided.

_____ **1.** Why did Congress still refuse to readmit southern states into the Union in 1865, when Vice President Andrew Johnson became president?

  **a.** The representatives of the new governments failed to declare secession illegal.

  **b.** The new governments failed to revise their constitutions by that year.

  **c.** The new governments refused to ban slavery in their respective states.

  **d.** The representatives of the new governments had been leaders of the Confederacy.

_____ **2.** Whom did white southerners call "carpetbaggers"?

  **a.** former Confederate leaders who joined the Republican Party

  **b.** African American Republicans who took over Confederate seats

  **c.** former slaves living in the north who voted with the Republicans

  **d.** northern-born Republican office-holders who had moved to the South

_____ **3.** Which statement describes working life at southern mills in the late 1800s?

  **a.** Skilled employees received constant training and were content with their work.

  **b.** Employees were overworked and suffered from asthma and brown-lung disease.

  **c.** Slow-moving machinery workers were bored but high wages satisfied them.

  **d.** Children were not allowed near the mills and most women could advance to higher-paying positions.

_____ **4.** The Freedmen's Bureau was an agency that

  **a.** infiltrated the Ku Klux Klan in southern states.

  **b.** worked to enforce Black Codes.

  **c.** gave relief for freedpeople and some poor southerners.

  **d.** gave jobs to freedpeople, but prohibited slaves from attending school.

Progress Assessment

_____ 5. Lincoln's main vision for Reconstruction was to
  a. quickly return the South to its previous way of life.
  b. see freed slaves living as equals with their white counterparts.
  c. reunite the nation as quickly and painlessly as possible.
  d. make it difficult for the southern states to reenter the Union.

_____ 6. Hiram Revels was the first African American to hold which post?
  a. Secretary of State
  b. U.S. Senator
  c. U.S. House Representative
  d. Supreme Court justice

_____ 7. Why was the Ku Klux Klan able to obtain a great deal of power in the South before 1870?
  a. Local governments did little to stop the group's violence.
  b. The Klan provided jobs for people who supported the group's beliefs.
  c. The Klan received public support from Congress to continue its work.
  d. Local governments had no legal right to prohibit the group's activities.

_____ 8. Jobs in which industry offered many southern workers an alternative to farming in the late 1800s?
  a. cotton
  b. steel
  c. construction
  d. shipping

_____ 9. At the urging of Radical Republicans, Congress passed a new bill that would
  a. limit African Americans' rights.
  b. abolish the Black Codes.
  c. give the Freedmen's Bureau more power.
  d. pardon those who committed crimes against African Americans.

_____ 10. To begin the process of Reconstruction, President Johnson first
  a. appointed a temporary governor for each state.
  b. established a temporary government for the entire South.
  c. banned Confederate officials from public office.
  d. allowed elections of state and federal representatives.

**PRACTICING SOCIAL STUDIES SKILLS** Study the political cartoon below and answer the question that follows.

_____ **11.** Which of the following aspects of the cartoon suggests that the artist supported Radical Republican ideas?

  **a.** the way the men are dressed

  **b.** the title of the cartoon

  **c.** the nicknames of the men

  **d.** the inclusion of the flag

**FILL IN THE BLANK** Read each sentence and fill in the blank with the word in the word pair that best completes the sentence.

**12.** To ensure that the Civil Rights Act of 1866 would not be overturned, Congress

proposed the _____ Amendment, which would grant citi-

zenship to African Americans. (**Fourteenth/Fifteenth**)

**13.** After President Andrew Johnson angered Congress by firing the secretary of war,

the House of Representatives voted to _____ the president,

hoping to remove him from office. (**depose/impeach**)

**14.** The Fifteenth Amendment granted African American men

_____ rights in the United States. (**voting/citizenship**)

**15.** The _____ was an agreement in which the Democrats accepted Republican Rutherford B. Hayes as president in exchange for the removal of federal troops from the South.
**(Civil Rights Act of 1875/Compromise of 1877)**

**16.** Abraham Lincoln's proposed plan for readmitting southern states to the Union was called the _____.

**(Ten Percent Plan/Civil Rights Act of 1866)**

**17.** Thaddeus Stevens was a leader of the _____ who wanted the federal government to be more involved in giving economic and political justice to African Americans and poor white southerners.
**(Freeedmen's Bureau/Radical Republicans)**

**18.** Common in southern states, _____ enforced segregation, or the separation of whites from African Americans in public places.
**(the Black Codes/Jim Crow laws)**

**TRUE/FALSE** Indicate whether each statement below is true or false by writing **T** or **F** in the space provided.

_____ **19.** After the Civil War the economy of the South was badly damaged and many banks and merchants went bankrupt.

_____ **20.** In the case of *Plessy* v. *Ferguson*, the U.S. Supreme Court decided that segregation was unconstitutional.

_____ **21.** The Thirteenth Amendment made slavery illegal throughout the United States.

_____ **22.** The Civil Rights Act of 1866 limited African Americans' rights.

_____ **23.** The Black Codes greatly increased the rights and freedom of African Americans in northern as well as southern states.

_____ **24.** In the election of 1868, Republican Ulysses S. Grant won the presidency with the help of African American votes.

_____ **25.** The Ku Klux Klan was formed because many white southerners opposed civil rights and disapproved of African American officeholders.

# Reconstruction

Chapter Test

## Form B

**SHORT ANSWER** On a separate sheet of paper, answer each of the following questions in complete sentences.

**1.** How did the Civil War affect life in the South?

**2.** What was the Thirteenth Amendment?

**3.** How did the Compromise of 1877 affect Reconstruction in the United States?

**4.** What factors led to the development of the Ku Klux Klan?

**5.** Why did Congressional Republicans want to pass the Fifteenth Amendment?

**6.** What were the Black Codes?

**PRACTICING SOCIAL STUDIES SKILLS** Study the map below and, on a separate sheet of paper, answer the question that follows.

### African American Representation in the South, 1870

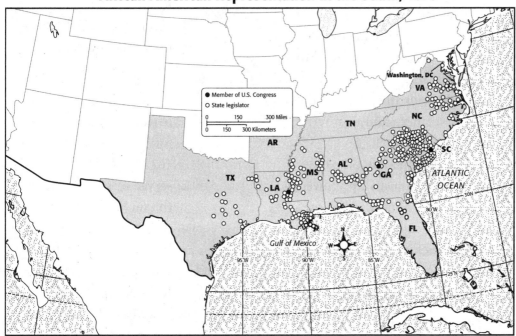

**7.** According to the map, which state had the highest concentration of African American state legislators in 1870?

Progress Assessment

Name _____ Class _____ Date _____

# The Nation Breaks Apart

**MULTIPLE CHOICE** For each of the following, write the letter of the best choice in the space provided.

_____ 1. What was the strategy of total war adopted by General Sherman?
  **a.** destroying civilian and economic resources
  **b.** executing all prisoners of war without a trial
  **c.** attacking the enemy both on land and from the sea
  **d.** emancipating slaves to reduce the work force

_____ 2. What was the significance of the development of ironclads?
  **a.** It shifted the majority of fighting from the land to the sea.
  **b.** It made the power of the Northern and Southern navies equal.
  **c.** It signified that the days of wooden warships powered by sails and wind were drawing to a close.
  **d.** It demonstrated to both sides that the war would not be ending soon.

_____ 3. Which group was angered by its exclusion from the benefits of the Fifteenth Amendment?
  **a.** women
  **b.** immigrants
  **c.** the lower classes
  **d.** ex-Confederate voters

_____ 4. Thomas "Stonewall" Jackson was a
  **a.** Union general whose strategy was to surround Confederates by building a stone wall.
  **b.** brave Confederate soldier who was buried beneath a stone wall in Richmond, Virginia.
  **c.** Confederate general who refused to back down during the First Battle of Bull Run.
  **d.** Union general who cautiously planned attacks.

_____ 5. Which of the following describes Ulysses S. Grant?
  **a.** led an army troop to victory during the War of 1812
  **b.** served in the French and Indian War and contributed to the victory
  **c.** led America to victory during the American Revolution
  **d.** served as a bold, restless commander of Union forces

Progress Assessment

**The Nation Breaks Apart,** *continued*                            Unit Test Form A

_____. **6.** Which of the following
African American units
played a key role in the attack
on South Carolina's Fort
Wagner?
  **a.** the 54th Massachusetts
  Infantry
  **b.** the 29th Connecticut
  Volunteer Cavalry
  **c.** the 8th Kansas Colored
  Heavy Artillery
  **d.** the 100th Tennessee
  Colored Infantry

_____ **7.** President Andrew Johnson's
plan for wealthy southerners
and former Confederate officials was to
  **a.** grant amnesty through
  presidential pardons.
  **b.** have them pay off
  Confederate debts.
  **c.** make them federal
  representatives.
  **d.** force them to surrender
  their land.

_____ **8.** The main problem for the
Confederate and Union
armies when preparing for
war was that
  **a.** the climate during many
  battles hurt soldiers'
  morale.
  **b.** civilians did not support
  either army.
  **c.** most soldiers were unreli-
  able mercenaries.
  **d.** most soldiers lacked supplies and were inexperi-
  enced and undisciplined.

_____ **9.** Which of the following
describes the situation in the
West in the war's early years.
  **a.** The Union succeeded
  in halting several
  Confederate attacks.
  **b.** The region remained in
  the hands of independent
  Native Americans.
  **c.** Pro-Confederate forces
  retreated from the region
  almost immediately.
  **d.** The Confederacy gained
  many territories thanks to
  the help of British troops.

_____ **10.** Which of the following best
describes the Emancipation
Proclamation?
  **a.** It discouraged enslaved
  Africans from escaping.
  **b.** It gave full control of slavery to the federal
  government.
  **c.** It had an immediate effect
  on abolishing slavery.
  **d.** It freed Confederate slaves.

_____ **11.** The Fifteenth Amendment
granted African American
men the right to
  **a.** bear arms.
  **b.** equal treatment.
  **c.** vote.
  **d.** peaceably assemble.

Progress Assessment

_____ **12.** The Fourteenth Amendment defined who could be considered a U.S. citizen. Which group did the Amendment exclude from U.S. citizenship?
   **a.** antislavery supporters
   **b.** Native Americans
   **c.** African Americans
   **d.** Confederacy supporters

_____ **13.** Which of the following best describes battlefield communication during the Civil War?
   **a.** Generals' wives would alert their husbands using their children as messengers.
   **b.** Civilians would alert soldiers by waving different colored flags.
   **c.** Drummers would signal troops with different beats.
   **d.** Generals received messages from civilians on horseback.

_____ **14.** Which of the following best describes the Ku Klux Klan?
   **a.** a secret society that paid public officials to harass African Americans
   **b.** a group of Native Americans who attacked women and African Americans
   **c.** a group of citizens who revolted against the "white man's government"
   **d.** a secret society that used disguises and attacked African Americans

_____ **15.** A direct effect of the Compromise of 1877 was the
   **a.** institution of a poll tax in the South.
   **b.** promotion of Reconstruction by the White House.
   **c.** removal of federal troops from the South.
   **d.** end of federal funding for Reconstruction reforms.

**TRUE/FALSE** Indicate whether each statement below is true or false by writing **T** or **F** in the space provided.

_____ **16.** The Union victory in the Siege of Vicksburg gave the Union full control of the valuable Mississippi River.

_____ **17.** Admiral David Farragut led key attacks on the southern ports of Vicksburg and New Orleans.

_____ **18.** President Lincoln proposed a plan to readmit the southern states even before the Civil War ended.

_____ **19.** General Robert E. Lee surrendered in April of 1865 after Union soldiers surrounded his troops, who had few supplies.

Progress Assessment

_____ **20.** The most successful industrial development in the New South involved paper production.

_____ **21.** President Abraham Lincoln's Reconstruction plan called for the establishment of military districts in the South.

_____ **22.** The Union army tried to get support from Great Britain through cotton diplomacy.

**FILL IN THE BLANK** Read each sentence and fill in the blank with the word in the word pair that best completes the sentence.

**23.** In 1864, under the leadership of General _____, the Union carried out its goal of destroying railroads by capturing Atlanta, Georgia, which was an important southern railroad link.
(**Thomas "Stonewall" Jackson/William Tecumseh Sherman**)

**24.** Confederate gunfire upon _____ in 1861 marked the official beginning of the Civil War. (**Fort Ticonderoga/Fort Sumter**)

**25.** The outcome of the Battle of Antietam shifted the advantage in the Civil War to the _____. (**North/South**)

**26.** A series of clashes known as the _____ forced the Union Army to retreat from near Richmond, Virginia in the summer of 1862.
(**Seven Days' Battles/Wilderness Campaign**)

**27.** In order to silence opposition to the Civil War, President Lincoln suspended the right of _____, which protects citizens from unlawful imprisonment. (**habeas corpus/double jeopardy**)

**28.** _____ organized medicine and supplies for troops on the battlefield and founded what would eventually become the American Red Cross.
(**Clara Barton/Dolley Madison**)

**29.** _____ was the name of the process used to reunite and rebuild the nation without slavery following the Civil War.
(**Reconstruction/Emancipation**)

**30.** The _____ was a secret society formed in 1866 by white southerners in Tennessee that used violence in opposition to civil rights for African Americans. (**Redeemers/Ku Klux Klan**)

**31.** The _____ Amendment, passed by Congress in 1865, made slavery illegal. (**Thirteenth/Fifteenth**)

**32.** The northern defeat in the _____, the first major battle of the Civil War, crushed the Union's hope of winning the war quickly. (**Battle of Gettysburg/First Battle of Bull Run**)

**33.** The Union victory in the _____ was a turning point in the war that marked General Lee's final attack in the North. (**Battle of Gettysburg/Battle of Antietam**)

**34.** In 1863 President Lincoln gave the _____, in which he praised the bravery of Union soldiers and expressed his commitment to winning the war. (**Gettysburg Address/Emancipation speech**)

**PRACTICING SOCIAL STUDIES SKILLS** Study the quotation below and answer the question that follows.

> "In the eye of the law, there is in the country no superior, dominant [controlling], ruling class of citizens . . . Our constitution is color-blind, and neither knows nor tolerates classes among citizens. In respect of civil rights, all citizens are equal before the law."
>
> —John Marshall Harlan, quoted in *Plessy* v. *Ferguson: A Brief History with Documents*, edited by Brook Thomas

_____ **35.** Why did Justice Harlan write a dissenting opinion against the Supreme Court's ruling in *Plessy* v. *Ferguson*?

   **a.** He did not want the Supreme Court's ruling on segregation to start a class war in the nation.

   **b.** He was blind to the unequal treatment under the law of African Americans and the poor.

   **c.** He was concerned that the Supreme Court's ruling would harm the nation's status as a world leader.

   **d.** He felt that any segregation went against the principle of equality stated in the Constitution.

**MATCHING** In the space provided, write the letter of the term or person that matches each description. Some answers will not be used.

_____ **36.** first African American senator; he helped organize African American troops in the Civil War

_____ **37.** organization that provided assistance to freedpeople and some poor people living in the South

_____ **38.** political group that wanted the federal government to become more involved in Reconstruction

_____ **39.** farming system used in the South in which a worker farms the land and gives the landowner a portion of the crop as payment for rent

_____ **40.** set of laws that divided the South into five districts under military control

_____ **41.** American leader who became president following Lincoln's assassination

_____ **42.** forced legal separation of the races introduced by Redeemer governments

_____ **43.** set of laws that limited the freedom and rights of African Americans

_____ **44.** law passed by Congress that gave African Americans the same legal rights as white Americans

_____ **45.** policy set forth by Redeemer governments in an effort to deny African Americans the right to vote

**a.** sharecropping

**b.** Reconstruction Acts

**c.** segregation

**d.** Radical Republicans

**e.** Andrew Johnson

**f.** Black Codes

**g.** poll tax

**h.** *Plessy* v. *Ferguson*

**i.** Freedmen's Bureau

**j.** Hiram Revels

**k.** Compromise of 1877

**l.** Civil Rights Act of 1866

**The Nation Breaks Apart**

# Unit Test

### Form B

**SHORT ANSWER** On a separate sheet of paper, answer each of the following questions in complete sentences.

1. What event in 1861 marked the beginning of the Civil War?

2. How did the Union naval blockade affect the South's economy during the Civil War?

3. Why did President Lincoln suspend the right of habeas corpus? What happened as a result?

4. Why did Congress refuse to support President Andrew Johnson's plan for Reconstruction?

5. How did the Redeemers attempt to limit the rights of African Americans in the United States?

6. How did the sharecropping system create a cycle of debt?

**PRACTICING SOCIAL STUDIES SKILLS** Study the map below and, on a separate sheet of paper, answer the question that follows.

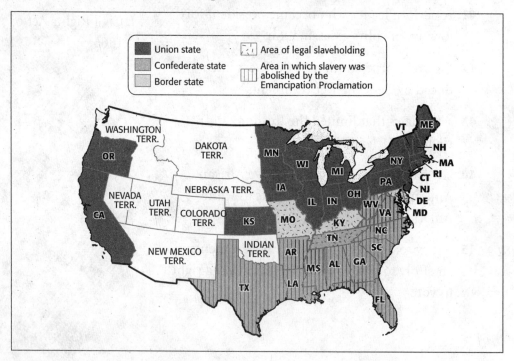

7. According to the map, in which states was slavery abolished by the Emancipation Proclamation?

Progress Assessment

**Americans Move West**

**MATCHING** In the space provided, write the letter of the term, place, or person that matches that description. Some answers will not be used.

_____ **1.** An undeveloped area

_____ **2.** A large deposit of gold and silver found in western Nevada

_____ **3.** Communities that grew suddenly when a mine opened

_____ **4.** Public land on which ranchers grazed huge herds; once occupied by Plains Indians

_____ **5.** Mexican ranch hands who cared for cattle and horses

_____ **6.** One of a cowboy's most important and dangerous duties

_____ **7.** Ran from San Antonio, Texas to the cattle town of Abilene, Kansas

_____ **8.** System of messengers on horseback that carried mail

_____ **9.** Completed on May 10, 1869

_____ **10.** Provided railroad companies with loans and large land grants that could be sold to pay for costs

**a.** boomtowns

**b.** cattle drive

**c.** Chisholm Trail

**d.** Comstock Lode

**e.** farmers

**f.** frontier

**g.** immigrants

**h.** open range

**i.** Pacific Railway Acts

**j.** Pony Express

**k.** settlers

**l.** transcontinental railroad

**m.** vaqueros

Progress Assessment

**Americans Move West**                                    Section Quiz

**FILL IN THE BLANK**   For each of the following statements, fill in the
blank with the appropriate word, phrase, or name.

1. For survival, Plains Indians depended on two animals, the horse and the

   _____.

2. The United States government tried to avoid disputes by negotiating the

   _____, signed with northern Plains nations in 1851.

3. New treaties between the United States and Plains Indians in 1861 created

   _____, areas of federal land set aside for American Indians.

4. In late 1866, _____ and a group of Sioux ambushed and
   killed 81 cavalry troops.

5. _____, a leader of the Lakota Sioux, protested demands by
   the U.S. government that his people sell their reservation land in the Black Hills.

6. The _____ was the U.S. Army's worst defeat in the battle
   over western lands, and the Sioux's last major victory.

7. The _____ was the forced 300-mile march of Navajo Indians
   to a reservation in New Mexico.

8. Near the border with Canada, U.S. troops overtook the

   _____ and relocated them to a reservation in Oklahoma.

9. A Chiricahua Apache named _____ and his small band of
   raiders avoided capture for many years.

10. The _____ was the last major engagement on the Great
    Plains.

Progress Assessment

**Americans Move West**

Section Quiz

**Section 3**

**MATCHING** In the space provided, write the letter of the term, place, or person that matches that description. Some answers will not be used.

_____ 1. Granted government owned land to small farmers

_____ 2. Granted more than 17 million acres of federal land to the states

_____ 3. Name given to the 20,000 to 40,000 African Americans who moved to Kansas seeking land

_____ 4. Nickname for Plains farmers

_____ 5. Method of farming that shifted the focus away from water-dependent crops such as corn

_____ 6. A decrease in the money supply and over-all lower prices

_____ 7. Supported a number of issues and social causes, including the movement for women's suffrage

_____ 8. A social and educational organization for farmers

_____ 9. Congressman from Nebraska who was well known for his support of populist ideas

_____ 10. Formed from the Farmers' Alliances at a convention in St. Louis, in February 1892

**a.** Annie Bidwell

**b.** Coinage Act of 1873

**c.** deflation

**d.** dry farming

**e.** Exodusters

**f.** Homestead Act

**g.** Laura Ingalls Wilder

**h.** Morill Act

**i.** National Grange

**j.** Populist Party

**k.** Republican Party

**l.** sodbusters

**m.** William Jennings Bryan

Progress Assessment

## Americans Move West

**MULTIPLE CHOICE** For each of the following, write the letter of the best choice in the space provided.

_____ **1.** The Chisholm Trail was used primarily by
   **a.** cowboys to drive cattle.
   **b.** the Pony Express to transport mail.
   **c.** Paiute Indians to hunt buffalo.
   **d.** the U.S. Army to build forts.

_____ **2.** By 1850, the western boundary of the American frontier had been pushed to the Pacific Ocean by the
   **a.** construction of the intercontinental railroad.
   **b.** discovery of silver and gold mines in Nevada.
   **c.** donation of the Great Plains to war veterans.
   **d.** admission of the state of California to the Union.

_____ **3.** The Oklahoma land rush signified the
   **a.** end of the frontier.
   **b.** strength of the Populist Party.
   **c.** rise of deflation.
   **d.** pointlessness of the Farmers' Alliance.

_____ **4.** Dry farming is best described as the
   **a.** cultivation of crops during droughts.
   **b.** conversion of fields into grazing land.
   **c.** growing of crops that do not need much water.
   **d.** development of fields far from water sources.

_____ **5.** What led up to the Long Walk of 1864?
   **a.** Geronimo surrendered to the U.S. Army.
   **b.** Raids by U.S. troops left the Navajo without food and shelter, forcing them to surrender.
   **c.** General Custer's troops attacked the Navajo.
   **d.** U.S. negotiators tricked the Navajo into selling their land in New Mexico, forcing them to move.

_____ **6.** Native Americans of the Plains survived by
   **a.** selling fur.
   **b.** gathering roots.
   **c.** breeding horses.
   **d.** hunting buffalo.

_____ **7.** The 11 million acres of land opened in the Oklahoma land rush belonged to the
  **a.** Lakota Sioux Indians.
  **b.** southern Plains Indians.
  **c.** Creek and Seminole Indians.
  **d.** Navajo and Nez Percé Indians.

_____ **8.** Which characteristic of the Texas longhorn made it significant to the Cattle Kingdom?
  **a.** little need for water and an ability to survive in harsh weather
  **b.** a diet of grain, which left grasslands available for grazing sheep
  **c.** meat that fetched a high price in overseas markets
  **d.** strength to handle north-ward cattle drives

_____ **9.** During western settlement in the 1850s reservations were set up to provide
  **a.** plots of land for miners and settlers.
  **b.** living space for Native Americans.
  **c.** small areas for Native Americans to breed livestock.
  **d.** temporary housing for cowboys on Native American land.

_____ **10.** Which of the following char-acterized the boomtowns of the West?
  **a.** high birth rates
  **b.** sudden growth
  **c.** tightly clustered houses
  **d.** underground gold mines

**TRUE/FALSE** Indicate whether each statement below is true or false by writing **T** or **F** in the space provided.

_____ **11.** William McKinley's victory in 1896 brought and end to both the Populist Party and the Farmers' Alliances.

_____ **12.** The Pacific Railway Acts were passed by the federal government in 1862 and 1864 to help finance construction of the transcontinental railroad.

_____ **13.** Plains Indians used the meat and hide of buffalo for food and clothing, but did not put the bones or horns to use.

_____ **14.** Most southern Plains Indians agreed to live on reservations in the Treaty of Medicine Lodge.

**PRACTICING SOCIAL STUDIES SKILLS** Read the quotation below and answer the question that follows.

> "Governor Stanford, president of the Central Pacific, took the sledge [hammer], and the first time he struck he missed the spike and hit the rail. What a howl went up! Irish, Chinese, Mexicans, and everybody yelled with delight."
>
> —Alexander Toponce, quoted in *A Treasury of Railroad Folklore,* edited by B.A. Botkin and Alvin F. Harlo

_____ **15.** What can be inferred from this passage about the completion of the first transcontinental railroad?
  **a.** Labor unions boycotted the railroad inauguration ceremony.
  **b.** Governor Stanford was an experienced railroad worker.
  **c.** The golden spike was hammered in during a workers' protest.
  **d.** A diverse crowd was present to witness the railroad's completion.

Progress Assessment

**MATCHING** In the space provided, write the letter of the term or person that matches each description. Some answers will not be used.

_____ **16.** connected the Union Pacific and Central Pacific railroad lines

_____ **17.** required states to sell land and build colleges of agriculture and engineering with the profits

_____ **18.** religious movement that predicted the arrival of paradise for Native Americans

_____ **19.** 300-mile march the Navajo were forced to go on to reach a reservation in New Mexico

_____ **20.** large group of African Americans who left the South to go to Kansas in 1879

_____ **21.** promoted the free and unlimited coinage of silver

_____ **22.** gave government-owned land to small farmers

_____ **23.** farmers working the tough soil of the Plains

_____ **24.** established private land ownership for Native Americans

_____ **25.** discovery that started the mining boom

**a.** Comstock Lode

**b.** Long Walk

**c.** Homestead Act

**d.** Morrill Act

**e.** golden spike

**f.** Ghost Dance

**g.** Dawes General Allotment Act

**h.** sodbusters

**i.** Exodusters

**j.** Populist Party

**k.** Annie Bidwell

**l.** Laura Ingalls Wilder

**Americans Move West**

# Chapter Test

## Form B

**SHORT ANSWER** On a separate sheet of paper, answer each of the following questions in complete sentences.

1. What happened in 1885 and 1886 to bring the Cattle Kingdom to an end?

2. How did the federal government help the construction of the transcontinental railroad?

3. What was the significance of the Treaty of Fort Laramie?

4. What was the Homestead Act? How did it lead people to move from regions such as New England?

5. What was the significance of the Dawes General Allotment Act?

6. Who was Sitting Bull?

**PRACTICING SOCIAL STUDIES SKILLS** Study the charts below and, on a separate sheet of paper, answer the question that follows.

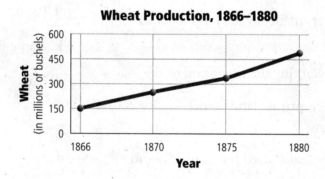

Wheat Production, 1866–1880

Wheat Prices, 1866–1880

7. What can you tell from these charts about the relationship between the amount of wheat produced and the cost of the wheat? Can you tell which caused which?

Progress Assessment

# The Industrial Age

Section Quiz

## Section 1

**FILL IN THE BLANK** For each of the following statements, fill in the
blank with the appropriate word, phrase, or name.

1. The _____ was a period of rapid growth in U.S. manufacturing during the late 1800s.

2. _____ is iron that has been made stronger by heat and the
   addition of other metals.

3. The _____ helped increase U.S. steel production by drasti-
   cally reducing the amount of time it took to transform iron ore into steel.

4. The Menlo Park, New Jersey research center of _____ came
   to be called the invention factory.

5. An exclusive right to make or sell an invention is called a

   _____.

6. In March 1876, _____ patented the telephone.

7. _____ and _____ built a light weight
   airplane with a small gas-powered engine.

8. The automobile became more widespread after _____ introduced the Model T in 1908.

9. The need for a reliable source of oil prompted _____ to
   prove that it was possible to pump crude directly from the ground.

10. The first _____ powered engine was produced by a German
    engineer in 1876.

Progress Assessment

**TRUE/FALSE** Mark each statement **T** if it is true or **F** if it is false. If false explain why.

_____ **1.** Vertical integration is accomplished by owning businesses involved in each step of a manufacturing process.

_____

_____

_____ **2.** Corporations are businesses that sell portions of ownership called stock shares.

_____

_____

_____ **3.** Andrew Carnegie and John D. Rockefeller were two of the most unsuccessful businessmen in U.S. history.

_____

_____

_____ **4.** Some business leaders used social Darwinism to justify their great personal wealth in light of the working and living conditions of their employees.

_____

_____

_____ **5.** Corporations and trusts stopped growing in size at the end of the 19th century largely because of the success of the Sherman Antitrust Act.

_____

_____

Progress Assessment

**The Industrial Age**

Section Quiz

**Section 3**

**MATCHING** In the space provided, write the letter of the term, place, or person that matches that description. Some answers will not be used.

_____ 1. A method for increasing worker efficiency that led to decreased costs and increased production for American industry

_____ 2. Published *The Principles of Scientific Management* in 1911

_____ 3. Mechanism of labor unions for achieving gains for the workers they represent

_____ 4. Irish immigrant who worked for better conditions for miners

_____ 5. Chicago labor strike of 1886 in support of an eight-hour workday; erupted in violence that resulted in the deaths of many

_____ 6. Invited only skilled laborers to be members; by 1904 it represented the interests of 1.5 million workers

_____ 7. Labor union that included both skilled and unskilled laborers

_____ 8. Immigrant laborer who would become the first president of the American Federation of Labor in 1895

_____ 9. Protest at a Carnegie Steel plant in Homestead, Pennsylvania resulting in the deaths of 16 people

_____ 10. Strike action that stopped traffic on many railroads

**a.** American Federation of Labor

**b.** collective bargaining

**c.** Frederick W. Taylor

**d.** Haymarket Riot

**e.** Homestead Strike

**f.** Knights of Labor

**g.** labor unions

**h.** Mary Harris Jones

**i.** organizations

**j.** production

**k.** Pullman Strike

**l.** Samuel Gompers

**m.** specialization

Progress Assessment

Name _____ Class _____ Date _____

# The Industrial Age

**MULTIPLE CHOICE** For each of the following, write the letter of the best choice in the space provided.

_____ **1.** New technologies in the steel industry in the late 1800s increased productivity in the
    **a.** textile industry.
    **b.** railroad industry.
    **c.** oil industry.
    **d.** electric industry.

_____ **2.** The Homestead Strike was a protest
    **a.** in Colorado demanding safer working conditions.
    **b.** in Chicago demanding an eight-hour workday.
    **c.** against the Pullman Palace Car Company's unsafe working conditions.
    **d.** against the Carnegie Steel Company's plan to cut jobs.

_____ **3.** The invention of the airplane led to increased demand for
    **a.** aluminum.
    **b.** lumber.
    **c.** coal.
    **d.** oil.

_____ **4.** How did the labor force change during the Second Industrial Revolution?
    **a.** Machines eliminated the jobs of many skilled craftspeople.
    **b.** Industries began to hire highly educated workers.
    **c.** Workers began to receive more benefits and higher wages.
    **d.** Experienced workers replaced children who had been working in mills.

_____ **5.** Andrew Carnegie dealt with striking union workers at his Pennsylvania steel factory in 1892 by
    **a.** firing every worker and replacing them with machines.
    **b.** firing half the workers and cutting pay for the rest.
    **c.** locking workers out of the factory and hiring strike breakers.
    **d.** agreeing to give workers higher wages.

Progress Assessment

_____ **6.** Of the following, which was an effect of the expansion of railroads across the United States?

    **a.** rapid growth of cities

    **b.** increase in steel prices

    **c.** decrease in interstate trade

    **d.** movement of city dwellers to the suburbs

_____ **7.** Which of the following was an effect of factory specialization in the late 1800s?

    **a.** Workers repeated the same steps over and over again, becoming tired, bored, and more likely to be injured.

    **b.** Factories produced only a single product, putting owners at greater financial risk if that product failed.

    **c.** Unions signed contracts with specific factories, eliminating violent conflicts over wages and working hours.

    **d.** Managers paid more attention to working conditions, attracting workers and creating greater competition for jobs.

_____ **8.** Collective bargaining is the

    **a.** practice used by employers to hire groups of laborers.

    **b.** practice used by employers to get the cheapest labor possible.

    **c.** idea that laborers working in groups are more productive in the workplace.

    **d.** idea that laborers acting together have greater success in negotiating with management.

_____ **9.** How did the telegraph differ from the telephone?

    **a.** The telegraph could work only in big cities.

    **b.** The telegraph was much more expensive than the telephone.

    **c.** The telegraph could carry only written messages.

    **d.** The telegraph could not send messages over long distances.

**PRACTICING SOCIAL STUDIES SKILLS** Study the political cartoon below and answer the question that follows.

[71880T] © Collection of the New-York Historical Society

_____ **10.** What does the cartoon illustrate?
   **a.** Rockefeller's diminishing control of the oil industry in America
   **b.** the U.S. government's control of big business
   **c.** Rockefeller's financial control of the U.S. government
   **d.** the U.S. government's failed attempt to regulate the steel industry

**FILL IN THE BLANK** Read each sentence and fill in the blank with the word in the word pair that best completes the sentence.

**11.** The telephone is the most well-known of _____'s inventions. **(Alexander Graham Bell/Thomas Edison)**

**12.** _____ own a corporation, but they do not make its day-to-day business decisions. **(CEOs/Stockholders)**

**13.** Terence V. Powderly became leader of the _____ in 1879. **(American Railway Union/Knights of Labor)**

**14.** Wilbur and Orville Wright built a lightweight airplane that ran on a

_____-powered engine. **(steam/gas)**

**15.** At a protest in Chicago's _____, a bomb killed eight police officers and injured many others. **(Haymarket Square/Lincoln Square)**

**The Industrial Age,** *continued*                    Chapter Test Form A

**MATCHING**  In the space provided, write the letter of the term or person that matches each description. Some answers will not be used.

_____ **16.** John D. Rockefeller's control of about 90 percent of the oil refining business

_____ **17.** owned businesses involved in each step of the manufacturing process in his industry

_____ **18.** led the American Federation of Labor

_____ **19.** the first national labor union

_____ **20.** made manufacturing more efficient with the moving assembly line

_____ **21.** inventor of the light bulb

_____ **22.** made it illegal to create monopolies

_____ **23.** made steel production quicker and cheaper, which created a booming railroad industry

_____ **24.** idea that those who were "fittest" would be successful

_____ **25.** encouraged managers to view workers as interchangeable parts of the production process

**a.** corporations

**b.** Frederick W. Taylor

**c.** Bessemer process

**d.** Andrew Carnegie

**e.** Knights of Labor

**f.** Thomas Edison

**g.** horizontal integration

**h.** Samuel Gompers

**i.** Henry Ford

**j.** social Darwinism

**k.** Grover Cleveland

**l.** Sherman Antitrust Act

Name _____ Class _____ Date _____

## The Industrial Age

## Chapter Test

### Form B

**SHORT ANSWER** On a separate sheet of paper, answer each of the following questions in complete sentences.

1. What was the cause of the Homestead strike? What was the effect of that strike?

2. What industry grew as a direct result of the reduced price of steel? What were some new developments in this industry?

3. How was the Knights of Labor different from the American Federation of Labor (AFL)?

4. What is the role of stockholders in a corporation?

5. What is specialization? What affect did it have on production and on workers during the Second Industrial Revolution?

6. How did Wilbur and Orville Wright revolutionize travel in the early 1900s?

**PRACTICING SOCIAL STUDIES SKILLS** Study the graph below and, on a separate sheet of paper, answer the question that follows.

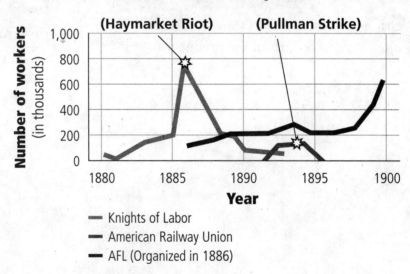

**Union Membership, 1880–1900**

7. In what year did membership in the Knights of Labor fall below membership in the AFL?

Progress Assessment

Name _____ Class _____ Date _____

# Immigrants and Urban Life

Section Quiz

**Section 1**

**MATCHING** In the space provided, write the letter of the term, place, or person that matches each description. Some answers will not be used.

_____ **1.** In the late 1800s, immigrants from Britain, Germany, Ireland, Scandinavia

_____ **2.** In the late 1800s, immigrants from southern and eastern Europe

_____ **3.** Area below a ship's deck where new immigrants traveled

_____ **4.** The busiest immigration processing center on the East Coast

_____ **5.** Where many Chinese immigrants entered the United States

_____ **6.** Started the Bank of Italy in San Francisco

_____ **7.** Organizations that offered immigrant families help in cases of sickness, unemployment, or death

_____ **8.** Workplaces with long hours and unhealthy working conditions

_____ **9.** Americans who feared too many new immigrants were being allowed into the country

_____ **10.** Banned Chinese people from immigrating to the United States for 10 years

**a.** Amadeo Giannini

**b.** Angel Island

**c.** benevolent societies

**d.** Chinese Exclusion Act

**e.** customs

**f.** Ellis Island

**g.** El Paso

**h.** nativists

**i.** new immigrants

**j.** old immigrants

**k.** Pauline Newman

**l.** steerage

**m.** sweatshops

Progress Assessment

**Immigrants and Urban Life**  Section Quiz

Section 2

**FILL IN THE BLANK** For each of the following statements, fill in the blank with the appropriate word, phrase, or name.

1. During the 1800s _____ and native-born Americans moved to cities in record numbers.

2. Many new _____ lines connecting the East and West Coasts ran through Chicago.

3. Thousands of Chicago residents found work in the city's

   _____ and meatpacking plants.

4. Architects such as Louis Sullivan began designing multistory buildings called

   _____.

5. _____ is public transportation designed to move lots of people.

6. Some cities built underground railroads, known as _____.

7. Many middle-class Americans who could afford it moved to the

   _____, residential neighborhoods outside of downtown.

8. In 1896 _____ added a color comic to his newspaper.

9. Giant retail shops, or _____, appeared in some cities.

10. Frederick Law Olmsted designed _____ in New York City.

Progress Assessment

## Immigrants and Urban Life

**MULTIPLE CHOICE** For each of the following, write the letter of the best choice in the space provided.

_____ **1.** What journalist and photographer became famous for exposing the horrible conditions in New York City tenements?
   **a.** Jane Addams
   **b.** Frederick Law Olmsted
   **c.** Jacob Riis
   **d.** Abraham Hyman

_____ **2.** In the late 1800s, Pittsburgh's prosperous steel mills brought about what serious problem?
   **a.** diseases
   **b.** overcrowding
   **c.** garbage
   **d.** air pollution

_____ **3.** This law required new buildings in New York to have better ventilation and running water.
   **a.** The Benevolent Act
   **b.** New York State Tenement House Act
   **c.** Chinese Exclusion Act
   **d.** The Settlement Act of 1901

_____ **4.** Settlement houses offered what kind of services in poor areas?
   **a.** education, recreation, and social activities
   **b.** trash removal
   **c.** mass transit
   **d.** pollution cleanup

_____ **5.** She visited sweatshops and wrote about the problems of child labor.
   **a.** Ellen Gates Starr
   **b.** Jane Addams
   **c.** Florence Kelley
   **d.** Pauline Newman

Progress Assessment

**Immigrants and Urban Life**

Chapter Test

Form A

**MULTIPLE CHOICE** For each of the following, write the letter of the best choice in the space provided.

_____ **1.** What did city governments do to try to improve city sanitation in the late 1800s?
  **a.** built public hospitals
  **b.** hired full-time firefighters
  **c.** built water purification systems
  **d.** forced steel factories to limit pollution

_____ **2.** The "old immigrants" who arrived in America during the 1800s were from
  **a.** eastern Europe.
  **b.** northern Europe.
  **c.** central Australia.
  **d.** central Asia.

_____ **3.** What was the main cause of pollution in Pittsburgh in the late 1800s?
  **a.** overcrowded tenements
  **b.** smoke from the steel mills
  **c.** garbage thrown in the river
  **d.** use of electricity for daytime lighting

_____ **4.** How frequently did immigration officials at Ellis Island reject new arrivals?
  **a.** never, as the government left it to social Darwinism to weed-out weak families
  **b.** often, because many immigrants contracted deadly diseases while traveling in steerage
  **c.** rarely, as records show less than two percent of arrivals were not allowed into the country
  **d.** often, because many nativists protested their arrival

_____ **5.** Because the transition into American culture was often difficult, many immigrant families
  **a.** chose to live in areas populated mostly by American families.
  **b.** returned to their native countries after a few years.
  **c.** moved into neighborhoods with people from the same country.
  **d.** kept their native customs secret.

Progress Assessment

_____ **6.** Which of the following was a major factor in Chicago's rapid growth?

  **a.** Many railroad lines connecting the East and West coasts ran through Chicago.

  **b.** Chicago's location on Lake Michigan made the city an international port.

  **c.** The city's large number of bakeries provided many jobs for new residents.

  **d.** Employers in Chicago paid their workers high salaries.

_____ **7.** What was the main change brought by the steel industry to American architecture of the late 1800s?

  **a.** Steel was used to build skyscrapers that needed limited city space.

  **b.** Every building was built with steel fire escapes.

  **c.** Residential neighborhoods called suburbs could be built cheaply.

  **d.** Steel could be combined with brick to create new buildings.

_____ **8.** Which of the following best describes Hull House?

  **a.** contributed to the survival of the immigrant population in Chicago and the nation as a whole by inspiring U.S. reform movements

  **b.** supplied monetary assistance to immigrants which helped them overcome discrimination by American citizens

  **c.** helped immigrants maintain their own cultures and taught Americans to embrace immigrants' cultures

  **d.** provided homes for immigrants and ended the problem of homelessness among immigrants in America

_____ **9.** Which industry was most closely associated with the term "sweatshops"?

  **a.** construction

  **b.** clothing

  **c.** steel

  **d.** transportation

**PRACTICING SOCIAL STUDIES SKILLS** Study the chart below and
answer the question that follows.

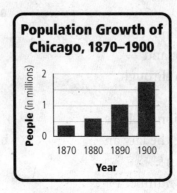

**Population Growth of
Chicago, 1870–1900**

_____ **10.** According to the chart, which of the following was true of Chicago's population in the late 1800s?
   **a.** The population tripled between 1870 and 1890.
   **b.** The population decreased slowly between 1870 and 1880.
   **c.** After 1890, the population stopped increasing.
   **d.** The largest increase occurred between 1890 and 1900.

**FILL IN THE BLANK** Read each sentence and fill in the blank with the
word in the word pair that best completes the sentence.

**11.** The majority of _____ immigrants were from southern and
eastern Europe. (**new/old**)

**12.** Lawrence Veiller's exhibit of photographs and maps helped get the

_____ passed.
(**New York City Building Code/New York State Tenement House Act**)

**13.** _____ were aid organizations that offered immigrants help
in cases of sickness and death. (**Settlement houses/Benevolent societies**)

**14.** Elevated trains are examples of _____, or public transportation designed for many passengers. (**mass transit/industrial transit**)

**15.** In the late 1800s the United States began to develop forms of

_____, or cultural activities shared by many people.

(**mass culture/popular entertainment**)

**16.** Many middle-class Americans who could afford it moved from cities to residential

neighborhoods outside of downtown known as _____.

**(tenements/suburbs)**

**17.** Most immigrants traveled in _____, where the cabins were

hot, cramped, and foul-smelling. **(steerage/second class)**

**18.** Americans who believed that the United States should not allow so many immi-

grants into the country were called _____.

**(nativists/protectionists)**

**TRUE/FALSE** Indicate whether each statement below is true or false by
writing **T** or **F** in the space provided.

_____ **19.** New immigrants were often forced to take low-paying industrial jobs
because they lacked the skills needed to obtain higher-paying jobs.

_____ **20.** The Chinese Exclusion Act marked the first time all members of a particu-
lar nationality were banned from entering the United States.

_____ **21.** Most of the victims of diseases such as cholera, influenza, and tuberculosis
in cities in the late 1800s were elderly.

_____ **22.** Crime was one of the effects of the overcrowded and unhealthy conditions
of city neighborhoods in the late 1800s.

_____ **23.** Florence Kelley helped pass laws that limited women's working hours and
prevented child labor.

_____ **24.** During the 1800s, the lack of jobs and adequate housing in the city forced
hundreds of immigrants to look for employment in the countryside.

_____ **25.** The efforts of nativists in the United States stopped immigrants from
southern and eastern Europe from entering the country in the late 1880s.

## Immigrants and Urban Life

**SHORT ANSWER** On a separate sheet of paper, answer each of the following questions in complete sentences.

1. In the late 1800s the populations of cities began to grow enormously. What major innovations and changes did cities use to respond to the resulting overcrowding?

2. In what ways did mass culture develop in the United States during the late 1800s?

3. What kinds of problems resulted from the overcrowding in city tenements?

4. Why did so many people want to immigrate to the United States?

5. What factors contributed to the rapid growth of the city of Chicago around 1900?

6. What requirement was placed on immigrants from China?

**PRACTICING SOCIAL STUDIES SKILLS** Study the bar graph below and, on a separate sheet of paper, answer the question that follows.

**Population Growth of Chicago, 1870–1900**

7. By about how many millions of people did the population of Chicago increase from 1880 to 1900?

Progress Assessment

# A Growing America

**MULTIPLE CHOICE** For each of the following, write the letter of the best choice in the space provided.

_____ **1.** Factory managers were encouraged to view workers as interchangeable parts by
  **a.** Terence V. Powderly, to create employment opportunities for all union members.
  **b.** Frederick W. Taylor, to increase efficiency and worker productivity.
  **c.** Henry Ford, to speed automobile production and make cars more widely available.
  **d.** Andrew Carnegie, to encourage the firing of disruptive workers and the hiring of obedient ones.

_____ **2.** Which of the following best describes Exodusters?
  **a.** settlers who moved west to establish religious communities
  **b.** former slaves who migrated in large numbers to Kansas from the South
  **c.** Native Americans who lived in shelters carved into limestone outcroppings
  **d.** miners who moved west in search of gold

_____ **3.** Andrew Carnegie managed to keep costs of production for his steel mills low by
  **a.** applying for government loans and taking advantage of corporate tax breaks.
  **b.** using assembly lines and other advanced manufacturing methods.
  **c.** purchasing machinery to produce steel instead of hiring workers.
  **d.** buying the businesses involved in each step of the manufacturing process.

_____ **4.** Which of the following applies to the Morrill Act?
  **a.** The West was open to several hundred federal employees.
  **b.** Farmers could own land if they promised to live on it for five years.
  **c.** More than 17 million acres of state land was granted to the federal government.
  **d.** States were required to sell land and build colleges with the profits.

Progress Assessment

_____ **5.** What was the main advantage of the Linotype machine?
   **a.** ability to print in color
   **b.** increased quality of publications
   **c.** ease of operation
   **d.** reduced time and cost of printing

_____ **6.** In the 1890s African Americans moved from the rural South to northern cities in order to
   **a.** change their identities.
   **b.** live in a place with many different cultures.
   **c.** escape discrimination and find jobs.
   **d.** escape religious persecution.

_____ **7.** How did the federal government assist railway companies in the construction of the transcontinental railroad?
   **a.** granted them millions of acres of public land that they could sell for cash
   **b.** used taxpayer dollars to pay-off debts incurred during construction
   **c.** did not charge them taxes on land and materials bought for the project
   **d.** promised them exclusive contracts to be the official carriers of the U.S. mail

_____ **8.** The poorly built, overcrowded apartment buildings often occupied by immigrants were called
   **a.** skyscrapers.
   **b.** tenements.
   **c.** settlement houses.
   **d.** benevolent societies.

_____ **9.** What was the main activity of cowboys in the late 1800s?
   **a.** managing their ranches
   **b.** breeding horses to sell at auctions
   **c.** maintaining order in cattle towns
   **d.** herding cattle to markets or to the plains for grazing

_____ **10.** What was the main cause for the deflation that occurred during the late 1800s?
   **a.** New European immigrants worked for low wages.
   **b.** Gold miners went on strike and stopped mining.
   **c.** Paper money began to be backed by silver in the treasury.
   **d.** The money supply grew more slowly than the nation's population.

_____ **11.** The airplane constructed by Wilbur and Orville Wright was powered by
   **a.** coal.
   **b.** wind.
   **c.** gas.
   **d.** steam.

Progress Assessment

_____ **12.** The mining boom began following the
  **a.** invention of dynamite by Alfred Nobel.
  **b.** discovery of the Comstock Lode.
  **c.** founding of the National Union of Miners.
  **d.** passage of the Homestead Act.

_____ **13.** The 1867 Treaty of Medicine Lodge
  **a.** settled the dispute in Texas between the U.S. army and the Comanche.
  **b.** dismantled U.S. forts built in Sioux territories.
  **c.** created reservations for southern Plains Indians.
  **d.** extended hunting grounds for southern Plains Indians.

_____ **14.** Which of the following best describes the work of Thomas Edison?
  **a.** uninspired
  **b.** practical
  **c.** impractical
  **d.** problematic

_____ **15.** Why were immigrants often forced to take low-paying industrial jobs?
  **a.** Immigrants lacked the skills needed to obtain higher-paying jobs.
  **b.** Americans refused to allow immigrants to farm.
  **c.** Hiring immigrants for other jobs was illegal.
  **d.** Immigrants did not have the equipment to work in any other fields.

_____ **16.** Who invented the telephone?
  **a.** Alexander Graham Bell
  **b.** Thomas Edison
  **c.** Orville Wright
  **d.** Henry Bessemer

_____ **17.** Labor unions were formed because
  **a.** immigrants refused to take less pay.
  **b.** women wanted higher pay than men.
  **c.** workers wanted better wages and working conditions.
  **d.** most factory managers would only hire children.

_____ **18.** Which city had the greatest population growth between 1850 and 1900?
  **a.** New York
  **b.** St. Louis
  **c.** Boston
  **d.** Chicago

Progress Assessment

_____ **19.** Which of the following best describes nativists?

**a.** people who wanted to live in nature, away from urban centers

**b.** Americans who wanted to revive Native American culture

**c.** children who were born in the United States to immigrant parents

**d.** Americans who believed that too many immigrants were coming into the country

_____ **20.** The golden spike was significant because it

**a.** created a monopoly of the Union Pacific and Central Pacific Railroads.

**b.** connected the Union Pacific and Central Pacific railroad lines.

**c.** united Irish, Chinese, and Mexican rail workers in a single union.

**d.** represented the laying of the first tie in the rail line to the Comstock Lode.

**FILL IN THE BLANK** Read each sentence and fill in the blank with the word in the word pair that best completes the sentence.

**21.** The Pony Express was put out of business because its messengers were outpaced

by _____. **(telegrams/telephones)**

**22.** The United States broke its promise to let the _____ Indians keep their land in Oregon. **(Nez Percé/Navajo)**

**23.** The belief known as _____ said that the "fittest" people would succeed in business and in their lives. **(social Darwinism/natural selection)**

**24.** The first event to lead to the end of the _____ was the rise in competition for land on the plains. **(reservations/open range)**

**25.** Henry Ford's idea of the _____ made the process of constructing automobiles faster and cheaper. **(moving assembly line/collective bargaining)**

**26.** Standard Oil developed _____ by buying nearly all other businesses in its field. **(horizontal integration/vertical integration)**

**27.** The _____ was a protest against the Carnegie Steel Company that intended to force the company not to cut jobs. **(Pullman Strike/Homestead Strike)**

Progress Assessment

**28.** The 300-mile march of the Navajo across the desert to a reservation in Bosque

Redondo, New Mexico, is known as the _____.

**(Long Walk/Trail of Tears)**

**29.** The passage of the _____ gave small farmers, unmarried
women, African Americans, and European immigrants a reason to move west in
the 1860s. **(Morrill Act/Homestead Act)**

**PRACTICING SOCIAL STUDIES SKILLS** Study the quotation below and
answer the question that follows.

> "What treaty that the whites have kept has the red man broken? Not
> one. What treaty that the white man ever made with us have they kept?
> Not one."
>
> —Sitting Bull, quoted in *Touch the Earth* by T.C. McLuhan

_____ **30.** The reader of this passage can conclude that Sitting Bull thought that
Native Americans
**a.** had been treated fairly by white society.
**b.** could defeat white society by using force.
**c.** should comply with demands of white society.
**d.** had always honored their word in treaties.

**MATCHING** In the space provided, write the letter of the term, person, or place that matches each description. Some answers will not be used.

_____ **31.** violated treaties with another country, but was renewed many times

_____ **32.** publisher and founder of the New York World newspaper

_____ **33.** focused on the needs of Chicago's immigrant families

_____ **34.** system of public transportation for large numbers of passengers

_____ **35.** busiest immigration center on the East Coast during the late 1800s

_____ **36.** exposed the living conditions of many New York residents in *How the Other Half Lives*

_____ **37.** overcrowded, low-standard apartment buildings

_____ **38.** neighborhood institutions supplying education and recreation for the poor

_____ **39.** visited sweatshops and wrote about the problems there

_____ **40.** immigrant organizations providing aid that few government agencies offered

**a.** Jacob Riis

**b.** tenements

**c.** Joseph Pulitzer

**d.** settlement houses

**e.** mass transit

**f.** Chinese Exclusion Act

**g.** Florence Kelley

**h.** benevolent societies

**i.** Frederick Law Olmstead

**j.** Hull House

**k.** Ellis Island

**l.** suburbs

**TRUE/FALSE** Indicate whether each statement below is true or false by writing **T** or **F** in the space provided.

_____ **41.** The Bessemer process sped up the procedure of refining oil.

_____ **42.** Horses and longhorn cattle were the most important animals to the Plains Indians.

_____ **43.** Thomas Edison developed a power system that could send electricity over long distances.

_____ **44.** The Massacre at Wounded Knee resulted in the death of Sioux leader Sitting Bull at the hands of reservation police.

_____ **45.** George Pullman lowered rents in the Pullman Palace Car company town when he cut his workers' pay.

_____ **46.** Populism failed because the government lacked power to enforce rail rate regulation.

_____ **47.** In the late 1870s, a Paiute Indian named Sarah Winnemucca gave lectures on problems of the reservation system.

_____ **48.** A corporation's stockholders are responsible for helping the corporation pay its business debts.

_____ **49.** The first national labor union, the Knights of Labor, was founded in the 1870s.

_____ **50.** Big business continued to grow in America despite the passage of the Sherman Antitrust Act, which was difficult to enforce.

**A Growing America**

# Unit Test

## Form B

**SHORT ANSWER** On a separate sheet of paper, answer each of the following questions in complete sentences.

1. How did the government respond to the Homestead and Pullman Strikes?

2. Who were the Exodusters and what does their name symbolize?

3. Large numbers of immigrants who had been displaced from their homes by war with the United States settled in the Southwest in the late 1800s. Which country did they leave?

4. In 1858, what event heightened tensions between the United States and Native Americans? How did it do so?

5. How did oil that was pumped from the ground become useable for cooking, heating, lighting, and running automobile and airplane engines?

6. How did nativists try to block immigrants from entering the United States?

**PRACTICING SOCIAL STUDIES SKILLS** Study the political cartoon below and, on a separate sheet of paper, answer the question that follows.

[#71880T] © Collection of the New-York Historical Society

7. How does the cartoonist show Rockefeller's power?

Progress Assessment

# The Progressive Spirit of Reform

## Section Quiz

### Section 1

**FILL IN THE BLANK** For each of the following statements, fill in the blank with the appropriate term, phrase, or name.

1. _____ were powerful organizations that used both legal and illegal methods to get their candidates elected to public office.

2. In the late 1800s a group of reformers known as _____ worked to improve society.

3. Journalists were nicknamed _____ because they "raked up" and exposed corruption.

4. Usually located in poor areas where immigrants lived, _____ houses worked to improve education, housing, and sanitation.

5. The _____ allowed Americans to vote directly for U.S. senators.

6. A _____ is a political measure that allows voters to remove elected officials from office before the end of their terms.

7. A procedure called an _____ allowed voters to propose a new law by collecting signatures on a petition.

8. A _____ allows voters to approve or reject a law that has already been proposed or passed by a government body.

9. The leader of New York City's political machine, _____ may have stolen up to $200 million from the city.

10. Wisconsin's Republican governor _____ decreased the power of political machines and used university professors and other experts to help write new laws and work in state agencies.

Progress Assessment

# The Progressive Spirit of Reform

**TRUE/FALSE** Mark each statement **T** if it is true or **F** if it is false. If false explain why.

_____ **1.** Because adult workers earned such good wages working in the factories, children did not have to work.

_____

_____

_____ **2.** In 1912 the state of New York passed the first minimum wage law.

_____

_____

_____ **3.** The Triangle Shirtwaist Fire and similar accidents led to the passage of laws improving factory safety standards.

_____

_____

_____ **4.** Workers' compensation laws guarantee a portion of lost wages to workers injured on the job.

_____

_____

_____ **5.** An economic system in which private businesses run most industries and competition determines the price of goods is called socialism.

_____

_____

Progress Assessment

# The Progressive Spirit of Reform

### Section Quiz

**Section 3**

**MATCHING** In the space provided, write the letter of the term, place, or person that matches the description. Some answers will not be used.

_____ **1.** This law banned the production, sale, and transportation of alcoholic beverages throughout the United States.

_____ **2.** This person founded what would become the NWP (National Woman's Party).

_____ **3.** This law granted American women the right to vote.

_____ **4.** Although born into slavery, he became a respected educator while in his twenties.

_____ **5.** This reformer wrote articles about the unequal education of African American children.

_____ **6.** These discriminatory laws imposed strict qualifications on voters unless their grandfathers had been allowed to vote.

_____ **7.** This state granted women the full right to vote in 1890.

_____ **8.** This reformer founded the NAACP in 1909.

_____ **9.** This school was founded for female students only in the 1800s.

_____ **10.** Progressive reform efforts overlooked this minority group.

**a.** Alice Paul

**b.** Booker T. Washington

**c.** Chinese

**d.** Eighteenth Amendment

**e.** German

**f.** grandfather clauses

**g.** Ida B. Wells

**h.** New York

**i.** Nineteenth Amendment

**j.** Smith College

**k.** W.E.B. Du Bois

**l.** Wyoming

**m.** Yale

Progress Assessment

## The Progressive Spirit of Reform

Section Quiz

**Section 4**

**MULTIPLE CHOICE** For each of the following, write the letter of the best choice in the space provided.

_____ 1. Who became president upon the death of William McKinley?
   a. William Howard Taft
   b. James A. Garfield
   c. Theodore Roosevelt
   d. Woodrow Wilson

_____ 2. This law prohibited the manufacture, sale, and transport of mislabeled or contaminated food and drugs.
   a. Pure Food and Drug Act
   b. Underwood Tariff Act
   c. Square Deal
   d. Federal Trade Commission

_____ 3. This measure allows the federal government to impose direct taxes on citizens' incomes.
   a. Fourteenth Amendment
   b. Sixteenth Amendment
   c. Tenth Amendment
   d. Eighteenth Amendment

_____ 4. Which is a formal process to settle disputes?
   a. administrative trust
   b. conservation
   c. regulation
   d. arbitration

_____ 5. Which of the following strengthened federal laws against monopolies?
   a. Clayton Antitrust Act
   b. Federal Trade Commission Act
   c. Regulation of the Economy Act
   d. Unfair Trade Act

Progress Assessment

# The Progressive Spirit of Reform

## Chapter Test

### Form A

**MULTIPLE CHOICE** For each of the following, write the letter of the best choice in the space provided.

_____ 1. City and county politics in the late 1800s were influenced by organizations called
   a. political machines.
   b. political mobs.
   c. voting leagues.
   d. voting drives.

_____ 2. William Howard Taft's main criticism of President Theodore Roosevelt was that he
   a. claimed more power for his presidency than the Constitution allowed.
   b. opposed big business regulation.
   c. hurt conservation efforts by leasing public lands to big business.
   d. encouraged the formation of monopolies.

_____ 3. Theodore Roosevelt's idea for balancing the interests of consumers, laborers, and businesspeople was called
   a. the Great Society.
   b. the Fair Play Accord.
   c. the Square Deal.
   d. the New Way.

_____ 4. Business leaders opposed granting women the right to vote mainly because they thought
   a. women voters would support minimum wage and child labor laws.
   b. women should focus on the prohibition of alcohol.
   c. women voters would support government anticorruption efforts.
   d. only married women should have a voice in government.

_____ 5. Politicians best confronted corruption in Washington during the Gilded Age by
   a. increasing security at the polls.
   b. passing a law that established a new system for granting federal jobs.
   c. recruiting honest, reform-minded candidates to run for office.
   d. identifying it as a partisan problem.

_____ **6.** Who encouraged African Americans to improve their economic and educational opportunities rather than fight discrimination directly?
   **a.** Ida B. Wells
   **b.** W.E.B. Du Bois
   **c.** Booker T. Washington
   **d.** Elizabeth Cady Stanton

_____ **7.** Which statement best describes the result of workplace laws passed during the Progressive movement?
   **a.** increased trust between labor and big business
   **b.** eased reformers' minds but were not always enforced
   **c.** caused big business to take operations abroad
   **d.** led to decreased government interference in the economy

_____ **8.** Journalists who wrote about problems in society during the Progressive age were known as
   **a.** Progressives.
   **b.** reformers.
   **c.** muckrakers.
   **d.** capitalists.

_____ **9.** Child labor continued even after the reforms of the early 1900s because
   **a.** greedy factory owners lied about workers' ages.
   **b.** poor families needed the income, however little.
   **c.** corruption made government monitoring useless.
   **d.** the courts established high child wage rates.

_____ **10.** What was the main reason for the rise in Mexican immigration between 1901 and 1930?
   **a.** Mexicans could cross the U.S. border with relative ease.
   **b.** Mexicans became a key part of the Southwest economy.
   **c.** Mexicans could occupy areas that once belonged to Mexico.
   **d.** Mexicans immigrated with their children and extended families.

_____ **11.** Which of these reforms allowed voters to overrule a law that government had proposed or passed?
   **a.** the recall
   **b.** direct primary
   **c.** the initiative
   **d.** the referendum

**PRACTICING SOCIAL STUDIES SKILLS** Study the map below and answer the question that follows.

### The Election of 1912

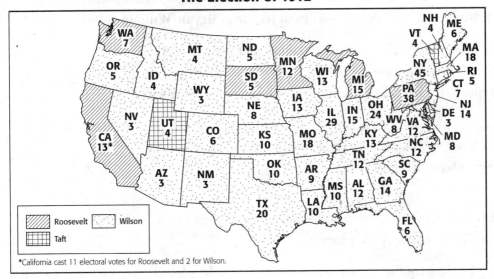

*California cast 11 electoral votes for Roosevelt and 2 for Wilson.

_____ **12.** Based on the information presented, which of these conclusions can be drawn?

    **a.** Roosevelt was the incumbent candidate, fighting to keep a seat he already held.

    **b.** Taft spent far less money on his campaign than the other candidates.

    **c.** It is possible for a state to split its electoral votes rather than give them all to one candidate.

    **d.** It is impossible for a candidate from a third party to beat a Democrat or a Republican.

**FILL IN THE BLANK** Read each sentence and fill in the blank with the term that best completes the sentence.

**13.** In its first decade, the _____ brought attention to racial inequality by using the courts to fight grandfather clauses that had been used to prevent African Americans in the South from voting. (**National Association for the Advancement of Colored People/National Urban League**)

**14.** During the Gilded Age, American reformers called for an end to

_____, the practice of giving government jobs to supporters

after a candidate wins an election. (**civil service/the spoils system**)

**15.** _____ founded the National Woman's Party (NWP). (**Alice Paul/Julia Ward Howe**)

**16.** _____'s reforms angered Progressives because they did not destroy trusts completely. (**William Jennings Bryan/William Howard Taft**)

**17.** A union member might have claimed that _____ was unfair because its emphasis on competition caused managers to consider profits more important than safe working conditions. (**capitalism/socialism**)

**18.** The _____ Amendment helped expand voting rights by allowing voters, and not state legislatures, to elect senators. (**Seventeenth/Eighteenth**)

**TRUE/FALSE** Indicate whether each statement below is true or false by writing **T** or **F** in the space provided.

_____ **19.** To help the conservation movement, Theodore Roosevelt signed a bill requiring manufacturers to limit the use of fossil fuels.

_____ **20.** The Triangle Shirtwaist Factory fire and other accidents led to passage of laws improving factory safety.

_____ **21.** A major aim of the Society of American Indians was to preserve Native Americans' traditional culture.

_____ **22.** Progressive reforms improved education for medical professionals.

_____ **23.** A procedure called an initiative allows voters to propose new laws by using petitions.

_____ **24.** Workers' compensation laws prohibited companies from paying wages to employees injured on the job.

_____ **25.** In the fight against discrimination, Ida B. Wells drew attention to the lynching of African Americans.

# The Progressive Spirit of Reform

## Chapter Test
### Form B

**SHORT ANSWER** On a separate sheet of paper, answer each of the following questions in complete sentences.

1. What is the difference between capitalism and socialism when it comes to owning industry and setting prices?

2. Which group did Elizabeth Cady Stanton and Susan B. Anthony found? Which group did Alice Paul found? How were the groups different?

3. Which group's efforts eventually led to the passage of the Eighteenth Amendment? What did that amendment do?

4. Why did the American Federation of Labor (AFL) outlast the Industrial Workers of the World (IWW)?

5. How did the National Association for the Advancement of Colored People (NAACP) first bring attention to racial inequality?

6. How did the Pendleton Civil Service Act help put an end to the spoils system?

**PRACTICING SOCIAL STUDIES SKILLS** Study the chart below and, on a separate sheet of paper, answer the questions that follow.

| The Progressive Amendments, 1909–1920 | | | |
|---|---|---|---|
| **Number** | **Description** | **Proposed by Congress** | **Ratified by States** |
| 16th | Federal income tax | 1909 | 1913 |
| 17th | Senators elected by people rather than state legislatures | 1912 | 1913 |
| 18th | Manufacture, sale, and transport of alcohol prohibited | 1917 | 1919 |
| 19th | Women's suffrage | 1919 | 1920 |

7. According to the chart, which of the Progressive amendments took the longest to ratify? What did that amendment do?

Progress Assessment

**America as a World Power**

**FILL IN THE BLANK** For each of the following statements, fill in the blank with the appropriate word, phrase, or name.

1. _____ is building an empire by founding colonies or conquering other nations.

2. The United States followed a limited policy of _____ , or avoiding involvement in the affairs of other countries.

3. In 1867 Secretary of State _____ arranged the purchase of Alaska from Russia for $7.2 million.

4. _____ became a United States territory in 1898.

5. U.S. President Millard Fillmore sent Commodore _____ to Japan to secure a peaceful trade relationship.

6. The _____ stated that all nations should have equal access to trade in China.

7. After Japan defeated China, other countries took advantage of China's weakness by seizing _____ , or areas where foreign nations controlled resources.

8. Many Chinese resented the power and control held by foreign nations; this hostility sparked the _____ .

9. In June 1900 Chinese nationalists took to the streets of _____ , China's capital, and laid siege to the walled settlement where foreigners lived.

10. China was forced to make a $333 million cash payment to foreign governments, $25 million of which went to the _____ .

# America as a World Power

## Section Quiz

### Section 2

**MULTIPLE CHOICE** For each of the following, write the letter of the best choice in the space provided.

_____ 1. What is the practice of printing sensational, often exaggerated stories called?
  a. isolationism
  b. arbitration
  c. capitalism
  d. yellow journalism

_____ 2. Which of the following stated that the United States had no interest in taking control of Cuba?
  a. McKinley Tariff
  b. Teller Amendment
  c. Open Door Policy
  d. Boxer Rebellion

_____ 3. Who led the Filipino rebels when they took control of Manila, the Philippine capital?
  a. Porfirio Díaz
  b. Emilio Aguinaldo
  c. Manuel Ramos
  d. Hidalgo Guadalupe

_____ 4. Which group opposed the peace treaty and the creation of an American colonial empire?
  a. Anti-Imperialist League
  b. Spheres of Influence
  c. Platt Amendment
  d. Open Door Policy

_____ 5. Which limited Cuba's right to make treaties and allowed the United States to intervene in Cuban affairs?
  a. Foraker Act
  b. Jones Act
  c. Platt Amendment
  d. Teller Amendment

Progress Assessment

**America as a World Power**

**MATCHING** In the space provided, write the letter of the term, person, or place that matches each description. Some answers will not be used.

_____ **1.** A link across the narrow neck of Central America that connects the Atlantic and Pacific oceans

_____ **2.** Established a new role for the U.S. as "police officer" of the Western Hemisphere

_____ **3.** Became president of the United States in 1909

_____ **4.** Influenced governments through economic, not military intervention

_____ **5.** A long, violent struggle for power in Mexico

_____ **6.** The first obstacle in building the Panama Canal

_____ **7.** Was fond of the saying, "speak softly and carry a big stick"

_____ **8.** Sent by President Wilson along with 15,000 U.S. soldiers into Mexico

_____ **9.** Rebel leader who killed 17 Americans in New Mexico

_____ **10.** Mexican dictator in 1910

**a.** channel

**b.** dollar diplomacy

**c.** Francisco "Pancho" Villa

**d.** John J. Pershing

**e.** Mexican Revolution

**f.** Monroe Doctrine

**g.** Panama Canal

**h.** Porfirio Díaz

**i.** progressive

**j.** Roosevelt Corollary

**k.** Theodore Roosevelt

**l.** William Howard Taft

**m.** yellow fever

Progress Assessment

**America as a World Power**

Chapter Test

Form A

**MULTIPLE CHOICE** For each of the following, write the letter of the best choice in the space provided.

_____ **1.** The growth of European imperialism from the late 1870s to 1914 was caused by the desire of
   **a.** countries to become isolationist.
   **b.** political leaders to improve the conditions of poorer countries.
   **c.** nations to become culturally varied by attracting new immigrants.
   **d.** countries to find sources of raw materials to help industrial growth.

_____ **2.** Why did President Roosevelt propose the Roosevelt Corollary?
   **a.** European nations were considering using force to collect debts from American nations.
   **b.** European nations had gone against the Monroe Doctrine.
   **c.** He did not want to get involved in European disputes.
   **d.** He did not agree with the Monroe Doctrine.

_____ **3.** What territories did the United States acquire in 1867?
   **a.** Alaska and the Midway Islands
   **b.** Alaska and Hawaii
   **c.** Hawaii and Samoa
   **d.** Hawaii and the Midway Islands

_____ **4.** The United States sought to open Japan's trade markets in the mid-1800s because it
   **a.** saw a chance to sell telegraph and railroad equipment to the Japanese.
   **b.** wanted to establish military bases in Japan.
   **c.** wanted to secure trade agreements with Japan before Europeans arrived.
   **d.** believed that trade with Japan would lead to trade with China.

Progress Assessment

_____ **5.** Supporters of isolationism believed that the United States should
   **a.** try to stop conflicts overseas.
   **b.** avoid interfering with other countries' affairs.
   **c.** increase military forces overseas.
   **d.** expand its territories in fuel-rich nations.

_____ **6.** Which of the following was an obstacle to the construction of the Panama Canal?
   **a.** tropical diseases such as malaria and yellow fever
   **b.** frequent attacks by Panamanian insurgents
   **c.** lack of food and water for the workers
   **d.** opposition of France, a major competitor

_____ **7.** The United States helped the Hawaiian sugar industry to prosper in the 1870s by
   **a.** allowing natives to manage Hawaiian shipyards.
   **b.** imposing high taxes on Hawaiian imports.
   **c.** allowing duty-free sugar shipments to the United States.
   **d.** sending American entrepreneurs to manage the plantations.

_____ **8.** The Anti-Imperialist League stood against
   **a.** the Spanish colonial empire.
   **b.** the territorial expansion of the United States.
   **c.** self-government in the Latin American colonies.
   **d.** the independence of Puerto Rico from the United States.

_____ **9.** Woodrow Wilson rejected Taft's dollar diplomacy because he believed
   **a.** the United States should avoid interfering with Latin American affairs.
   **b.** the United States had a moral obligation to promote democracy in Latin America.
   **c.** military force should be avoided.
   **d.** it would hurt the U.S. economy.

_____ **10.** The Mexican Revolution was started because of
   **a.** a revolt against a harsh dictator.
   **b.** strict immigration laws.
   **c.** loss of jobs.
   **d.** conflicts with Venezuela.

**PRACTICING SOCIAL STUDIES SKILLS** Study the quotation below and answer the question that follows.

> "We have cherished the policy of noninterference with affairs of foreign governments wisely inaugurated [begun] by Washington, keeping ourselves free from entanglement, either as allies or foes, content to leave undisturbed with them the settlement of their own domestic concerns."
>
> —President William McKinley,
> First Inaugural Address, 1897

_____ **11.** Which of the following policies is illustrated by McKinley's statement?
   **a.** imperialism
   **b.** isolationism
   **c.** Open Door Policy
   **d.** Dollar Diplomacy

**FILL IN THE BLANK** Read each sentence and fill in the blank with the term that best completes the sentence.

**12.** After the death of her brother, _____ proposed a new constitution that would return power to the Hawaiian monarchy, causing a revolt. (**Queen Liliuokalani/High Chiefess Kaahumanu**)

**13.** _____ arrived in Japan in 1853, and a year later convinced the Japanese to open trade with the United States. (**Commodore Matthew Perry/Millard Fillmore**)

**14.** Areas where foreign nations control trade and natural resources are called

_____. (**sites of imperialism/spheres of influence**)

**15.** President Roosevelt helped Panamanian rebels throw off Columbian rule

because Columbia's leaders would not allow the United States to lease

_____ for a canal. (**the Isthmus of Panama/Cristobal**)

**MATCHING** In the space provided, write the letter of the term, person, or place that matches each description. Some answers will not be used.

_____ **16.** warned that in cases of "wrongdoing" by Latin American countries, the United States might exercise "international police power"

_____ **17.** introduced dollar diplomacy, the practice of influencing governments through economic, not military, intervention

_____ **18.** stated that the United States had no interest in taking control of Cuba

_____ **19.** military general ordered by Woodrow Wilson to capture Francisco "Pancho" Villa in Mexico

_____ **20.** exaggerated news stories to attract readers

_____ **21.** limited Cuba's right to make treaties and permitted U.S. involvement in Cuban affairs

_____ **22.** his *New York World* published sensational stories that led to American support for Cuba

_____ **23.** arranged the purchase of Alaska from Russia in 1867

_____ **24.** Filipino rebel leader who took control of the Philippine capital, Manila, with the help of U.S. reinforcements

_____ **25.** waterway linking Atlantic and Pacific oceans

**a.** Teller Amendment

**b.** Liliuokalani

**c.** Platt Amendment

**d.** Panama Canal

**e.** Theodore Roosevelt

**f.** John J. Pershing

**g.** Joseph Pulitzer

**h.** yellow journalism

**i.** William H. Seward

**j.** William Howard Taft

**k.** William McKinley

**l.** Emilio Aguinaldo

**m.** Isthmus of Panama

# America as a World Power

Chapter Test

**Form B**

**SHORT ANSWER** On a separate sheet of paper, answer each of the
following questions in complete sentences.

1. In which two regions did the United States expand its influence in the late 1800s
and early 1900s?

2. What series of events led to the Spanish-American War?

3. What were reasons for the United States to end its policy of isolationism and get
involved in conflicts between other nations?

4. What caused Emilio Aguinaldo's transition from U.S. ally to U.S. foe in the
Philippines?

5. By about how many miles did the Panama Canal reduce the journey from San
Francisco to New York City?

**PRACTICING SOCIAL STUDIES SKILLS** Study the chart below and
answer the question that follows.

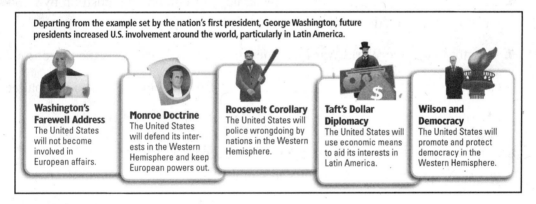

Departing from the example set by the nation's first president, George Washington, future
presidents increased U.S. involvement around the world, particularly in Latin America.

**Washington's Farewell Address**
The United States will not become involved in European affairs.

**Monroe Doctrine**
The United States will defend its interests in the Western Hemisphere and keep European powers out.

**Roosevelt Corollary**
The United States will police wrongdoing by nations in the Western Hemisphere.

**Taft's Dollar Diplomacy**
The United States will use economic means to aid its interests in Latin America.

**Wilson and Democracy**
The United States will promote and protect democracy in the Western Hemisphere.

6. What can you tell from this chart about how the American mission in the Western
Hemisphere changed over time? Describe the changes.

Progress Assessment

**FILL IN THE BLANK** For each of the following statements, fill in the blank with the appropriate word, phrase, or name.

1. _____ is a strong sense of pride and loyalty to one's own nation or culture.

2. European nations focused their resources on _____, or the aggressive strengthening of armed forces.

3. On June 28, 1914, _____, heir to the throne of Austria-Hungary, was assassinated while visiting Sarajevo.

4. The alliance between Austria-Hungary and Germany came to be known as the

   _____.

5. The _____ stretched from the North Sea all the way to Switzerland.

6. _____ was a new strategy of defending a position by fighting from the protection of deep ditches.

7. A factor that made World War I deadlier than previous wars was the use of modern technology like _____ that could fire 400 to 600 bullets a minute.

8. After a year of vicious fighting, the war had become a _____, or situation in which neither side can win a decisive victory.

9. The powerful British navy _____ the ports of the Central Powers and laid explosive mines in the North Sea.

10. The Germans used submarines called _____ to launch torpedoes against Allied supply ships, causing heavy losses.

Progress Assessment

# World War I

**MATCHING** In the space provided, write the letter of the term, person, or place that matches each description. Some answers will not be used.

_____ **1.** sunk by a German U-boat killing 1,200 people, including 128 Americans

_____ **2.** sent by German foreign minister to Mexico; decoded and published by American newspapers

_____ **3.** asked Congress to declare war on Germany in April 1917

_____ **4.** required men between the ages of 21 and 30 to register to be drafted

_____ **5.** organized rallies and parades and published posters and pamphlets to support the war

_____ **6.** restricted free speech and allowed the government to arrest war opponents

_____ **7.** provided billions of dollars for loans to the Allies

_____ **8.** oversaw the production and distribution of steel, copper, cement, and rubber

_____ **9.** voted against the United States' entering World War I

_____ **10.** helped workers and management avoid strikes and reach agreements, established a minimum wage and limited work hours

**a.** Committee on Public Information

**b.** Espionage Act of 1917

**c.** Jane Addams

**d.** Jeannette Rankin

**e.** Liberty bonds

**f.** *Lusitania*

**g.** National War Labor Board

**h.** prices

**i.** Selective Service Act

**j.** *Sussex*

**k.** War Industries Board

**l.** Woodrow Wilson

**m.** Zimmerman Note

Progress Assessment

**World War I**

**TRUE/FALSE** Mark each statement **T** if it is true or **F** if it is false. If false explain why.

_____ **1.** By the time U.S. troops arrived in Europe, the Allies were close to defeat.

_____

_____

_____ **2.** The American Expeditionary Force (AEF) did not join the French and British units, but fought as a separate force.

_____

_____

_____ **3.** In November 1917 a group of Germans known as the Kaisers overthrew the Russian government and seized power.

_____

_____

_____ **4.** Allied forces attacked and defeated the Germans at the town of Saint-Mihiel on the border of France and Germany in September 1918.

_____

_____

_____ **5.** The armistice, or truce, went into effect on the 9th hour of the 9th day of the 9th month of 1918.

_____

_____

Progress Assessment

**World War I**

Section Quiz

**Section 4**

**MULTIPLE CHOICE** For each of the following, write the letter of the best choice in the space provided.

_____ **1.** What was the international assembly created to settle disputes and encourage democracy called?
   **a.** the Zimmerman Note
   **b.** the League of Nations
   **c.** the International Treaty
   **d.** the Navigation Act

_____ **2.** Payments for war damages are known as
   **a.** retaliations.
   **b.** separatism.
   **c.** nationalism.
   **d.** reparations.

_____ **3.** The conference and final peace settlement of World War I was the
   **a.** League of Nations.
   **b.** Treaty of Versailles.
   **c.** International Treaty.
   **d.** Zimmerman Note.

_____ **4.** This Republican senator declared: "No peace that satisfied Germany in any degree can ever satisfy us."
   **a.** Henry Cabot Lodge
   **b.** Georges Clements
   **c.** David Lloyd George
   **d.** John J. Pershing

_____ **5.** The flu epidemic started in an army training camp in
   **a.** North Carolina.
   **b.** Chicago.
   **c.** Kansas.
   **d.** Nebraska.

Progress Assessment

**World War I**

**MULTIPLE CHOICE** For each of the following, write the letter of the best choice in the space provided.

_____ **1.** The Treaty of Versailles was signed by representatives of the United States, France, Britain, and
   **a.** Germany.
   **b.** Italy.
   **c.** Russia.
   **d.** Belgium.

_____ **2.** In World War I, the new strategy of trench warfare was an effective way to
   **a.** exchange secret messages.
   **b.** camouflage the soldiers in the wilderness.
   **c.** isolate soldiers suffering from contagious diseases.
   **d.** defend a position by fighting from within deep ditches.

_____ **3.** Which statement describes one of Woodrow Wilson's most significant accomplishments?
   **a.** He was awarded a Purple Heart for his bravery during World War I.
   **b.** He served as a general in the Civil War.
   **c.** He won the Nobel Peace Prize for his role in founding the League of Nations.
   **d.** He did not support the Treaty of Versailles.

_____ **4.** The purpose of the Liberty bonds issued by the U.S. government before World War I was to
   **a.** relieve the tax burden on working families.
   **b.** suppress anti-war propaganda.
   **c.** support the Allies.
   **d.** aid in the reconstruction of European cities.

_____ **5.** How did the Bolsheviks affect Russia's involvement in World War I?
   **a.** They refused to pay the army, ending Russia's military role in the war.
   **b.** They forced the czar to sign a treaty to make Russia cease fighting.
   **c.** Their overthrow of the czar sparked a civil war, which led to Russia's withdrawal from World War I.
   **d.** They forced the United States to send aid to Russia in exchange for Russia's allegiance.

Progress Assessment

_____ **6.** The aggressive strengthening of armed forces is known as

    **a.** militarism.

    **b.** nationalism.

    **c.** communism.

    **d.** capitalism.

_____ **7.** The influenza outbreak of 1918 was so deadly because it

    **a.** spread through water supplies.

    **b.** spread through the air, quickly and unknowingly.

    **c.** spread slowly, causing chronic illnesses.

    **d.** targeted children and the elderly.

_____ **8.** Which nation was the last to surrender to the Allied Forces in 1918?

    **a.** Austria-Hungary

    **b.** Bulgaria

    **c.** Germany

    **d.** the Ottoman Empire

_____ **9.** When American soldiers arrived in Europe in 1917, the

    **a.** Russians were advancing against Germany.

    **b.** Allies were dangerously near defeat.

    **c.** Germans were retreating from Paris.

    **d.** Allies were pummeling the German Navy at sea.

_____ **10.** How did the convoy system help the Allies at sea?

    **a.** It hurt German troops, making them vulnerable to Allied attacks.

    **b.** It allowed the Allies to infiltrate enemy trenches with air missiles.

    **c.** It helped the Allies encode and send messages that the Germans could not crack.

    **d.** It allowed destroyers to escort and protect groups of Allied merchant ships.

_____ **11.** The Selective Service Act passed in 1917 required

    **a.** the segregation of military units.

    **b.** the ban of any kind of anti-war campaign.

    **c.** the training of African American men as officers.

    **d.** men between the ages of 21 and 30 to register to be drafted.

Progress Assessment

**PRACTICING SOCIAL STUDIES SKILLS** Study the graph below and
answer the question that follows.

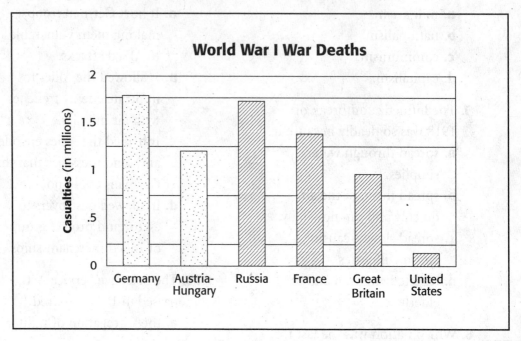

**World War I War Deaths**

_____ **12.** Approximately how many casualties did the Central Powers have in World
War I?
   **a.** 6 million
   **b.** over 5 million
   **c.** at least 3 million
   **d.** 1.5 million

**FILL IN THE BLANK** Read each sentence and fill in the blank with the
word in the word pair that best completes the sentence.

**13.** By 1916 World War I had become a _____, a situation in
which neither side can win a decisive victory. (**quagmire/stalemate**)

**14.** Because of a labor shortage during World War I, U.S. factories hired more than a

million _____. (**women/non-union workers**)

**15.** The spark that ignited World War I occurred when _____,
heir to the throne of Austria-Hungary, was killed by a Serb nationalist.
(**Archduke Francis Ferdinand/Franz Josef**)

**16.** Woodrow Wilson's _____ were a list of specific proposals for
postwar peace. (**Fourteen Points/State of the Union speeches**)

**17.** One cause of tension in Europe in the early 1900s was the rise of a sense of pride

in one's country, or _____. (**nationalism/isolationism**)

**MATCHING** In the space provided, write the letter of the term, place, or
person that matches each description. Some answers will not be used.

_____ **18.** secret telegram in which Germany offered to
help Mexico regain territory in the United
States if Mexico joined the Central Powers

_____ **19.** truce that ended active warfare and paved
the way for a peace treaty

_____ **20.** British passenger liner sunk by Germans

_____ **21.** leader of Republican opposition in the U.S.
Senate to the Treaty of Versailles

_____ **22.** German submarines used to attack Allied
and neutral ships

_____ **23.** payments for war damages

_____ **24.** Russian peace treaty with the Central Powers

_____ **25.** U.S. troops who fought in Europe in World
War I

**a.** the *Lusitania*

**b.** U-boats

**c.** American
Expeditionary Force
(AEF)

**d.** Treaty of Brest-Litovsk

**e.** Zimmermann Note

**g.** Henry Cabot Lodge

**h.** reparations

**j.** armistice

**k.** Sedition Act of 1918

**l.** militarism

**m.** the *Maine*

# World War I

**SHORT ANSWER** On a separate sheet of paper, answer each of the following questions in complete sentences.

1. What chain of events led to Russia's withdrawal from the war?

2. What name was given to the U.S. soldiers who were sent to fight in World War I?

3. What chain of events led to World War I?

4. About how many soldiers died in World War I?

5. If the Allies had lost the First Battle of the Marne in 1914, what might have happened?

6. What reason did President Wilson give for bringing America into the war in 1917?

**PRACTICING SOCIAL STUDIES SKILLS** Study the chart below and, on a separate sheet of paper, answer the question that follows.

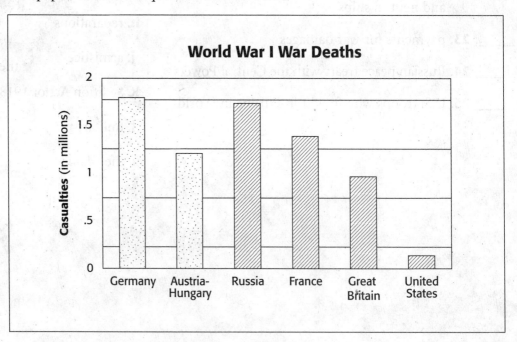

7. According to the chart, which countries suffered the most casualties—the Central Powers, or the Allied Powers? What can you infer about the loss of life caused by World War I?

Progress Assessment

# The Beginning of Modern America

Unit Test

## Form A

**MULTIPLE CHOICE** For each of the following, write the letter of the best choice in the space provided.

_____ 1. Republicans objected to the Treaty of Versailles mainly because they
   **a.** did not want Poland restored as a nation.
   **b.** felt its demands for reparations were too harsh.
   **c.** didn't want the League of Nations to have the power to use military force.
   **d.** thought that Russia should be included in the peace treaty process.

_____ 2. Why was the U.S. purchase of Alaska in 1867 called "Seward's Folly"?
   **a.** Americans didn't want to own a territory so close to Russia.
   **b.** Americans thought Alaska was nothing but a frozen wasteland.
   **c.** The United States had already annexed Samoa, and did not need another Pacific territory.
   **d.** Americans thought two-cents per acre was too expensive.

_____ 3. What was President Wilson's top priority when he first took office?
   **a.** pass reform legislation to improve social conditions
   **b.** raise tariffs to boost the economy
   **c.** decrease regulations on big businesses
   **d.** improve relations with other countries

_____ 4. What was the greatest effect of muckrakers' writing during the Progressive movement?
   **a.** brought racial discrimination to light, turning the movement's attention to a neglected issue
   **b.** brought social and economic issues to the public eye, uniting the movement
   **c.** angered politicians and business leaders, making the movement's work more difficult
   **d.** served as a valuable record of events, creating a model for future generations

Progress Assessment

_____ **5.** What was the final event that
ended World War II?
   **a.** stalemate
   **b.** armistice
   **c.** Treaty of Versailles
   **d.** neutrality

_____ **6.** Many Native Americans
resisted adopting white culture because they
   **a.** wanted to preserve their
   traditional culture.
   **b.** wanted to stay on their
   reservations.
   **c.** thought it would invite
   conflict from other minority groups.
   **d.** did not trust the federal
   court system.

_____ **7.** Which territory was annexed
by the United States because
of the economic value of its
sugarcane plantations?
   **a.** Alaska
   **b.** the Midway Islands
   **c.** Hawaii
   **d.** Samoa

_____ **8.** One of the goals of the
Fourteen Points was to
   **a.** create secret alliances.
   **b.** reduce free shipping.
   **c.** increase armies and navies.
   **d.** resolve colonial claims.

_____ **9.** What caused the Mexican
Revolution?
   **a.** mass immigration to the
   United States
   **b.** poverty and landlessness
   **c.** the harsh rule of a dictator
   **d.** the dominance of
   American business

_____ **10.** Which of the following did
Theodore Roosevelt do to
help the conservation
movement?
   **a.** He signed a bill requiring
   manufacturers to limit the
   use of fossil fuel.
   **b.** He put millions of acres
   of public lands in private
   hands.
   **c.** He suggested that natural
   history be taught in all
   public schools.
   **d.** He doubled the number of
   national parks and created
   wildlife reservations.

_____ **11.** Why did employers hire child
laborers?
   **a.** Children had more energy
   than adults.
   **b.** Children were easier to
   train than adults.
   **c.** Children worked for less
   pay than adults.
   **d.** Children could work longer hours than adults.

_____ **12.** Theodore Roosevelt can best be described as
  **a.** a senator from New York.
  **b.** a strong leader with an aggressive foreign policy.
  **c.** a hero in the Civil War.
  **d.** the first president to die in battle.

_____ **13.** The United States gained construction rights for the Panama Canal by
  **a.** attacking Panama with U.S. warships.
  **b.** annexing Panama to the United States.
  **c.** signing an agreement with the Colombian Senate.
  **d.** encouraging a local uprising against the Colombian government.

_____ **14.** Which incident finally brought the United States into World War I, ending its neutrality?
  **a.** U.S. investment in Allied nations, amounting to $2 billion which would be lost if the Central Powers won the war
  **b.** Germany's attack on the British passenger liner *Lusitania*, in which 128 Americans were killed
  **c.** Germany's attack on the French passenger ship *Sussex*, in which four Americans were killed
  **d.** discovery of the Zimmermann Note, in which Germany promised to help Mexico recapture land it had lost in the Mexican-American War

_____ **15.** Which of the following was a factor leading to a shortage of labor in the United States during World War I?

**a.** American factories were working nonstop to provide weapons and supplies for the Allied forces, and they needed new workers to meet this huge demand.

**b.** Women were not allowed to replace male workers because they were limited to a 40-hour work week.

**c.** Many of the young men who would normally have taken factory jobs went off to Europe after 1917 to protest the war.

**d.** Immigrants who had provided a steady source of factory labor were not available because they had returned to their native countries.

_____ **16.** When the United States entered World War I, General John J. Pershing insisted that the American Expeditionary Force

**a.** fight as a separate army.

**b.** join British units.

**c.** accept only experienced volunteers.

**d.** enter the conflict as soon as possible.

_____ **17.** Which was one of the costs of World War I?

**a.** America had borrowed a lot of money from France and Great Britain, and was now in debt.

**b.** The deaths of millions of people and great financial disaster affected many parts of Europe.

**c.** Losing the war caused food riots and starvation in Russia.

**d.** State and local governments were forced to impose quarantines.

**PRACTICING SOCIAL STUDIES SKILLS** Study the graph below and
answer the question that follows.

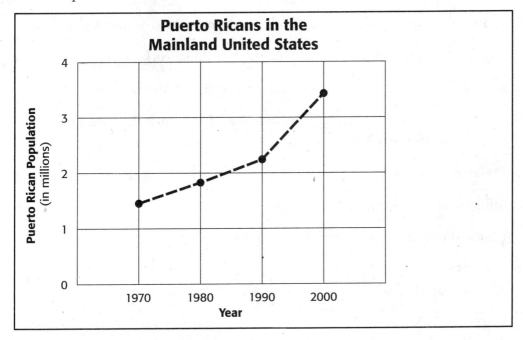

_____ **18.** About how many Puerto Ricans moved to the mainland United States
between 1980 and 2000?

**a.** 0.5 million

**b.** 1 million

**c.** 1.5 million

**d.** 3 million

**FILL IN THE BLANK** Read each sentence and fill in the blank with the
word in the word pair that best completes the sentence.

**19.** _____ spread from the late 1870s to 1914 because countries
wanted to find sources of raw materials to help industrial growth.
(**Mercantilism/Imperialism**)

**20.** In May 1915, a German U-boat sank the _____, a British
passenger liner. (***Maine/Lusitania***)

**21.** The use of _____ warfare, a new military strategy, was a
large part of what made World War I so long and deadly. (**germ/trench**)

**22.** The _____ allowed people to approve or reject a law that the government had already passed. (**referendum/ballot initiative**)

**23.** In 1902 President Roosevelt threatened to take over the coal mines unless the managers agreed to settle their disputes with striking workers through a formal process called _____. (**arbitration/mediation**)

**24.** The _____ Amendment gave women the right to vote. (**Nineteenth/Seventeenth**)

**25.** President William Howard Taft used economic rather than military tactics to influence other governments, a policy called _____. (**dollar diplomacy/the power of the purse**)

**26.** The term _____ identifies the practice of exaggerating news stories in order to sell newspapers. (**sphere of influence/yellow journalism**)

**27.** In 1918 a worldwide _____ broke out, killing approximately 30 million people around the world. (**influenza epidemic/bacterial infection**)

**28.** In July 1918, German generals launched their final offensive—a last attempt to cross the _____ River. (**Marne/Rhine**)

**29.** One cause of tension in Europe in the early 1900s was the rise of a sense of pride in one's country, or _____. (**nationalism/isolationism**)

**TRUE/FALSE** Indicate whether each statement below is true or false by writing **T** or **F** in the space provided.

_____ **30.** Chinese resentment of power held by foreign nations sparked the Boxer rebellion.

_____ **31.** The Teller Amendment, which was in effect until 1934, required Cuba to sell or lease land to the United States.

_____ **32.** The Roosevelt Corollary to the Monroe Doctrine stated that if Caribbean and South American countries did not pay their debts to European countries, the United States would get involved.

_____ **33.** The United States managed to rid the Panama Canal route of malaria before construction began.

_____ **34.** The Anti-Imperialist League claimed that newly acquired territories such as Guam and Puerto Rico should be granted the right of self-government.

_____ **35.** The Supreme Court's ruling in the case of *Lochner* v. *New York* meant it was unconstitutional for the state to limit workers to a ten-hour workday.

_____ **36.** The National War Labor Board, set up in 1918, banned strikes during wartime, resulting in more than one million striking workers losing their jobs.

_____ **37.** The Selective Service Act of 1917 required able-bodied men ages 21 to 30 to register to be drafted.

_____ **38.** Nearly one million soldiers were killed at Verdun and the Somme, but these two battles had very little effect on the western front.

_____ **39.** Several representatives of Russia and the Central Powers attended the Paris Peace Conference, and expressed their ideas for the peace treaty.

_____ **40.** The American Open Door Policy stated that all nations should have equal access to trade in China.

**MATCHING** In the space provided, write the letter of the term, person, or place that matches each description. Some answers will not be used.

_____ **41.** restricted free speech in the United States during wartime

_____ **42.** led the socialist union known as the Industrial Workers of the World

_____ **43.** co-founded the National Association for the Advancement of Colored People (NAACP)

_____ **44.** set up a merit system for assigning government jobs backed by President Chester A. Arthur

_____ **45.** may have stolen up to $200 million from New York City while boss of Tammany Hall

_____ **46.** allowed Americans to vote directly for U.S. senators

_____ **47.** group of reformers who worked to improve society during the late 1800s

_____ **48.** fought for local and state laws banning the sale of alcohol

_____ **49.** he and his wife's death led to World War I

_____ **50.** drew attention to the lynching of African Americans

**a.** William Marcy Tweed

**b.** Eighteenth Amendment

**c.** Pendleton Civil Service Act

**d.** Progressives

**e.** W.E.B. Du Bois

**f.** William "Big Bill" Haywood

**g.** Women's Christian Temperance Union

**h.** Seventeenth Amendment

**i.** National Consumers' League

**j.** Archduke Francis Ferdinand

**k.** Ida B. Wells

**l.** Sedition Act of 1918

　　　　　　　　Progress Assessment

# The Beginning of Modern America

Unit Test

Form B

**SHORT ANSWER** On a separate sheet of paper, answer each of the following questions in complete sentences.

**1.** How did the recall, the initiative, and the referendum change American politics?

**2.** Why were so many children working dangerous jobs instead of going to school during the Gilded Age?

**3.** To which nations did the United States send troops around the turn of the 20th century?

**4.** Why were U.S. actions in Hawaii and the Philippines not a threat to U.S. isolationism?

**5.** Why do you think General Pershing did not want American troops to fight in French or British regiments?

**6.** Why were tanks such a powerful new weapon of war?

**PRACTICING SOCIAL STUDIES SKILLS** Study the chart below and, on a separate sheet of paper, answer the question that follows.

**SUPREME COURT DECISIONS**

**Schenck v. United States (1919)**

**Background of the Case** Charles Schenck was arrested for violating the Espionage Act. He had printed and distributed pamphlets urging resistance to the draft. Schenck argued that the First Amendment, which guarantees freedom of speech and freedom of the press, gave him the right to criticize the government.

**The Court's Ruling**
The Supreme Court ruled that the pamphlet was not protected by the First Amendment and that the Espionage Act was constitutional.

**The Court's Reasoning**
The Supreme Court decided that under certain circumstances, such as a state of war, Congress could limit free speech. The Court created a test to distinguish between protected and unprotected speech. Unprotected speech would have to present "a clear and present danger" to national security. For example, the First Amendment would not protect a person who created a panic by yelling "Fire!" in a crowded theater.

**Why It Matters**
Schenck v. United States was important because it was the first case in which the Supreme Court interpreted the First Amendment. The Court concluded that certain constitutional rights, such as free speech, could be limited under extraordinary conditions, such as war. Later rulings by the Court narrowed the test of "clear and present danger" to speech advocating violence. The nonviolent expression of ideas and opinions—however unpopular—was thereby protected.

**7.** Use this chart, along with information you learned in this unit, to describe why *Schenck* v. *United States* (1919) was such an important ruling. Describe how the ruling was influenced by U.S. actions around the world from the 1880s to 1917. List the military and economic actions that might have led Americans to protest their government's policies.

Progress Assessment

**The Roaring Twenties**

**MATCHING** In the space provided, write the letter of the term or person that matches each description. Some answers will not be used.

_____ **1.** Senator from Ohio and Republican candidate for president

_____ **2.** Massachusetts governor and Republican vice presidential candidate

_____ **3.** Idea that tax cuts for wealthy Americans would "trickle down" to less-well-off Americans

_____ **4.** Secretary of the Interior Albert Fall's acceptance of large sums of money and valuable gifts in exchange for government oil reserves

_____ **5.** Agreement that outlawed war, signed by the United States and 14 other nations

_____ **6.** Inventor and business leader from Detroit

_____ **7.** Sturdy and reliable car nicknamed the Tin Lizzie

_____ **8.** System that used conveyer belts to move parts of cars from one group of workers to another

_____ **9.** Purchasing method that allowed people to pay a small amount of the price every month until an item was paid for

_____ **10.** Secretary of commerce who became president in 1928

**a.** Alfred E. Smith

**b.** moving assembly line

**c.** Calvin Coolidge

**d.** factories

**e.** Henry Ford

**f.** Herbert Hoover

**g.** installment plan

**h.** Kellogg-Briand Pact

**i.** Model T

**j.** prosperity

**k.** Teapot Dome Scandal

**l.** trickle-down theory

**m.** Warren G. Harding

Progress Assessment

Name _____ Class _____ Date _____

## The Roaring Twenties

Section Quiz

**Section 2**

**FILL IN THE BLANK** For each of the following statements, fill in the blank with the appropriate word, phrase, or name.

1. Young women known as _____ challenged traditional ideas of how women were supposed to behave.

2. The _____ was a time of fear of Communists and radicals.

3. The _____ Union was founded in 1920 to defend people's civil rights.

4. _____ are people opposed to organized government.

5. The _____ Act of 1921 limited the total number of immigrants allowed into the United States.

6. In 1933 the government passed the _____, which ended prohibition.

7. The belief in an exact, word-for-word interpretation of the Bible is known as

_____.

8. The _____ was a movement in which large numbers of African Americans began leaving the South to take jobs in northern factories.

9. The _____ was a racist group that terrorized African Americans and harassed Catholics, Jews, and immigrants.

10. _____ encouraged black people around the world to express pride in their culture and become economically independent.

Progress Assessment

## The Roaring Twenties

**FILL IN THE BLANK** For each of the following statements, fill in the blank with the appropriate word, phrase, or name.

1. In the 1920s _____ allowed people all over the country to listen to the same programs.

2. *The Jazz Singer* was the first _____, or motion picture with sound.

3. An explosion in the popularity of jazz music gave the 1920s the nickname of the

   _____.

4. _____ was a trumpet player known for his method of stepping out from the band to perform a solo.

5. The period of African American artistic accomplishment in the 1920s was known

   as the _____.

6. _____ was a famous writer who produced poems, plays, and novels about African American life.

7. Writers who criticized American society in the 1920s became known as the

   _____.

8. A community of American _____, or people who leave their home country to live elsewhere, developed in Paris in the 1920s.

9. _____'s novel *The Great Gatsby* focused on what he saw as a loss of morality behind the fun and free-spirited times of the Jazz Age.

10. Sinclair Lewis was the first American to receive the _____ in literature.

Progress Assessment

Name _____ Class _____ Date _____

# The Roaring Twenties

**MULTIPLE CHOICE** For each of the following, write the letter of the best choice in the space provided.

_____ **1.** Warren G. Harding's campaign strategy was based on a promise to
   **a.** return to prewar isolationism.
   **b.** restore normalcy, or stability and prosperity.
   **c.** end political corruption.
   **d.** increase government involvement in big business.

_____ **2.** Why were some American writers of the 1920s called the "Lost Generation"?
   **a.** They returned to Paris where most of them were originally from.
   **b.** They expressed feelings of separation from American society.
   **c.** They appreciated the Jazz Age and its rebellious youth culture.
   **d.** They expressed the pain of racism experienced by African Americans.

_____ **3.** 1927 was a fundamental year in motion pictures, because it brought the first
   **a.** color film.
   **b.** film with sound.
   **c.** full-length feature.
   **d.** still-frame animation.

_____ **4.** What was the main reason Herbert Hoover was elected by a large majority of votes?
   **a.** Hoover was a veteran of World War I.
   **b.** Hoover promised to continue the economic boom.
   **c.** Hoover would have been the first Catholic president.
   **d.** Hoover ran a campaign that focused on city dwellers.

_____ **5.** The Scopes Trial represented the conflict between
   **a.** Anarchists and Communists about political reform.
   **b.** scientists and environmentalists about the environment.
   **c.** fundamentalist beliefs and scientific ideals about evolution.
   **d.** the government and U.S. citizens about prohibition.

Progress Assessment

_____ **6.** Ernest Hemingway was one of a group of writers in the 1920s whose writing
   **a.** described the effects of prohibition.
   **b.** criticized American society.
   **c.** focused on Communist ideals.
   **d.** described the lives of jazz musicians in Paris.

_____ **7.** The effects of Prohibition included
   **a.** strained relations with Canada, because so much illegal alcohol was shipped across the Canadian border.
   **b.** more expensive home-made alcohol, such as moonshine, which was sold in speakeasies.
   **c.** the rise of organized crime, as gangs became more powerful with the money they got from selling illegal weapons.
   **d.** increased government corruption, as local police and politicians took bribes from gangsters to ignore the movement and sale of alcohol.

_____ **8.** One of the main goals of Marcus Garvey's black nationalism was for African Americans to
   **a.** fight against the violence of the Ku Klux Klan.
   **b.** have their own businesses and communities.
   **c.** receive government funds for their businesses.
   **d.** avoid conflict with the Ku Klux Klan by limiting the spread of their culture.

_____ **9.** Until 1924, Native Americans did not have access to adequate legal protection from the government because they
   **a.** were not citizens of the United States.
   **b.** had refused to fight during World War I.
   **c.** were not allowed to leave the reservations.
   **d.** had become the smallest and least powerful minority.

**PRACTICING SOCIAL STUDIES SKILLS** Study the charts below and
answer the question that follows.

**Motor Vehicle Prices and Production, 1908–1924**

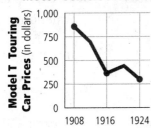 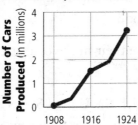

_____ **10.** According to the charts, what can you infer about the sale and production
of the Model T between 1908 and 1924?

    **a.** As prices were lowered, production of the Model T also dropped.

    **b.** Prices increased as sales increased. ·

    **c.** Because the Model T was affordable, more people could buy it, causing
production to rise.

    **d.** Prices diminished dramatically, but fewer people could afford to buy
the Model T.

**TRUE/FALSE** Indicate whether each statement below is true or false by
writing **T** or **F** in the space provided.

_____ **11.** Trumpeter Louis Armstrong invented the jazz solo, when one musician
steps out from the band to play alone.

_____ **12.** Immigration to the United States fell dramatically in the 1920s because of
the millions of people killed in Europe during World War I.

_____ **13.** The Teapot Dome scandal caused people to question the judgment and
honesty of government officials.

_____ **14.** In the 1920s, high school attendance fell as young people flocked to the
cities to take advantage of high-paying jobs and the nightclubs of the new
youth culture.

_____ **15.** After World War I, the U.S. economy suffered a downturn that led to hard
times as the 1920s began.

**MATCHING** In the space provided, write the letter of the term, person, or place that matches each description. Some answers will not be used.

_____ **16.** young women who challenged society's ideas about womanhood

_____ **17.** people who leave their home countries to live elsewhere

_____ **18.** 1928 pact in which the United States and other countries agreed not to engage in war

_____ **19.** affordable automobile invented by Henry Ford

_____ **20.** flourishing of African American literature and art in the 1920s

_____ **21.** system that uses conveyor belts to move parts to different groups of workers

_____ **22.** fear of Communist infiltration after the Russian Revolution

_____ **23.** ended Prohibition in 1933

_____ **24.** Republican candidate for vice president in 1920

_____ **25.** painter famous for creating detailed paintings of flowers

**a.** Twenty-first Amendment

**b.** moving assembly line

**c.** Red Scare

**d.** Georgia O'Keeffe

**e.** expatriates

**f.** flappers

**g.** Harlem Renaissance

**h.** Langston Hughes

**i.** Kellogg-Briand Pact

**j.** Model T

**k.** Calvin Coolidge

**l.** Warren G. Harding

Progress Assessment

**The Roaring Twenties**

Chapter Test

**Form B**

**SHORT ANSWER** On a separate sheet of paper, answer each of the following questions in complete sentences.

1. What first set the economic boom of the 1920s in motion?

2. What were the pros and cons of a job on the Ford assembly line?

3. Why did some Americans see Alfred Smith's Catholicism as a threat?

4. Why were flappers controversial in 1920s society?

5. How would you describe the Sacco and Vanzetti case? Why were Sacco and Vanzetti found guilty of robbery and murder?

6. What was Marcus Garvey's plan for African Americans, known as "black nationalism"?

**PRACTICING SOCIAL STUDIES SKILLS** Study the information below and, on a separate sheet of paper, answer the question that follows.

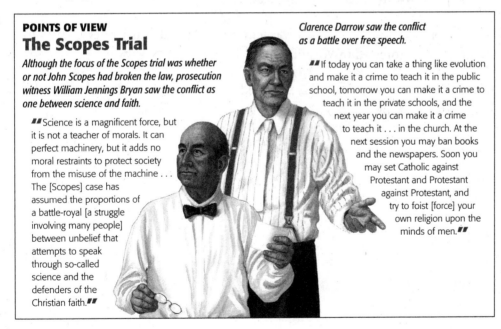

**POINTS OF VIEW**
**The Scopes Trial**

*Although the focus of the Scopes trial was whether or not John Scopes had broken the law, prosecution witness William Jennings Bryan saw the conflict as one between science and faith.*

**"**Science is a magnificent force, but it is not a teacher of morals. It can perfect machinery, but it adds no moral restraints to protect society from the misuse of the machine . . . The [Scopes] case has assumed the proportions of a battle-royal [a struggle involving many people] between unbelief that attempts to speak through so-called science and the defenders of the Christian faith.**"**

*Clarence Darrow saw the conflict as a battle over free speech.*

**"**If today you can take a thing like evolution and make it a crime to teach it in the public school, tomorrow you can make it a crime to teach it in the private schools, and the next year you can make it a crime to teach it . . . in the church. At the next session you may ban books and the newspapers. Soon you may set Catholic against Protestant and Protestant against Protestant, and try to foist [force] your own religion upon the minds of men.**"**

7. Sum up Bryan's or Darrow's arguments in your own words.

Progress Assessment

## The Great Depression

**FILL IN THE BLANK** For each of the following statements, fill in the blank with the appropriate word, phrase, or name.

1. For most of the 1920s, the stock market was a _____, or one with rising stock values.

2. People who could not afford a stock's full price began _____, or purchasing on credit with a loan.

3. A market with declining stock prices is known as a _____.

4. On Tuesday, October 29, 1929, a day that became known as

   _____, the stock market crashed.

5. The _____ is the up-and-down pattern of consumer purchasing and the production of goods.

6. _____ did not believe that it was the federal government's role to provide direct relief to Americans.

7. The _____ was a group of World War I veterans and their families who protested in Washington, D.C.

8. General _____ used force, including tear gas and tanks, to scatter the veterans.

9. _____ won the 1932 presidential election by a landslide.

10. The Temporary _____ Administration gave unemployment assistance to many out-of-work New Yorkers.

Progress Assessment

# The Great Depression

Section Quiz

## Section 2

**MATCHING** In the space provided, write the letter of the term or person that matches each description. Some answers will not be used.

_____ 1. New programs to battle the Depression and aid economic recovery

_____ 2. Radio addresses given by Roosevelt in which he spoke directly to the American people

_____ 3. Government program that hired people to build dams and generators, bringing electricity and jobs to poor communities in the Tennessee River Valley

_____ 4. The nation's first female cabinet member

_____ 5. Helped farmers refinance their mortgages in order to keep their farms

_____ 6. First Lady and an active supporter of the New Deal programs

_____ 7. Provided some financial security for the elderly, disabled, children, and the unemployed

_____ 8. Organized workers into unions based on industry, not skill

_____ 9. When striking workers stay in the factories so they can't be replaced by new workers

_____ 10. New Deal critic who proposed a program called "Share Our Wealth," which would have taxed rich Americans to help the poor

**a.** Congress of Industrial Organizations

**b.** Eleanor Roosevelt

**c.** Farm Credit Administration

**d.** fireside chats

**e.** Frances Perkins

**f.** Huey Long

**g.** Judicial Procedures Reform Act

**h.** New Deal

**i.** sit-down strike

**j.** Social Security Act

**k.** Tennessee Valley Authority

**l.** unions

**m.** Wagner Act

Progress Assessment

**TRUE/FALSE** Mark each statement **T** if it is true or **F** if it is false. If false explain why.

_____ **1.** Parts of the Great Plains farms were destroyed because of rains and flooding.

_____

_____

_____ **2.** The Great Depression affected families all over the United States.

_____

_____

_____ **3.** Mary McLeod Bethune was one of several African Americans who President Roosevelt appointed to his administration.

_____

_____

_____ **4.** Big band leaders like Duke Ellington, Benny Goodman, and Count Basie helped make swing music popular.

_____

_____

_____ **5.** Even today, New Deal critics believe that Roosevelt's programs ended the Great Depression.

_____

_____

Progress Assessment

Name _____ Class _____ Date _____

# The Great Depression

**MULTIPLE CHOICE** For each of the following, write the letter of the best choice in the space provided.

_____ **1.** Critics who thought the New Deal went too far claimed which of the following?
  **a.** The government should nationalize the country's wealth and natural resources.
  **b.** The new laws gave the president too much authority.
  **c.** The enormous expansion of the federal government was a step toward communism.
  **d.** The cost of the new programs could bankrupt some businesses.

_____ **2.** Businesses were hurt by the stock market crash because they
  **a.** lost their savings in failed banks and had to close or cut back.
  **b.** had lent money to foreign countries and were not paid back.
  **c.** had no workers to make goods.
  **d.** were forced to cut back production but could not fire workers.

_____ **3.** Which group suffered most in the Dust Bowl?
  **a.** scientists
  **b.** unskilled laborers
  **c.** industrial workers
  **d.** farmers

_____ **4.** Americans regained faith in banks after President Roosevelt signed the Emergency Banking Relief Act into law because the act
  **a.** allowed only healthy banks to remain open.
  **b.** gave people the right to withdraw all their money without a penalty or waiting period.
  **c.** authorized the government to immediately deposit $1 billion in banks to guarantee deposits.
  **d.** required the federal government to pay back in full the customers of any bank that failed.

Progress Assessment

_____ **5.** Herbert Hoover lost the election in 1932 mainly because Americans

   **a.** thought he would raise taxes.

   **b.** thought he would spend too much government money.

   **c.** lost confidence in him or blamed him for the Depression.

   **d.** worried about his priority on foreign policies instead of domestic issues.

_____ **6.** The TVA is significant because it hired people to

   **a.** deliver food to the poverty-stricken Dust Bowl residents.

   **b.** build dams and generators that provided electricity.

   **c.** work on farms to help stabilize agriculture.

   **d.** work in the automobile industry to increase mass production.

_____ **7.** What problems did President Roosevelt have with the Supreme Court?

   **a.** The Court would not give him adequate funding for the New Deal programs.

   **b.** He directly accused the Supreme Court of causing the stock market crash.

   **c.** The Court issued a series of rulings declaring many New Deal programs unconstitutional.

   **d.** He was not given the chance to nominate new Supreme Court justices.

_____ **8.** Which of the following is a lasting effect of the New Deal?

   **a.** workplace safety

   **b.** clean air and water

   **c.** whistleblowers in corrupt corporations

   **d.** the protection of the savings of bank customers

_____ **9.** Which of the following best describes Black Tuesday?

   **a.** Half a million workers lost their jobs.

   **b.** Hoover lost the election.

   **c.** The stock market crashed.

   **d.** Over 2,000 banks closed.

**PRACTICING SOCIAL STUDIES SKILLS** Study the graph below and
answer the question that follows.

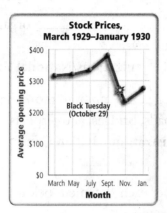

Stock Prices,
March 1929–January 1930

_____ **10.** People who invested in which month would have been hurt most by Black
    Tuesday?
    **a.** May
    **b.** July
    **c.** September
    **d.** November

**FILL IN THE BLANK** Read each sentence and fill in the blank with the
term that best completes the sentence.

**11.** People who could not afford to buy stocks at full price began

_____. (**buying on margin/paying back loans**)

**12.** _____ wrote *The Grapes of Wrath*, the story of a family of
farmers forced to move in search of work. (**Woody Guthrie/John Steinbeck**)

**13.** _____ authorized $1.2 billion in aid to different financial
institutions in the first year of the Depression, but refused to give direct assistance
to individual Americans. (**Herbert Hoover/Franklin D. Roosevelt**)

**14.** Grass and trees were planted in the Dust Bowl to try to stop

_____. (**soil erosion/tornadoes**)

**15.** One of the major causes of the Great Depression was the

_____ goods at a time when the market for goods was

shrinking. (**overproduction of/increased taxes on**)

**16.** _____ was an African American educator appointed to Roosevelt's administration. (**Dorothea Lange/Mary McLeod Bethune**)

**17.** A group called the _____ organized workers into unions based on industry, not skill level.
(**Congress of Industrial Organizations/National Youth Administration**)

**18.** The _____ employed more than 8.5 million people from 1935 to 1943, building roads, bridges, and airports.
(**Works Progress Administration/Civilian Conservation Corps**)

**TRUE/FALSE** Indicate whether each statement below is true or false by writing **T** or **F** in the space provided.

_____ **19.** The up and down pattern in the economy is known as the business cycle.

_____ **20.** As first lady, Eleanor Roosevelt convinced her husband to create the National Youth Administration to help young workers stay in school.

_____ **21.** Woody Guthrie's lively, upbeat songs offered an escape from the loss and struggle suffered by so many people during the Depression.

_____ **22.** The passage of the Social Security Act was the first time the federal government took direct responsibility for many citizens' economic well-being.

_____ **23.** The Bonus Army demanded that Hoover authorize early payment of their military bonuses to help ease the need caused by the Depression.

_____ **24.** The Second New Deal was made up of programs the Roosevelt administration introduced when the Supreme Court struck down programs of the first New Deal.

_____ **25.** After the Supreme Court blocked several New Deal programs, President Roosevelt tried to pass an act that would allow him to appoint six new Supreme Court justices immediately.

# The Great Depression

**SHORT ANSWER** On a separate sheet of paper, answer each of the following questions in complete sentences.

**1.** What was buying on margin, and why was it popular in the 1920s?

**2.** What two actions made President Hoover unpopular by the 1932 election?

**3.** What were Roosevelt's fireside chats, and why were they influential?

**4.** How were unions impacted by the New Deal?

**5.** How did First Lady Eleanor Roosevelt show her support for equal rights for African Americans?

**6.** In what two ways did Americans find some relief from their troubles during the Depression?

**PRACTICING SOCIAL STUDIES SKILLS** Study the chart below and, on a separate sheet of paper, answer the questions that follow.

## Unemployment, 1929–1941

**7.** How could this chart be used to prove that Roosevelt's programs stopped the Great Depression? How could it be used to prove the opposite?

Name _____ Class _____ Date _____

# World War II

**MATCHING**  In the space provided, write the letter of the term, place, or person that matches each description. Some answers will not be used.

_____ **1.** Leader who gained complete control of Italy in 1922

_____ **2.** Political system in which the government is seen as more important than individuals

_____ **3.** Fiery speaker who inspired huge audiences by vowing to restore Germany to prosperity and a position of international power

_____ **4.** Dictator of the Soviet Union in 1929

_____ **5.** Alliance formed by Germany, Italy, and later joined by Japan

_____ **6.** Policy of avoiding war with an aggressive nation by giving in to its demands

_____ **7.** British leader during World War II

_____ **8.** Alliance between Britain and France

_____ **9.** Allowed the president to aid any nation he believed was vital to U.S. defense

_____ **10.** Where the U.S. fleet was attacked by the Japanese in December 1941

**a.** Adolf Hitler

**b.** Allied Powers

**c.** appeasement

**d.** Axis Powers

**e.** Benito Mussolini

**f.** Blitzkrieg

**g.** fascism

**h.** Joseph Stalin

**i.** Lend-Lease Act

**j.** Luftwaffe

**k.** Nazis

**l.** Pearl Harbor

**m.** Winston Churchill

Progress Assessment

**FILL IN THE BLANK** For each of the following statements, fill in the
blank with the appropriate word, phrase, or name.

1. _____ contributed to the war effort by running 24 hours a
   day, producing ships, tanks, jeeps, and ammunition.

2. _____ workers were soon doubling the war production of
   Germany, Japan, and all other Axis Power countries combined.

3. To oversee the conversion of factories to war production the government created

   the _____.

4. The government urged _____ to fill positions left by men
   leaving home to fight in the war.

5. To protest the unfair treatment of African Americans, labor leader

   _____ began to organize a march to Washington, D.C.

6. The Tuskegee Airmen were _____ pilots who trained at the
   Tuskegee Army Air Field in Alabama.

7. In Los Angeles, groups of sailors attacked Mexican Americans wearing distinctive

   clothing, beginning the _____.

8. Executive Order 9066 began the process of _____, or forced
   relocation and imprisonment of Japanese Americans.

9. Men from the ages of 18 to 38 were required to register for the

   _____.

10. To finance the war effort, the government increased _____
    and sold war bonds.

**World War II**

**TRUE/FALSE** Mark each statement **T** if it is true or **F** if it is false. If false explain why.

_____ **1.** By the time the U.S. entered the war, the Axis Powers were in trouble of losing the war.

_____

_____

_____ **2.** The British stopped the Afrika Korps in July 1942 at the Battle of El Alamein.

_____

_____

_____ **3.** The first step in the mission to liberate Western Europe was the invasion of German-occupied France.

_____

_____

_____ **4.** The invasion took place on June 6, 1944 and was known as D-Day, or "dooms day".

_____

_____

_____ **5.** By the end of D-Day, the Allies had stopped the German advance and slowly began driving back German forces.

_____

_____

Progress Assessment

# World War II

**MATCHING** In the space provided, write the letter of the term, person, or place that matches each description. Some answers will not be used.

_____ 1. Commanded the American and Filipino forces in the Philippines

_____ 2. Where more than 600 Americans and 10,000 Filipinos were starved and beaten by Japanese soldiers

_____ 3. Admiral who led the U.S. Pacific Fleet

_____ 4. Conflict in which American and Japanese aircraft carriers and fighter planes clashed but neither side won a clear victory

_____ 5. Began on June 4, 1942, when U.S. aircraft carriers launched their attack on Japanese planes while they were refueling on deck

_____ 6. Strategy to capture only the most important islands

_____ 7. The largest navel battle in history

_____ 8. Conflict in which Japanese soldiers were dug into caves and resulted in thousands of deaths for Japanese and U.S. forces

_____ 9. Island where over 100,000 Japanese soldiers were when some of the deadliest battles of the war in the Pacific occurred

_____ 10. Japanese strategy to purposely crash piloted planes into enemy ships

**a.** Bataan Death March

**b.** Battle of the Coral Sea

**c.** Battle of Leyte Gulf

**d.** Battle of Midway

**e.** Chester Nimitz

**f.** Douglas MacArthur

**g.** Guadalcanal

**h.** island-hopping

**i.** Iwo Jima

**j.** kamikaze

**k.** mainland

**l.** Okinawa

**m.** Pearl Harbor

# World War II

**MULTIPLE CHOICE** For each of the following, write the letter of the best choice in the space provided.

_____ **1.** The Allies gained victory in Europe with the surrender of what country?
  **a.** France
  **b.** Germany
  **c.** China
  **d.** Russia

_____ **2.** What was the program of mass murder used by Hitler and the Nazis in their effort to exterminate the entire Jewish population of Europe?
  **a.** Doom's Day Project
  **b.** Manhattan Project
  **c.** the Rhine Project
  **d.** the Holocaust

_____ **3.** Hitler's "final solution" was
  **a.** genocide, or the extermination of an entire group of people.
  **b.** to force Jews into urban centers called ghettos.
  **c.** the last battle against the Allied Forces.
  **d.** a pact between Germany and the Soviet Union.

_____ **4.** The secret program to develop the atomic bomb was known as the
  **a.** Manhattan Project.
  **b.** Holocaust.
  **c.** Enola Gay.
  **d.** D-Day Solution.

_____ **5.** On August 6, 1945, a B-29 bomber dropped the first atomic bomb on what Japanese city?
  **a.** Nagasaki
  **b.** Tokyo
  **c.** Hiroshima
  **d.** Osaka

**World War II**

# Chapter Test

### Form A

**MULTIPLE CHOICE** For each of the following, write the letter of the best choice in the space provided.

_____ **1.** Why did Great Britain and France finally declare war on Germany in September 1939?
   **a.** Hitler signed a non aggression pact with Stalin, threatening the Allies.
   **b.** Hitler signed an alliance with Mussolini, forming the Axis Powers.
   **c.** They had pledged to defend Poland against Hitler, who attacked it from the west.
   **d.** They had formed an international army to fight Hitler, whose forces trapped thousands of soldiers in Czechoslovakia.

_____ **2.** What was significant about America's Selective Training and Service Act in 1940?
   **a.** It oversaw the conversion of factories to war production.
   **b.** It was the first peacetime draft in the country's history.
   **c.** It allowed Americans to serve in foreign countries.
   **d.** It required both men and women to serve in the army.

_____ **3.** Why did Hitler direct his anger towards intellectuals, Communists, and Jews in the 1930s?
   **a.** He felt they threatened his authority.
   **b.** He blamed them for Germany's economic problems and its defeat in World War I.
   **c.** They opposed the National Socialist Party, keeping it from winning a majority in Parliament.
   **d.** He was fearful they would band together and start another world war.

_____ **4.** Harry Truman took over as president because President Roosevelt
   **a.** died of a stroke in April 1945.
   **b.** lost his re-election bid in 1944.
   **c.** chose not to run for a fourth term in 1944.
   **d.** focused his efforts on aid to war-torn European countries rather than on domestic issues.

Progress Assessment

**5.** The first priority of President Roosevelt and Winston Churchill to defeat the Axis Powers was to
   **a.** place "Asia first."
   **b.** defeat the Germans.
   **c.** attack Italian forces in West Africa.
   **d.** aid Japan in the fight against China.

**6.** Why did Japan plan a large-scale attack against the U.S. naval fleet at Pearl Harbor?
   **a.** It wanted to give itself time to secure control of East Asia before the U.S. military could respond.
   **b.** It wanted to retaliate against the United States for freezing Japanese bank accounts.
   **c.** It wanted to punish the United States for sending billions of dollars in aid to Chinese Nationalists.
   **d.** It wanted to defend its German and Soviet allies against a U.S. invasion.

**7.** The Bataan Death March caused the death of
   **a.** soldiers in the Japanese invasion of Hong Kong.
   **b.** thousands of U.S. soldiers in the Pacific Fleet led by Chester Nimitz.
   **c.** 600 Americans and thousands of Filipinos.
   **d.** General Douglas MacArthur.

**8.** What Tuskegee Airman later became the first African American general in the U.S. Air Force?
   **a.** A. Philip Randolph
   **b.** Benjamin O. Davis
   **c.** Dorie Miller
   **d.** Daniel Inouye

**9.** The United States was expected to be responsible for most of the postwar rebuilding because it
   **a.** had to make reparations for dropping bombs on Hiroshima and Nagasaki.
   **b.** escaped much destruction and was then the strongest power in the world.
   **c.** was given millions of dollars by Germany after Germany surrendered.
   **d.** had promised to help European countries at the beginning of the war.

**10.** What American general was forced to retreat from the Philippines in March 1942?
   **a.** Hideki Tojo
   **b.** Chester Nimitz
   **c.** Louis Ortega
   **d.** Douglas MacArthur

**PRACTICING SOCIAL STUDIES SKILLS** Study the quotation below and answer the question that follows.

> "The cold, the snow, and the darkness were enough to set young nerves on edge. The thud of something as innocuous [harmless] as snow plopping to the ground from a tree branch could be terrifying. Was it snow? Was it maybe a German patrol? Should you fire at the sound and risk giving away your position, or worse, hitting one of your own men? But did the Germans have us surrounded?"
>
> —Dave Nutt, quoted in *Citizen Soldiers*, by Stephen Ambrose

_____ **11.** What purpose could this quotation serve in a research paper?
   **a.** It could illustrate the way in which World War II-era American soldiers were outfitted for war.
   **b.** It could provide an example of how U.S. inexperience affected the outcomes of battles with Germany.
   **c.** It could describe in detail the preparations taken by Allied soldiers for the Battle of the Bulge.
   **d.** It could bring to life the thoughts of an anxious soldier on patrol in unfamiliar territory.

**FILL IN THE BLANK** Read each sentence and fill in the blank with the term that best completes the sentence.

**12.** The Allied Powers included the United States, Great Britain, the Soviet Union, and

_____. (**China/Italy**)

**13.** The Battle of _____ in the Philippines was the largest naval battle in history. (**Leyte Gulf/the Coral Sea**)

**14.** In April 1943, Jewish people in the _____ rose up against the Germans, and it took nearly a month for the Nazis to crush the uprising. (**Warsaw Ghetto/Treblinka death camp**)

**15.** Executive Order 9066 allowed the government to begin the process of

_____, or forced relocation and imprisonment, of Japanese-

Americans. (**deportation/internment**)

**MATCHING** In the space provided, write the letter of the term, person, or place that matches each description. Some answers will not be used.

_____ **16.** fascist Italian leader who allied with Hitler to form the Axis Powers

_____ **17.** organized a march on Washington in 1941 to demand equal pay for black workers

_____ **18.** counterattack launched by Germans after the D-Day invasion

_____ **19.** tactic of purposely crashing piloted planes into enemy ships

_____ **20.** battle in the Soviet Union during which German forces froze or starved to death

_____ **21.** policy of avoiding war with an aggressive nation by giving in to its demands

_____ **22.** president who ordered use of atomic bombs on Japan

_____ **23.** extermination of an entire group of people

_____ **24.** invasion on June 6, 1944, in which thousands of Allied soldiers were killed or wounded

_____ **25.** policy allowing the United States to aid any nation vital to its defense

**a.** kamikaze

**b.** Lend-Lease Act

**c.** Battle of Stalingrad

**d.** Harry S. Truman

**e.** A. Philip Randolph

**f.** Battle of El Alamein

**g.** Benito Mussolini

**h.** Battle of the Bulge

**i.** D-Day

**j.** genocide

**k.** appeasement

**l.** Daniel Inouye

**World War II**

## Chapter Test
### Form B

**SHORT ANSWER** On a separate sheet of paper, answer each of the
following questions in complete sentences.

**1.** What actions did Hitler take in the late 1930s that set the stage for war?

**2.** What was the Battle of Britain?

**3.** What were war bonds, and how did they help the war effort?

**4.** How did Dorie Miller, an African-American Navy cook, become a hero?

**5.** Why did the Allies agree not to make a separate peace with the Axis?

**6.** Describe the Japanese conquests in the Pacific in the months following Pearl
Harbor.

**PRACTICING SOCIAL STUDIES SKILLS** Study the chart below and, on a
separate sheet of paper, answer the questions that follow.

## Causes and Effects
## of World War II

**Causes**

• Global and local economic problems

• Totalitarian governments

• Germany's aggression in Europe

• Japanese aggression in Asia and
the Pacific

**Effects**

• Millions of deaths worldwide

• Widespread destruction of cities
and industries

• The Holocaust

• Rise of the United States as the
leading world power

**7.** Give two examples of each cause and effect of the war. Which cause do you think
was most important? Which effect?

## Boom Times and Challenges

**MULTIPLE CHOICE** For each of the following, write the letter of the best choice in the space provided.

_____ 1. Immediately following the attacks of December 7, 1941, Congress voted to
  **a.** freeze all Japanese funds in U.S. banks and end trade with Japan.
  **b.** declare war on Japan and enter World War II.
  **c.** institute the internment of all Japanese-born U.S. citizens.
  **d.** institute a draft of all Japanese-American men over eighteen.

_____ 2. What did Herbert Hoover promise the American public during his presidential campaign?
  **a.** to raise funds for the veterans
  **b.** to raise funds for war hospitals
  **c.** to send food and supplies to war-torn Europe
  **d.** to maintain economic prosperity

_____ 3. What is one way that World War II affected the American economy?
  **a.** The unemployment rate skyrocketed.
  **b.** Factories ran 24 hours a day producing military supplies.
  **c.** The effects of the Depression became more severe.
  **d.** Agricultural production suffered because there were fewer consumers.

_____ 4. How did fundamentalism affect society in the 1920s?
  **a.** Its ideals clashed with scientific theories such as evolution.
  **b.** It supported the teaching of science, which led to new technological developments.
  **c.** It called attention to important issues such as race, equality, and religion.
  **d.** It passed laws that allowed schools to teach evolution.

_____  **5.** Why did the drop in stock prices in October 1929 ultimately lead the stock market to crash?

    **a.** Investors who had bought stocks on margin panicked, selling off all their stocks.

    **b.** Business leaders began selling off shares in their own companies, panicking investors.

    **c.** Banks refused to issue credit to middle-class investors, causing demand for stocks to plummet.

    **d.** The stock market shut down for one week, leading furious investors to cash in their stocks.

_____  **6.** What did critics think about Roosevelt's "court-packing" bill?

    **a.** He was going to put every New Deal law in jeopardy.

    **b.** He was violating the Judiciary Act of 1789.

    **c.** He was blurring the separation of powers required in a democratic republic.

    **d.** He was trying to shift the balance of power defined in the U.S. Constitution.

_____  **7.** How did sonar technology help the Allied war effort during World War II?

    **a.** It helped Allied pilots avoid anti-aircraft fire.

    **b.** It helped Allied ships find and destroy German U-boats.

    **c.** It allowed Allied pilots to fly bombing raids at night.

    **d.** It allowed long-range Allied planes to drop bombs in France.

_____  **8.** Why was island hopping so important to the Allies' victory in World War II?

    **a.** Japanese forces were limited and surrendered quickly.

    **b.** It allowed the Allies to isolate Japanese forces on bypassed islands.

    **c.** It helped secure more U.S. territory.

    **d.** It allowed the Allies to limit casualties.

_____ **9.** Why was D-Day so important?

    **a.** Once the French beaches were secured, Allied troops could move toward Paris and establish a free government under de Gaulle.

    **b.** Once the French beaches were secured, Allied troops could begin their drive east toward Germany.

    **c.** It tricked the Germans by opening up a front where they least expected it—in France, not Italy.

    **d.** It prevented England from experiencing further air attacks.

_____ **10.** V-E Day on May 8, 1945, marked

    **a.** the Allied invasion of France.

    **b.** Japan's surrender.

    **c.** Germany's surrender.

    **d.** the end of the war in the Pacific.

_____ **11.** Hitler's rebuilding of the German military violated the

    **a.** Monroe Doctrine.

    **b.** Treaty of Versailles.

    **c.** Munich Conference.

    **d.** Geneva Convention.

_____ **12.** Why was the Battle of Stalingrad a turning point in the war?

    **a.** German troops surrendered and Axis powers began to retreat from the Soviet Union.

    **b.** Hitler sent more troops to defeat the Soviet Union.

    **c.** It proved to the Allied powers that Germany could defeat the Soviet forces.

    **d.** Long-range Allied planes dropped bombs on Soviet factories, railroads, and cities.

_____ **13.** What was the Holocaust?

    **a.** the Nazis' attempt to exterminate the entire Jewish population of Europe

    **b.** Hitler's attempt to overthrow the United States through military force

    **c.** the liberation of a country that had previously been Communist-controlled

    **d.** a German military strategy of controlling key portions of land

_____ **14.** Why was the United States unable to prevent the Japanese advance that led to the Bataan Death March?
- **a.** Japan's attack on Pearl Harbor left the U.S. Pacific Fleet so weakened that American and Filipino soldiers were forced to surrender.
- **b.** American and Filipino soldiers were forced to march to prison camps and could not fight.
- **c.** Japan conquered the British colonies of Hong Kong and Singapore, making it impossible for British troops to support the U.S. Pacific Fleet.
- **d.** American and Filipino soldiers were weakened because they were starved and beaten by the Japanese.

_____ **15.** What was the result of the Battle of the Coral Sea?
- **a.** The Japanese clearly lost.
- **b.** The United States suffered its worst loss of the war.
- **c.** The Japanese assault was halted although there was no clear victor.
- **d.** The United States failed to halt the Japanese attack of Port Moresby.

_____ **16.** The Dust Bowl was created by
- **a.** loose topsoil that was blown away by hurricanes.
- **b.** a severe drought in the Great Plains that lasted almost ten years.
- **c.** severe rains that flooded the soil and washed away many crops.
- **d.** problems with irrigation systems throughout the Midwest.

_____ **17.** What caused the sharp rise in unemployment after World War I?
- **a.** Factories using Ford's new assembly line technology needed fewer workers.
- **b.** The millions of workers who went on strike for higher wages were fired.
- **c.** Veterans returning from the war could not get their old jobs back.
- **d.** The government cancelled billions of dollars' worth of contracts, so factories cut back production.

**PRACTICING SOCIAL STUDIES SKILLS** Study the quotation below and answer the question that follows.

> "As soon as he said that we were now eligible to volunteer, that room exploded into a fury of yells and motion. We went bursting out of there and ran—ran!—the three miles to the draft board."
>
> —Daniel Inouye

_____ **18.** This quotation shows that young Japanese Americans
   **a.** were promised great financial rewards for military participation.
   **b.** had serious reservations about aiding the American war effort.
   **c.** were extremely excited about joining the United States military.
   **d.** felt betrayed by the U.S. government's practice of internment.

**FILL IN THE BLANK** Read each sentence and fill in the blank with the word in the word pair that best completes the sentence.

**19.** _____ won the 1920 presidential election with his call for a return to "normalcy." (**Warren G. Harding/James M. Cox**)

**20.** The Ku Klux Klan harassed Catholics, Jews, and _____, as well as African Americans. (**immigrants/women**)

**21.** _____ became famous for painting flowers and the American Southwest. (**Edward Hopper/Georgia O'Keeffe**)

**22.** After the United States destroyed four Japanese aircraft carriers at the Battle of

_____, Admiral Nimitz said Pearl Harbor had been partially

avenged. (**Midway/the Bulge**)

**23.** _____ let people buy expensive items without having to save up for years. (**Credit cards/Installment plans**)

**24.** The Great Depression was characterized by the longest

_____ in the history of the American economy.

(**inflation/recession**)

**25.** In 1928 the United States and 14 other countries signed the

_____. (**Treaty of Versailles/Kellogg-Briand Pact**)

**26.** The _____ and Roosevelt's fireside chats helped restore
Americans' faith in banks in 1933.
**(Social Security Act/Emergency Banking Relief Act)**

**27.** 1925 saw the election of the first two _____ governors in the
history of the United States. **(female/African American)**

**28.** The _____ was founded in 1920 to defend people's civil
rights at a time when minorities, immigrants, and suspected radicals were being
attacked. **(ACLU/NAACP)**

**29.** Charles Lindbergh dominated national news in 1927 when he completed the first

_____ across the Atlantic Ocean.

**(nonstop solo flight/solo flight without instruments)**

**TRUE/FALSE** Indicate whether each statement below is true or false by
writing **T** or **F** in the space provided.

_____ **30.** It is generally agreed that the New Deal expanded the role of the federal
government.

_____ **31.** The Eighteenth Amendment put an end to the prohibition era.

_____ **32.** Several veterans were killed when General MacArthur used force to evict
the Bonus Army from its shantytown.

_____ **33.** The 1920s became known as the Roaring Twenties because of the thousands of new automobiles filling the streets with their loud engines.

_____ **34.** Henry Ford allowed installment plans so that his employees could buy
Ford cars at the price it cost to make them.

_____ **35.** In 1928 the United States and fourteen other nations signed a pact that
they would not engage in war.

_____ **36.** The Red Scare began in April 1919, when U.S. postal workers found
bombs hidden in packages addressed to famous Americans and assumed
Communists had sent them.

_____ **37.** The zoot-suit riots occurred in June 1944 when Mexican-American farm
workers attacked groups of sailors who jeered at them.

_____ **38.** Hitler's National Socialist Party gained popularity and Hitler became Germany's chancellor in 1933.

_____ **39.** The first atomic bomb was dropped over Nagasaki in August 1945.

_____ **40.** Unable to stop Japan's advance in the Philippines, U.S. General MacArthur left the islands, while over 70,000 American and Filipino soldiers were taken prisoner by the Japanese.

_____ **41.** The Soviets fought to hold on to Stalingrad even after Joseph Stalin told them to abandon the city and go to Kursk to reinforce the army there.

**MATCHING** In the space provided, write the letter of the term, person, or place that matches each description. Some answers will not be used.

_____ **42.** period immediately after Roosevelt's inauguration

_____ **43.** critic of the New Deal who wanted the government to take over the country's wealth and natural resources

_____ **44.** African American educator appointed to the Roosevelt administration

_____ **45.** strategy of protest in which workers occupy the factories where they work

_____ **46.** veterans and their families who protested in Washington, D.C., in 1932

_____ **47.** wrote songs of loss and sorrow during the Depression

_____ **48.** secretary of labor and first female cabinet member

_____ **49.** region of the Great Plains that was hit by a severe drought in the early 1930s

_____ **50.** welcomed African American and Hispanic members, as well as women and immigrants

**a.** Congress of Industrial Organizations

**b.** Eleanor Roosevelt

**c.** Frances Perkins

**d.** Bonus Army

**e.** Hundred Days

**f.** John Steinbeck

**g.** Dust Bowl

**h.** Mary McLeod Bethune

**i.** sit-down strikes

**j.** Woody Guthrie

**k.** Charles Edward Coughlin

# Boom Times and Challenges

**SHORT ANSWER** On a separate sheet of paper, answer each of the following questions in complete sentences.

1. How did the rise of the automobile industry change American society and business?

2. What is the business cycle?

3. Why did American farmers experience hard times well before the start of the Great Depression?

4. Why were radios such an important part of life for Americans during the Depression?

5. What was the policy of appeasement? Did it succeed or not?

6. Why was there a good chance for the Axis Powers to win the war in the summer of 1940?

**PRACTICING SOCIAL STUDIES SKILLS** Read the quotation below and, on a separate sheet of paper, answer the question that follows.

> "[I] learned to use an electric drill . . . and I soon became an outstanding riveter . . . The war really created opportunities for women. It was the first time we got a chance to show that we could do a lot of things that only men had done before."
>
> —Winona Espinosa, quoted in *Ordinary Americans,* edited by Linda Monk

7. Use this quotation, along with information you learned in this unit, to explain why and how women's roles changed during World War II.

# Early Years of the Cold War

**MATCHING** In the space provided, write the letter of the term that matches each description. Some answers will not be used.

_____ 1. Where Roosevelt, Churchill, and Stalin met to discuss postwar plans

_____ 2. Trial of high-ranking Nazi officials for war crimes

_____ 3. Organization dedicated to finding peaceful solutions to international conflicts

_____ 4. Used to describe the long struggle for global power between the U.S. and the Soviet Union

_____ 5. Means to prevent the Soviet Union from expanding its influence around the world

_____ 6. Resulted in western Europe receiving more than $13 billion in U.S. loans for economic recovery

_____ 7. Alliance of the United States, nine Western European countries, Iceland, and Canada

_____ 8. Offered veterans money for school, and loans for houses, farms, and businesses

_____ 9. Policy of providing aid to help foreign countries fight communism

_____ 10. Included a higher minimum wage, creation of national insurance plan, and expanded Social Security benefits for the elderly

**a.** Cold War

**b.** containment

**c.** Fair Deal

**d.** General Assembly

**e.** GI Bill of Rights

**f.** Marshall Plan

**g.** North Atlantic Treaty Organization

**h.** Nuremberg trials

**i.** Taft-Hartley Act

**j.** Truman Doctrine

**k.** United Nations

**l.** Warsaw Pact

**m.** Yalta Conference

Progress Assessment

Name _____ Class _____ Date _____

# Early Years of the Cold War

**FILL IN THE BLANK** For each of the following statements, fill in the blank with the appropriate word, phrase, or name.

1. On October 1, 1949, led by _____, the Communists officially established the People's Republic of China.

2. The _____ was a line dividing North and South Korea.

3. From 1950 to 1953 the United States fought Communist _____ in the Korean War.

4. Cold War fears led to the _____ in the late 1940s and 50s.

5. Wisconsin senator _____ raised fears to a fevered pitch in 1950 by charging that Communists were working inside the State Department.

6. In 1950 President Truman approved work on the _____, a weapon more powerful than the atomic bomb.

7. In what became a nuclear _____ both the U.S. and the Soviet Union rushed to build more weapons.

8. In October 1957 the Soviet Union launched _____, the world's first artificial satellite.

9. President Eisenhower and Secretary of State John Foster Dulles supported the strategy of _____, or willingness to go to the brink of war to oppose communism.

10. Eisenhower used covert, or secret, operations to deal with _____ around the world.

Progress Assessment

Name _____ Class _____ Date _____

**Early Years of the Cold War**

Section Quiz

**Section 3**

**TRUE/FALSE** Mark each statement **T** if it is true or **F** if it is false. If false explain why.

_____ **1.** In the 1950s millions of Americans earned more money than ever before.

_____

_____

_____ **2.** Many businesses and workers moved to the Sun Belt because it offered a warm climate year-round and low tax rates.

_____

_____

_____ **3.** The postwar years were so happy and productive that all Americans were satisfied with American society.

_____

_____

_____ **4.** In the 1950s there were many jobs options for women, even after marriage.

_____

_____

_____ **5.** Some of the new forms of popular culture enjoyed by Americans were shopping in malls, eating at fast-food restaurants, watching television, and listening to new styles of music.

_____

_____

Progress Assessment

**Early Years of the Cold War**

Chapter Test

Form A

**MULTIPLE CHOICE** For each of the following, write the letter of the best choice in the space provided.

_____ **1.** Which benefits did the G.I. Bill of Rights offer to veterans?
   **a.** exemption from rationing of food and gasoline
   **b.** money for school, loans for houses, farms, and businesses
   **c.** guaranteed acceptance into state universities and colleges
   **d.** monthly allowances for the unemployed

_____ **2.** What was the original purpose of the United Nations?
   **a.** hunger prevention
   **b.** conflict resolution
   **c.** terror prevention
   **d.** disaster relief

_____ **3.** President Truman sent U.S. military forces to South Korea to
   **a.** take over the fighting from the North Korean troops.
   **b.** give South Korean troops cover and support.
   **c.** defend U.S. diplomats against the South Korean army.
   **d.** protect the Chinese border to prevent the conflict from spreading.

_____ **4.** In the 1950s the federal government began an urban renewal program mainly to
   **a.** encourage community-owned urban businesses.
   **b.** discourage families from moving to the suburbs.
   **c.** improve city services and urban housing.
   **d.** decrease federal funding for highway construction.

_____ **5.** What is one reason why some American women were discouraged during the postwar years?
   **a.** People expected them to go to college regardless of their career goals.
   **b.** There were not enough jobs to go around.
   **c.** Only low salaries were offered for teaching and nursing jobs.
   **d.** Society seemed to assume that a woman's principal role was as a wife and mother.

Progress Assessment

_____ **6.** During the 1950s, musicians such as Elvis Presley helped what type of music become popular?
   **a.** classical
   **b.** rock n' roll
   **c.** jazz
   **d.** Bebop

_____ **7.** One of the first decisions made by the United Nations was to
   **a.** divide Palestine into separate Arab and Jewish states.
   **b.** officially condemn the 1949 war on Israel.
   **c.** send peacekeeping troops to Palestine.
   **d.** protest the division of Palestine.

_____ **8.** The term Cold War came to be used to describe the
   **a.** conflict between Israel and its Arab neighbors.
   **b.** resentment toward Germany that lingered following World War II.
   **c.** struggle for global power between the United States and the Soviet Union.
   **d.** campaign to purge the U.S. government of known Communists.

_____ **9.** Major gains early on by the UN forces in Korea were undermined when
   **a.** President Truman fired General MacAurther for disrespect of authority.
   **b.** China sent hundreds of thousands of troops to join the North Korean army.
   **c.** illness forced General MacArthur to resign his command of UN forces.
   **d.** the Soviet Union sent hundreds of thousands of troops to join the North Korean army.

_____ **10.** Dwight D. Eisenhower said the first task of his administration would be to
   **a.** build a hydrogen bomb.
   **b.** end the Korean War.
   **c.** put a stop to inflation.
   **d.** root out Communist spies.

**PRACTICING SOCIAL STUDIES SKILLS**  Study the charts below and
answer the question that follows.

## Postwar Boom, 1945–1960

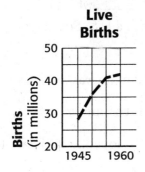
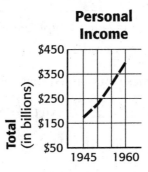

_____ **11.** According to the charts, which of the following statements is true for the
period between 1945 and 1960?
  **a.** As live births increased, personal income decreased.
  **b.** As live births decreased, personal income increased.
  **c.** Live births and personal income increased during the time period.
  **d.** Live births and personal income decreased during the time period.

**FILL IN THE BLANK**  Read each sentence and fill in the blank with the
term that best completes the sentence.

**12.** President Truman appointed Eleanor Roosevelt as one of the first U.S. delegates to

the _____. (**United Nations/Potsdam Conference**)

**13.** A new _____ swept America in the 1940s and 1950s, when
Americans again became preoccupied with fear of Communists.
(**Red Scare/Cold War**)

**14.** In the 1950s many people moved to the _____, where tax
rates were often low. (**inner city/Sun Belt**)

**15.** The 1952 novel _____ focused on the isolation from mainstream society felt by many African Americans.
(***The Catcher in the Rye/Invisible Man***)

**16.** A crisis involving the _____, which began when Britain, France, and Israel invaded Egypt, ended with a U.S.-Soviet agreement to condemn the invasion. (**Suez Canal/Red Sea**)

**17.** Some social critics complained that suburban life was too heavily based on

_____. (**McCarthyism/consumer culture**)

**18.** The new foreign policy the United States developed to deal with the Cold War was

based on the goal of _____. (**containment/nonalignment**)

**TRUE/FALSE** Indicate whether each statement below is true or false by writing **T** or **F** in the space provided.

_____ **19.** Suburban neighborhoods welcomed diverse populations, and soon became models of integration.

_____ **20.** In 1946 the United States sent troops to Greece to help its monarchy put down a Communist rebellion.

_____ **21.** Many Republicans did not support Truman in the 1948 presidential election because of his support for civil rights laws.

_____ **22.** The first hydrogen bombs were dropped by the United States during World War II.

_____ **23.** In 1950 Senator Joseph McCarthy claimed to know of Communists who were aiding the Soviet Union from inside the U.S. State Department.

_____ **24.** The United States joined nine Western European countries, along with Iceland and Canada, to form the North Atlantic Treaty Organization.

_____ **25.** In October 1957, the Soviet Union launched *Sputnik*, the world's first artificial satellite.

# Early Years of the Cold War

Chapter Test

**Form B**

**SHORT ANSWER** On a separate sheet of paper, answer each of the following questions in complete sentences.

**1.** Describe the Berlin Airlift of 1948–1949. Why did it begin and how did it end?

**2.** Who were the Dixiecrats?

**3.** What was the Suez Crisis of 1956?

**4.** Why did Americans accept Joseph McCarthy and his anti-Communist campaign at first?

**5.** What factors made the suburbs so appealing to Americans in the 1950s?

**6.** In what ways did Americans begin to share more experiences in the 1950s?

**PRACTICING SOCIAL STUDIES SKILLS** Study the chart below and, on a separate sheet of paper, answer the question that follows.

## Postwar Boom, 1945–1960

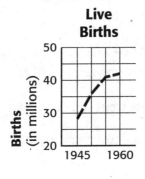

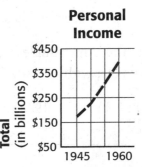

**7.** Look at the chart. What cause-and-effect relationships can you infer from the data?

# The Civil Rights Movement

**FILL IN THE BLANK** For each of the following statements, fill in the blank with the appropriate word, phrase, or name.

1. Early civil rights leaders focused on ending _____ in America's public schools.

2. Before becoming the first African American Supreme Court justice, _____ was an attorney for the NAACP.

3. On May 17, 1954, the Supreme Court issued a unanimous ruling in _____, ruling that segregation in public schools was illegal.

4. The _____ was a small group of African American students selected to integrate Central High School.

5. _____ was a seamstress and NAACP worker arrested for refusing to give up her seat on a bus.

6. In the _____ boycott, thousands of African Americans stopped riding the buses.

7. African American leaders turned to _____, a young Baptist minister with a reputation as a powerful speaker.

8. On February 1, 1960, students went into Woolworth and staged a _____, a demonstration in which protesters sit down and refuse to leave.

9. The student protesters practiced the strategy of _____ resistance.

10. The leaders of the student protests formed the _____ to train protesters and organize civil rights demonstrations.

# The Civil Rights Movement

Section Quiz

## Section 2

**MATCHING** In the space provided, write the letter of the term or person that matches each description. Some answers will not be used.

_____ **1.** Became the youngest person ever elected president of the United States

_____ **2.** Series of protests in which African American and white bus riders traveled together throughout the South

_____ **3.** Massive demonstration for civil rights held on August 28, 1963

_____ **4.** Vice President who was quickly sworn in after the assassination of the president

_____ **5.** Banned segregation in public places

_____ **6.** Gave the federal government new powers to protect African Americans' voting rights

_____ **7.** Program of domestic reforms

_____ **8.** Movement which called for African American power and independence

_____ **9.** Nation of Islam leader who argued that integration would never solve African Americans' problems

_____ **10.** Created to help low income families get better housing

**a.** Black Power

**b.** Civil Rights Act of 1964

**c.** Congress of Racial Equality

**d.** Department of Housing and Urban Development

**e.** Eugene "Bull" Connor

**f.** Freedom Rides

**g.** Great Society

**h.** John F. Kennedy

**i.** Lyndon B. Johnson

**j.** Malcolm X

**k.** March on Washington

**l.** Stokely Carmichael

**m.** Voting Rights Act of 1965

Progress Assessment

## The Civil Rights Movement

Section Quiz

**Section 3**

**FILL IN THE BLANK** For each of the following statements, fill in the blank with the appropriate word, phrase, or name.

1. The _____ population grew to 4 million by 1960 and organized for civil rights.

2. _____ was one of many Hispanic American activists who worked to improve economic opportunities.

3. The _____ union was committed to the goal of better pay and working conditions for migrant workers.

4. The *Feminine Mystique* by _____ described the dissatisfaction some women felt with their traditional role as homemaker.

5. The _____ was formed to fight for equal educational and career opportunities for women.

6. Approved by Congress in 1972, the _____ outlawed all discrimination based on sex.

7. _____, a conservative activist, founded the group STOP ERA.

8. The _____ was founded in 1968 to fight for Native Americans' rights.

9. In 1970 Judy Heumann and other activists created _____ to make people aware of challenges facing disabled people.

10. The _____ Act of 1975 required public schools to give a quality education to children with disabilities.

Progress Assessment

Name _____ Class _____ Date _____

# The Civil Rights Movement

# Chapter Test

## Form A

**MULTIPLE CHOICE** For each of the following, write the letter of the best choice in the space provided.

_____ **1.** As a leading figure in the Black Power movement, Malcom X argued that African Americans should
   **a.** embrace integration as the best means to achieve equality.
   **b.** engage in strictly nonviolent protest to overcome discrimination.
   **c.** support efforts to achieve equality through the political process.
   **d.** work for social and political independence.

_____ **2.** Martin Luther King Jr. delivered his famous "I Have a Dream" speech
   **a.** at the Voting Rights March in Selma, Alabama.
   **b.** in support of Malcolm X, and the Nation of Islam.
   **c.** from a jail cell in Birmingham, Alabama.
   **d.** at the March on Washington, a massive civil rights demonstration.

_____ **3.** The Southern Christian Leadership Conference was founded by
   **a.** Thurgood Marshall.
   **b.** Jo Ann Robinson.
   **c.** Martin Luther King Jr.
   **d.** Rosa Parks.

_____ **4.** President Johnson called his program of domestic reforms the
   **a.** Fair Deal.
   **b.** Great Society.
   **c.** New Frontier.
   **d.** Johnson Plan.

_____ **5.** The Student Nonviolent Coordinating Committee (SNCC) was created to
   **a.** fight for school segregation in the South.
   **b.** protect African American students at Central High School.
   **c.** continue the peaceful struggle for civil rights.
   **d.** protest the arrest of Rosa Parks.

Progress Assessment

_____ **6.** How did the Montgomery bus boycott end?

    **a.** The Supreme Court ruled that separate-but-equal busses had to be provided for African Americans.

    **b.** Montgomery's leaders finally agreed to integrate the bus system.

    **c.** The Supreme Court ruled that segregation on public transportation was illegal.

    **d.** Montgomery's leaders decided to shut down the city bus system.

_____ **7.** Betty Friedan became a leader of the modern women's rights movement in 1966 when she

    **a.** established the group Disabled in Action.

    **b.** prevented ratification of the Equal Rights Amendment.

    **c.** became the first woman to run for the vice presidency.

    **d.** helped found the National Organization for Women.

_____ **8.** What prevented the Little Rock Nine from integrating Central High School on September 4, 1957?

    **a.** Congress passed legislation barring forced desegragation of public schools.

    **b.** President Eisenhower ordered that the students not attend the school until the protests died down.

    **c.** White students organized a nonviolent sit-in at the entrance to the school, preventing class meetings.

    **d.** Arkansas governor Orval Faubus used National Guard troops to block the students from entering the school.

_____ **9.** Stokely Carmichael was a founder of the

    **a.** Black Power movement.

    **b.** American Indian Movement.

    **c.** United Farm Workers.

    **d.** Nation of Islam.

Progress Assessment

**PRACTICING SOCIAL STUDIES SKILLS** Study the quotation below and answer the question that follows.

> "Man holds in his mortal hands the power to abolish all forms of human poverty and all forms of human life."
>
> —John F. Kennedy, from his inaugural address

_____ **10.** Which statement offers the best paraphrase of Kennedy's quote?
   **a.** People have the ability to help society, but also the ability to destroy it.
   **b.** Human beings must not interfere with the laws of nature.
   **c.** The civil rights movement is the most vital aspect of American society.
   **d.** People of all nations must learn to coexist before peace can be achieved.

**TRUE/FALSE** Indicate whether each statement below is true or false by writing **T** or **F** in the space provided.

_____ **11.** The Freedom Rides were repeatedly disrupted by attacks by white mobs.

_____ **12.** Phyllis Schlafly was a women's rights activist who supported the Equal Rights Amendment.

_____ **13.** Cesar Chavez helped Hispanic American workers win better wages and benefits.

_____ **14.** Judy Heumann and other activists created Disabled in Action to make people aware of challenges facing people with disabilities.

_____ **15.** President Kennedy was not in favor of the civil rights movement and took steps to break it apart.

**MATCHING** In the space provided, write the letter of the term or person that matches each description. Some answers will not be used.

_____ **16.** union committed to the goal of better pay and working conditions for migrant farm wokers

_____ **17.** NAACP attorney who argued for Linda Brown in *Brown* v. *Board of Education*

_____ **18.** gave the federal government new powers to protect African Americans' voting rights

_____ **19.** form of nonviolent protest

_____ **20.** founded in 1968 to fight for Native Americans' rights

_____ **21.** first African American woman elected to the U.S. Congress

_____ **22.** implemented a series of domestic reforms called the Great Society

_____ **23.** arrested for refusing to give her seat to a white passenger

_____ **24.** helped ban discrimination against people with disabilities

_____ **25.** youngest person ever elected president of the United States

**a.** Disabled in Action

**b.** American Indian Movement

**c.** Freedom Rides

**d.** Rosa Parks

**e.** John F. Kennedy

**f.** United Farm Workers

**g.** Thurgood Marshall

**h.** sit-in

**i.** Shirley Chisholm

**j.** Lyndon B. Johnson

**k.** Voting Rights Act of 1965

**l.** Malcolm X

        Progress Assessment

# The Civil Rights Movement

Chapter Test

**Form B**

**SHORT ANSWER** On a separate sheet of paper, answer each of the
following questions in complete sentences.

1. Describe the 1955–56 Montgomery bus boycott. How did both black and white
   activists react to it?

2. Who took part in the sit-ins, what was their goal, and what happened as a result
   of their actions?

3. What were the components and goals of Kennedy's New Frontier?

4. Describe the Civil Rights Act of 1964. What did it do?

5. How did Cesar Chavez help migrant farm workers?

6. What was the Equal Rights Amendment? Why was it never put into effect?

**PRACTICING SOCIAL STUDIES SKILLS** Study the time line below and,
on a separate sheet of paper, answer the question that follows.

## Civil Rights Movement, Key Events

**1955** An African American tailor's assistant named Rosa Parks refused to give up her seat on a Montgomery, Alabama, bus, sparking a citywide bus boycott that would last more than a year.

**1963** Four young girls die in the racially motivated bombing of a Birmingham, Alabama, church. The deaths lead to riots and civil unrest during which police attack African Americans. Televised images of the events shocked many people.

**1950** ———————————————————————— **1965**

**1960** The first sit-in at a lunch counter occurs in Greensboro, North Carolina. During these sit-ins, young African Americans sat at segregated lunch counters along with their white counterparts and asked to be served.

**1964** Civil rights leader Martin Luther King Jr. receives the Nobel Peace Prize for his work in nonviolent demonstrations against segregation.

7. Look at the time line. What inference can you make about how civil rights activism changed over time?

Progress Assessment

Name _____ Class _____ Date _____

# The Vietnam War Years

**MATCHING** In the space provided, write the letter of the term or person that matches each description. Some answers will not be used.

_____ 1. Committed to the Cold War policy of stopping the spread of communism

_____ 2. Sent volunteers to developing countries to help with digging wells and building schools

_____ 3. Cuban rebel who led a revolution against an unpopular dictator

_____ 4. Barrier of concrete and barbed wire between East and West Berlin

_____ 5. Occurred when American U-2 spy planes discovered Soviets installing nuclear missiles in Cuba

_____ 6. Banned the testing of new nuclear weapons above ground

_____ 7. One of the first people to walk on the moon

_____ 8. One of the leading Vietnamese nationalists

_____ 9. Fear that if one country became Communist, nearby countries would also

_____ 10. Guerilla forces supplied and funded by North Vietnamese Communists

**a.** Berlin Wall

**b.** Cold War

**c.** Cuban Missile Crisis

**d.** domino theory

**e.** Fidel Castro

**f.** Geneva Accords

**g.** Ho Chi Minh

**h.** John F. Kennedy

**i.** Limited Nuclear Test Ban Treaty

**j.** Neil Armstrong

**k.** Nikita Khrushchev

**l.** Peace Corps

**m.** Vietcong

Progress Assessment

# The Vietnam War Years

Section Quiz

## Section 2

**TRUE/FALSE** Mark each statement **T** if it is true or **F** if it is false. If false explain why.

_____ **1.** President Kennedy committed the United States to total victory in Vietnam.

_____

_____

_____ **2.** In the Vietnam War, much of the war was fought in the jungles and villages of South Vietnam.

_____

_____

_____ **3.** The Tet Offensive was a series of surprise attacks all over South Vietnam.

_____

_____

_____ **4.** As casualty rates increased, support for the Vietnam War declined.

_____

_____

_____ **5.** On search-and-destroy missions U.S. patrols searched Vietnamese cities.

_____

_____

Progress Assessment

# The Vietnam War Years

**FILL IN THE BLANK** For each of the following statements, fill in the blank with the appropriate word, phrase, or name.

1. As the Vietnam War continued, growing numbers of _____ began to criticize the war.

2. College students formed the _____ whose members protested the draft and companies that made weapons used in Vietnam.

3. _____ were members of a counterculture that emphasized individual freedom, nonviolence, and communal sharing.

4. Republican nominee _____ promised to restore order to American society and bring "peace with honor" to Vietnam.

5. National security adviser, _____ helped create a plan to pull U.S. troops out of Vietnam.

6. _____ was the strategy of pulling out U.S. troops and allowing the South Vietnamese army to take over the fighting.

7. The _____ lowered the federal voting age from 21 to 18.

8. On January 27, 1973, the U.S. signed a _____ called the Paris Peace Accords.

9. The _____ of 1973 requires the president to get congressional approval before committing U.S. troops to an armed struggle.

10. The _____ Memorial is a black granite memorial listing the names of the dead and missing American soldiers.

Progress Assessment

**The Vietnam War Years**

Chapter Test

Form A

**MULTIPLE CHOICE** For each of the following, write the letter of the best choice in the space provided.

_____ **1.** What 1964 event led to a rapid expansion of U.S. involvement in Vietnam?

  **a.** The French lost control of Vietnam to the Vietcong.

  **b.** A group of South Vietnamese army officers killed Ngo Dinh Diem.

  **c.** U.S. ships off the North Vietnamese coast reported being attacked.

  **d.** Laos and Cambodia fell to Ho Chi Minh's fascist rule.

_____ **2.** How did the hippie counterculture express its ideals in the 1960s?

  **a.** emigrated from the United States

  **b.** supported individual freedom, nonviolence, and communal sharing

  **c.** defended government authority

  **d.** respected the generation that came before it

_____ **3.** The Vietcong fought against

  **a.** North Vietnam.

  **b.** the United States.

  **c.** France.

  **d.** Japan.

_____ **4.** What was one effect of the My Lai massacre?

  **a.** Americans began to perceive the Johnson Administration as honest.

  **b.** The Johnson Administration lost the support of wealthy Americans.

  **c.** Support for the war among college students nearly doubled.

  **d.** Many Americans began to question U.S. involvement in the war.

_____ **5.** Which of the following best describes the domino theory?

  **a.** If atomic weapons were used once to end a war, they would be used to end all subsequent wars.

  **b.** If the United States waged one war against communism, it would have to wage other wars.

  **c.** If one nation became Communist, nearby countries would also fall to communism.

  **d.** If the Soviets took over one Asian nation, they would take over the entire continent.

Progress Assessment

_____ **6.** What did President Kennedy intend to do by establishing the Peace Corps?
   **a.** bring a nonviolent end to racial segregation in the United States
   **b.** design a treaty that would end the conflict with Cuba
   **c.** provide young people with a chance to express their views
   **d.** help developing countries with tasks such as building schools

_____ **7.** What does "escalation" mean with respect to President Johnson's policy toward Vietnam between 1965 and 1968?
   **a.** slow withdrawal
   **b.** increased involvement
   **c.** frequent surprise attacks
   **d.** full disclosure of information

_____ **8.** During the Vietnam War, hawks and doves disagreed mainly over whether
   **a.** funding domestic programs was more important than winning the Cold War.
   **b.** U.S. forces should use a nuclear bomb to force the Vietcong to surrender.
   **c.** the United States should have a draft.
   **d.** protesting the war was unpatriotic.

_____ **9.** The Vietnam War ended when
   **a.** the United States and North Vietnam signed the Hanoi Accords in 1973.
   **b.** North Vietnamese forces captured Saigon in 1975.
   **c.** Communist dictators took over Laos and Cambodia in 1977.
   **d.** North Vietnam returned all American prisoners of war in 1979.

_____ **10.** What did President Nixon do on April 30, 1970 to infuriate many Americans?
   **a.** began slowly withdrawing U.S. troops from Vietnam without the knowledge of Congress or the people
   **b.** announced that he had sent U.S. troops into Cambodia, expanding the war he had promised to end
   **c.** authorized the use of force by National Guard troops against students on college campuses
   **d.** admitted that the U.S. government and his administration had been lying about progress in the war

**PRACTICING SOCIAL STUDIES SKILLS** Study the map below and answer the question that follows.

### French Indochina

_____ **11.** Which of the following statements about French Indochina is true?

    **a.** The Annamite Mountains formed the area's eastern boundary.

    **b.** The island of Hainan was within its territory.

    **c.** Burma was located on its northwest border.

    **d.** The Gulf of Tonkin formed the area's western boundary.

**FILL IN THE BLANK** Read each sentence and fill in the blank with the term that best completes the sentence.

**12.** The _____ was successful in improving U.S. relations with Latin America. (**Central Intelligence Agency/Peace Corps**)

**13.** By the end of 1967, U.S. military leaders claimed they were nearing victory in

Vietnam, but the _____ in January 1968 proved they were

wrong. (**Tet Offensive/Tonkin Gulf Resolution**)

**14.** The _____ revealed that U.S. officials had been lying to the
American people about the progress of the Vietnam War for years.
(**Pentagon Papers/War Powers Act**)

**15.** After the _____, the United States and the Soviet Union
signed a treaty that banned aboveground testing of new nuclear weapons.
(**Tonkin Gulf Resolution/Cuban missile crisis**)

**MATCHING** In the space provided, write the letter of the term or person that matches each description. Some answers will not be used.

_____ **16.** lowered the federal voting age from 21 to 18          **a.** Yuri Gagarin

_____ **17.** strategy calling for the South Vietnamese          **b.** Tonkin Gulf
              Army to take over fighting the war in                   Resolution
              Vietnam

                                                                  **c.** Ho Chi Minh
_____ **18.** commanded U.S. ground forces in Vietnam

                                                                  **d.** William
_____ **19.** requires the president to get congressional           Westmoreland
              approval before committing U.S. troops to an
              armed struggle
                                                                  **e.** Alan Shepard Jr.

_____ **20.** increased involvement of U.S. military forces     **f.** Twenty-sixth
              in the Vietnam War                                      Amendment

_____ **21.** first person to travel into space
                                                                  **g.** Operation Rolling
_____ **22.** designed the Vietnam Veterans Memorial                Thunder

_____ **23.** authorized the president to take "all neces-      **h.** Neil Armstrong
              sary measures to repel any armed attack
              against the forces of the United States"            **i.** War Powers Act

_____ **24.** Communist leader of North Vietnam                 **j.** Vietnamization

_____ **25.** one of the first people to walk on the moon       **k.** escalation

                                                                  **l.** Maya Ying Lin

**The Vietnam War Years**

Chapter Test

**Form B**

**SHORT ANSWER** On a separate sheet of paper, answer each of the following questions in complete sentences.

**1.** What is the story behind the creation of the Berlin Wall?

**2.** How did the Cuban Missile Crisis begin, and how did it end?

**3.** How did the Vietcong and North Vietnamese Army make up for their inferior firepower?

**4.** What happened at My Lai and how did it affect American public opinion?

**5.** What two factors led to a Nixon victory in the 1968 presidential election?

**6.** What happened after U.S. forces left Vietnam?

**PRACTICING SOCIAL STUDIES SKILLS** Study the primary source below and, on a separate sheet of paper, answer the question that follows.

---

"I think these few minutes were the time of gravest concern for the President. Was the world on the brink of a holocaust? Was it our error? A mistake? Was there something further that should have been done? Or not done? . . . The minutes in the Cabinet Room ticked slowly by. What could we say now—what could we do?

Then it was 10:25—a messenger brought in a note . . . 'Mr President . . . some of the Russian ships have stopped dead in the water . . . Six ships . . . have stopped or have turned back toward the Soviet Union' . . .

Then we were back to the details. The meeting droned on. But everyone looked like a different person. For a moment the world had stood still, and now it was going around again."

—Robert F. Kennedy, from *Thirteen Days: A Memoir of the Cuban Missile Crisis*

---

**7.** What does this primary source passage reveal about the readiness of the United States and the Soviet Union for war? Explain your answer.

Progress Assessment

Name _____ Class _____ Date _____

**Postwar America**

# Unit Test

## Form A

**MULTIPLE CHOICE** For each of the following, write the letter of the best choice in the space provided.

_____ 1. Which of the following American astronauts were the first to walk on the moon?
   a. John Glenn and Virgil "Gus" Grissom
   b. Alan Shepard and Donald "Deke" Slayton
   c. Neil Armstrong and Edwin "Buzz" Aldrin
   d. Roger Chaffee and William Anders

_____ 2. An issue for Native Americans in the 1960s was the
   a. lack of voting rights in federal elections.
   b. lack of control over tribal lands.
   c. forced attendance at segregated reservation schools.
   d. forced confinement on tribal lands.

_____ 3. What did William Levitt's homes have in common with Henry Ford's Model T cars?
   a. They were designed to be simple and affordable.
   b. Each worker who built them did only one task.
   c. They contributed to a decline in city services.
   d. Only white citizens were allowed to buy them.

_____ 4. What led President Kennedy to move slowly on civil rights legislation?
   a. unwillingness to anger Republicans and conservative Democrats in Congress
   b. anger over African Americans' lack of support in the election
   c. lack of faith in the goals of the civil rights movement
   d. inability to pass legislation due to a limited budget

_____ 5. Beat writers Allen Ginsberg and Jack Kerouac encouraged young people to
   a. get educated at good universities.
   b. start families in the suburbs.
   c. question mainstream society.
   d. become familiar with technology.

_____ 6. The 1954 Geneva Accords resulted in
   a. open trade between Vietnam and France.
   b. an alliance between Vietnam and China.
   c. an entirely Communist Vietnam.
   d. the temporary creation of North and South Vietnam.

Progress Assessment

_____ **7.** Work by the organization Disabled in Action led to the Rehabilitation Act of 1973, which

   **a.** banned federal agencies from discriminating against people with disabilities.

   **b.** provided medical assistance to disabled Americans.

   **c.** provided financial assistance to disabled government workers.

   **d.** established equal education for children with disabilities.

_____ **8.** The Korean War ended in 1953 with

   **a.** Soviet troops guarding the North Korean border.

   **b.** China pulling out its troops and ending its support for North Korea.

   **c.** the defeat of North Korea, which retreated north.

   **d.** North and South Korea once again divided near the 38th parallel.

_____ **9.** The "iron curtain" was the

   **a.** tension between Arabs and Jews over Palestine.

   **b.** division between Soviet controlled countries and the Western world.

   **c.** punishment of the Nazis.

   **d.** policy of providing aid to foreign countries to contain communism.

_____ **10.** The 1975 Voting Rights Act and the 1968 Elementary and Secondary Education Act both called for

   **a.** access to education for migrant workers.

   **b.** choice of schools for Hispanic Americans.

   **c.** bilingual services for people speaking English as a second language.

   **d.** desegregated schools and polling places, and laws to protect minority students.

_____ **11.** An effort toward healing the wounds of the Vietnam War was made with the

   **a.** dedication of the Vietnam Veterans Memorial.

   **b.** passage of the War Powers Act.

   **c.** construction of the Berlin Wall.

   **d.** signing of the Limited Nuclear Test Ban Treaty.

_____ **12.** Kennedy allowed the Soviet Union to build the Berlin Wall because he was

   **a.** focused on winning the space race.

   **b.** preoccupied by the Cuban threat.

   **c.** intent on strengthening relations with Russia.

   **d.** unwilling to go to war over the issue.

_____ **13.** What were students protesting against at Kent State
University in the early 1970s?
- **a.** lack of U.S. military spending
- **b.** the secret bombing of Cambodia
- **c.** McGovern's loss to Nixon
- **d.** passage of the Twenty-first Amendment

_____ **14.** NOW was established to fight
for
- **a.** access for the disabled.
- **b.** opportunities for women.
- **c.** education for Hispanics.
- **d.** voting rights for African Americans.

_____ **15.** Eleanor Roosevelt changed
the role of the first lady by
- **a.** acting as a public figure.
- **b.** campaigning for her husband.
- **c.** hosting White House din- ners for foreign dignitaries.
- **d.** running for Congress.

_____ **16.** The "duck and cover" drills of
the 1950s were held in prepa-
ration for
- **a.** artificial satellites.
- **b.** nuclear attack.
- **c.** acid rain.
- **d.** terrorist attacks.

_____ **17.** What did U.S. forces do to
disrupt the Ho Chi Minh
Trail?
- **a.** created open, easily defen- sible areas to serve as safe havens for U.S. military operations
- **b.** cut off food and water supplies to force Vietcong troops out of tunnels
- **c.** dropped napalm and Agent Orange to kill troops, destroy supplies, and down forests
- **d.** infiltrated Vietcong forces using Vietnamese- American soldiers fluent in the language

**FILL IN THE BLANK** Read each sentence and fill in the blank with the
word in the word pair that best completes the sentence.

**18.** To help migrant farm workers, _____ formed a union that
later became the United Farm Workers. (**Cesar Chavez/Saul Alinsky**)

**19.** The _____ bus boycott was organized to protest Rosa Parks'
arrest for refusing to give her seat on a bus to a white person.
(**Tuskegee/Montgomery**)

**20.** _____ launched STOP ERA to stop ratification of the Equal Rights Amendment, saying it would hurt families by encouraging women to focus on careers rather than motherhood. (**Phyllis Schlafly/Shirley Chisholm**)

**21.** In Greensboro, South Carolina, African American students organized a

_____ at Woolworth's segregated lunch counter.

(**sit-in/boycott**)

**22.** The Freedom Rides were organized to stop the segregation of

_____. (**city bus lines/interstate bus stations**)

**23.** Many Democrats opposed the candidacy of _____ in the 1968 presidential election, as they disliked his connection with President Johnson and the Vietnam War. (**Robert F. Kennedy/Hubert Humphrey**)

**24.** In the 1972 presidential election, voters aged 18 to 21 voted for the first time as a

result of the passage of the _____ Amendment.

(**Twenty-first/Twenty-sixth**)

**25.** School segregation in the United States was ruled unconstitutional in the 1954

Supreme Court decision _____.

(*Plessy* v. *Ferguson*/*Brown* v. *Board of Education*)

**26.** On July 2, President Johnson signed the _____ of 1964, which banned segregation in public places as well as workplace discrimination. (**Equal Rights Amendment/Civil Rights Act**)

**27.** _____ activists believed African Americans should focus on controlling their own, segregated communities. (**CORE/Black Power**)

**28.** President Nixon's plan to pull U.S. soldiers from Vietnam and turn the fight-

ing over to the South Vietnamese Army was called _____.

(**Vietnamization/escalation**)

**29.** _____ delivered a passionate speech about equality during the March on Washington. (**Malcolm X/Martin Luther King Jr.**)

**TRUE/FALSE** Indicate whether each statement below is true or false by writing **T** or **F** in the space provided.

_____ **30.** Most of the battles against North Vietnam were fought in the jungles and villages of South Vietnam.

_____ **31.** In 1955 Rosa Parks was arrested for refusing to give up her seat to a white passenger.

_____ **32.** Malcolm X was a civil rights leader who believed in a policy of nonviolent resistance.

_____ **33.** The Voting Rights Act of 1965 outlawed discrimination in the workplace.

_____ **34.** The 1961 Bay of Pigs invasion was led by Cuban exiles trained by the CIA to invade Cuba and overthrow Castro.

_____ **35.** President Lyndon Johnson had no question about what happened in the Gulf of Tonkin when he declared the incident an act of war.

_____ **36.** Students for a Democratic Society (SDS) promoted "dropping out" of traditional society and starting a nonviolent counterculture.

_____ **37.** Young men from poor families that needed financial support could get deferments, which meant they would not be drafted to fight in Vietnam.

_____ **38.** After the Tet Offensive, nearly half of the American public believed that the United States should never have become involved in the Vietnam War.

_____ **39.** The Vietcong were a South Vietnamese guerilla force allied with the United States.

**PRACTICING SOCIAL STUDIES SKILLS** Study the quotation below and answer the question that follows.

> "The wrongs which we seek to condemn and punish have been so calculated, so malignant and devastating, that civilization cannot tolerate their being ignored because it cannot survive their being repeated."
>
> —Robert H. Jackson, on the Nuremberg Trials

_____ **40.** According to Robert Jackson, who served as chief American attorney during the Nuremberg Trials, the main purpose of the trials was to
   **a.** seek help from other countries in persecuting the Nazis.
   **b.** keep genocides like the Holocaust from happening again.
   **c.** treat the Nazis just as they had treated the Jews.
   **d.** appease Holocaust survivors with the creation of the State of Israel.

**MATCHING** In the space provided, write the letter of the term that matches each description. Some answers will not be used.

_____ **41.** nuclear weapon of enormous destructive power

_____ **42.** first artificial satellite launched into space

_____ **43.** creative young people who caused others to question the rules of mainstream America

_____ **44.** policy to help foreign countries fight communism

_____ **45.** plan for the economic recovery of European nations after World War II

_____ **46.** where Allied leaders planned for the postwar world

_____ **47.** led Communists in establishing the People's Republic of China

_____ **48.** willingness to go to the edge of war to oppose communism

_____ **49.** policy of social improvement promoted by President Truman in 1949

_____ **50.** strategy to prevent Communist countries from expanding their influence

**a.** Marshall Plan

**b.** hydrogen bomb

**c.** Yalta Conference

**d.** containment

**e.** brinkmanship

**f.** Fair Deal

**g.** beats

**h.** Truman Doctrine

**i.** *Sputnik*

**j.** Mao Zedong

**k.** GI Bill of Rights

**l.** Nuremberg Trials

## Postwar America

**SHORT ANSWER** On a separate sheet of paper, answer each of the following questions in complete sentences.

**1.** What factors contributed to the growth of suburbs in the 1950s?

**2.** What factors led to the Korean War? How was China involved?

**3.** Explain the origins of segregated schools and why they were unequal.

**4.** Describe the "Freedom Summer" of 1964.

**5.** Why was the space race so important at the height of the Cold War?

**6.** Why was there confusion about events that occurred in the Gulf of Tonkin?

**PRACTICING SOCIAL STUDIES SKILLS** Study the images below and, on a separate sheet of paper, answer the question that follows.

### A Society Divided

Some young Americans supported the war in Vietnam. Many saw it as the only way to stop the spread of communism.

Other young Americans protested the war. They believed the United States should not be involved in a violent conflict far from home.

(l) © David J. & Janice L. Frent Collection/CORBIS; (cl) © Leif Skoogfors/CORBIS; (cr) © Dick Swanson/Time Life Pictures/Getty Images; (r) David J. & Janice L. Frent Collection/CORBIS

**7.** Use the pictures, along with information you learned in this unit, to explain the differing views Americans had about Vietnam.

Progress Assessment

Name _____ Class _____ Date _____

# Searching for Order

**MATCHING** In the space provided, write the letter of the term, place, or person that matches each description. Some answers will not be used.

_____ 1. Americans who opposed antiwar protests and supported Nixon's plan for ending the Vietnam War

_____ 2. Nixon's plan to limit the power of the federal government

_____ 3. Economic condition of combined stagnant economic growth and high inflation

_____ 4. Group that worked to control the production and sale of oil to keep prices high

_____ 5. German term meaning "actual politics"

_____ 6. Led to a treaty limiting U.S. and Soviet nuclear weapons

_____ 7. Term meaning "less hostile relations"

_____ 8. Break-in that exploded into a massive political scandal

_____ 9. Michigan congressman appointed vice president

_____ 10. Term meaning "freedom from punishment"

**a.** détente

**b.** embargo

**c.** energy crisis

**d.** Gerald Ford

**e.** New Federalism

**f.** Organization of Petroleum Exporting Countries

**g.** pardon

**h.** realpolitik

**i.** Silent Majority

**j.** stagflation

**k.** Strategic Arms Limitation Talks

**l.** Watergate

**m.** Whip Inflation Now

Progress Assessment

Name _____ Class _____ Date _____

# Searching for Order

**FILL IN THE BLANK** For each of the following statements, fill in the blank with the appropriate word, phrase, or name.

1. In 1972 a law known as _____ banned discrimination on the basis of sex in educational programs that receive federal funds.

2. _____ is the practice of giving special consideration to non-whites or women to make up for past discrimination.

3. In 1976, the Democrats nominated _____, a little-known former governor of Georgia for president.

4. After being elected president, Carter favored policies that promoted

   _____, the basic rights and freedoms of all people.

5. _____ is a system of laws requiring racial segregation.

6. Economic penalties to encourage reform are known as

   _____.

7. In 1979 the _____ invaded the central Asian country of Afghanistan.

8. President Carter responded to the invasion of Afghanistan by breaking off

   arms control talks and refusing to allow U.S. athletes to participate in the 1980

   _____ in Moscow.

9. The _____ was a peace agreement between Egyptian president Anwar el-Sadat and Israeli Prime Minister Menachem Begin.

10. The seizure of Americans from the U.S. embassy in Tehran created the

    _____ crisis which lasted for more than a year.

Progress Assessment

# Searching for Order

**TRUE/FALSE** Mark each statement **T** if it is true or **F** if it is false. If false explain why.

_____ **1.** President Reagan's approach to government was based on liberal ideas.

_____

_____

_____ **2.** Reagan's economic policies were known as "Reaganomics" and were based on the theory of supply-side economics.

_____

_____

_____ **3.** President Reagan was an outspoken critic of communism and the Soviet Union.

_____

_____

_____ **4.** Congressional hearings found evidence of illegal activity by President Reagan in the Iran-Contra affair.

_____

_____

_____ **5.** In 1987 Reagan signed the Intermediate-Range Nuclear Forces Treaty with Soviet leader Boris Yeltsin.

_____

_____

Progress Assessment

**Searching for Order**

**MULTIPLE CHOICE** For each of the following, write the letter of the best choice in the space provided.

_____ **1.** What did the 1972 law known as Title IX do?
  **a.** banned discrimination based on sex in federally funded educational programs
  **b.** increased African American enrollment in colleges
  **c.** gave funding to schools that chose students using affirmative action
  **d.** granted scholarships to women studying medicine at state universities

_____ **2.** How did the rivalry between China and the Soviet Union affect the United States?
  **a.** U.S. officials became less concerned that the two countries would unite to spread communism.
  **b.** The United States was forced to double its production of nuclear weapons.
  **c.** It became impossible for the United States to establish peaceful relations with either country.
  **d.** The United States began to encourage Chinese immigration.

_____ **3.** Which is an example of how the Nixon administration practiced realpolitik?
  **a.** bringing Sadat and Begin together to reach a Middle East peace agreement
  **b.** placing economic sanctions on nations that committed human rights violations
  **c.** backing several harsh military governments because they were friendly to U.S. interests
  **d.** criticizing student protesters and calling on them to stop antiwar activities

_____ **4.** Spiro Agnew resigned as vice president in 1974 because he was
  **a.** unwilling to testify before the Senate Watergate committee.
  **b.** involved in the Watergate burglary cover-up.
  **c.** dismayed at the corruption revealed in Nixon's administration.
  **d.** suspected of taking bribes and failing to pay taxes.

Progress Assessment

_____ **5.** The majority of immigrants to the United States in the 1970s
  **a.** came for educational opportunities.
  **b.** were adults over age 65.
  **c.** came from the Americas and Asia.
  **d.** were Protestant rather than Catholic or Jewish.

_____ **6.** Nixon's New Federalism was a plan to
  **a.** provide federal aid to struggling businesses.
  **b.** limit the power of the federal government.
  **c.** focus the government on civil rights legislation.
  **d.** reduce dependence on foreign oil by developing alternative fuels.

_____ **7.** Bob Woodward and Carl Bernstein's articles revealed that the Committee to Reelect the President had
  **a.** bribed voting officials in the 1972 election.
  **b.** hidden illegal campaign contributions.
  **c.** lied about Nixon's past voting record.
  **d.** stolen money from the Democratic campaign.

_____ **8.** Why did Congress resist President Ford's 1974 Whip Inflation Now campaign?
  **a.** Stagflation was no longer a problem for the country.
  **b.** Congress wanted to increase spending to help the poor and unemployed.
  **c.** Americans were pressuring the government to focus on foreign relations.
  **d.** The program would have cut the budget for Cold War defense.

_____ **9.** Many Americans voted for Jimmy Carter because of his
  **a.** promise to run an open government and remove the taping system from the Oval Office.
  **b.** outspokeness in calling for Nixon's resignation.
  **c.** status as a Washington outsider.
  **d.** suggestion that he would reverse the pardon that had been granted to Nixon.

_____ **10.** Rachel Carson was the
  **a.** secret informant in the Watergate investigation.
  **b.** defendant in the case that legalized abortion.
  **c.** first woman admitted to Harvard University.
  **d.** author of a book about the dangers of pollution.

_____ **11.** The Camp David Accords
  **a.** reopened trade between the United States and Russia.
  **b.** established peace between Egypt and Israel.
  **c.** restricted the use of harmful chemicals.
  **d.** ended apartheid in South Africa.

**PRACTICING SOCIAL STUDIES SKILLS** Study the map below and answer the question that follows.

**The Election of 1976**

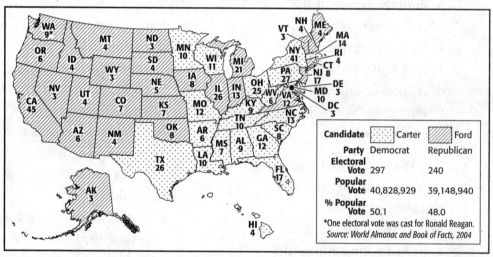

_____ **12.** In which region was Carter most victorious in the election of 1976?
  **a.** the West
  **b.** the South
  **c.** the East
  **d.** the North

**FILL IN THE BLANK** Read each sentence and fill in the blank with the term that best completes the sentence.

**13.** Nixon used the term _____ to describe Americans who opposed anti-war protests and supported his plan for bringing the Vietnam War to an end. (**Silent Majority/détente**)

**14.** One way Carter hoped to reduce American dependence on foreign oil was by

expanding the use of _____ power. (**nuclear/coal**)

**15.** President Carter called for _____, or economic penalties, to
encourage reform in South Africa. (**sanctions/tariffs**)

**16.** _____ economics called for sharp tax cuts, with the goal of
increasing the amount of money people and businesses have to invest.
(**Demand-side/Supply-side**)

**17.** In Nicaragua, the United States supported a rebel group known as the

_____. (**Contras/Guerillas**)

**18.** President Nixon was able to improve U.S. relations with the U.S.S.R. by first

improving U.S. relations with _____. (**China/Cuba**)

**19.** President Reagan appointed _____ to be the first female
Supreme Court justice. (**Sandra Day O'Connor/Ruth Bader Ginsberg**)

**TRUE/FALSE** Indicate whether each statement below is true or false by
writing **T** or **F** in the space provided.

_____ **20.** The Senate committee on Watergate approved seven articles of impeachment against Nixon.

_____ **21.** Ford pardoned Nixon because he believed Americans were ready to for-
give Nixon for his involvement in the Watergate scandal.

_____ **22.** Détente broke down because Carter refused to let U.S. athletes participate
in the 1980 Summer Olympics in Moscow.

_____ **23.** Reagan did not sign the Intermediate-Range Nuclear Forces Treaty
because it would have removed all nuclear weapons from Europe.

_____ **24.** In 1973 OPEC members banned oil sales to the United States in response
to U.S. support for Israel during the Yom Kippur War.

_____ **25.** Just two months into his term, President Reagan was shot and severely
wounded in an assasination attempt by John Hinckley Jr.

## Searching for Order

**SHORT ANSWER** On a separate sheet of paper, answer each of the following questions in complete sentences.

1. What factors led to the 1973 oil embargo?

2. Why did the Nixon administration authorize the Watergate break-in?

3. What is the purpose of affirmative action, and what position did each side take in the debate over it?

4. What agreement was reached at Camp David in 1978?

5. What was "Reaganomics" and what did it do to balance the budget?

6. What was the Iran-Contra affair?

**PRACTICING SOCIAL STUDIES SKILLS** Study the information below and, on a separate sheet of paper, answer the question that follows.

# SUPREME COURT DECISIONS

**United States v. Nixon (1974)**

**Background of the Case** During the Watergate investigation, a special prosecutor asked for the tapes of President Nixon's Oval Office conversations. Nixon claimed that he did not have to obey court orders to turn over the tapes, because of executive privilege. On July 8, 1974, the case went before the Supreme Court.

**The Court's Ruling**
The Supreme Court announced its unanimous decision on July 24. It stated, "the legitimate [lawful] needs of the judicial process may outweigh presidential privilege." Nixon could not use executive privilege to avoid the subpoenas.

**The Court's Reasoning**
The Court decided to hear the case more quickly than most cases because of its importance to the functioning of government and the interest of the American public. The Supreme Court ruled that to claim executive privilege

a president would have to show a compelling national security reason. Nixon had no such reason for refusing to hand over the tapes.

**Why It Matters**
The Supreme Court ruling showed that, despite their unique and important position, presidents do have to obey the law. It also showed that the government could use the powers defined in the Constitution to prevent one branch from becoming too powerful. Less than a week later, the House Judiciary Committee voted to impeach Nixon.

7. Why was *United States* v. *Nixon* such an important ruling both in 1974 and since then? Explain your answer, using the term "executive privilege."

Progress Assessment

# America Looks to the Future

## Section Quiz

### Section 1

**FILL IN THE BLANK** For each of the following statements, fill in the blank with the appropriate word, phrase, or name.

1. The Soviet Union broke apart and the Cold War ended during the presidency of

   _____.

2. In 1989 Germans tore down the _____ and within a year reunited Germany into one democratic country.

3. In August 1990 _____, dictator of Iraq, invaded neighboring oil-rich Kuwait.

4. The U.S.-led Coalition easily defeated Iraq in _____.

5. General _____, the chairman of the joint chiefs of staff, was the highest-ranking African American to ever serve in the U.S. military.

6. As Democratic presidential nominee, Arkansas governor

   _____ told voters he would focus on improving the

   economy.

7. Once elected, President Clinton convinced Congress to support the

   _____ Agreement, which eliminated trade barriers between

   the United States, Canada, and Mexico.

8. In 1998 Bill Clinton became only the second president in U.S. history to be

   _____.

9. _____ was the first woman appointed to be secretary of

   state.

10. A major issue in the 1990s was _____, or the use of violence by individuals or small groups to advance political goals.

Progress Assessment

**America Looks to the Future**                     Section Quiz

                                                    **Section 2**

**MULTIPLE CHOICE** For each of the following, write the letter of the best choice in the space provided.

_____ **1.** Who won the disputed 2000 presidential election?
  **a.** Bill Clinton
  **b.** George W. Bush
  **c.** Colin Powell
  **d.** Al Gore

_____ **2.** In 2001 terrorists attacked the World Trade Center on what date?
  **a.** October 11
  **b.** August 11
  **c.** November 11
  **d.** September 11

_____ **3.** The hijackers were members of a fundamentalist Islamic terrorist group called
  **a.** al Qaeda.
  **b.** Iraqis United.
  **c.** Kuwait Alliance.
  **d.** Operation Afghanistan.

_____ **4.** Who is the wealthy Saudi Arabian leader of al Qaeda?
  **a.** Boris Yeltsin
  **b.** Osama bin Laden
  **c.** Saddam Hussein
  **d.** Mikhail Gorbachev

_____ **5.** What are chemical, biological, or nuclear weapons that can kill thousands called?
  **a.** trade barriers
  **b.** chemical networks
  **c.** weapons of mass destruction
  **d.** napalm

# America Looks to the Future

## Section Quiz

### Section 3

**MATCHING** In the space provided, write the letter of the term that matches each description. Some answers will not be used.

_____ 1. When most people have jobs providing services rather than producing goods

_____ 2. Growing connections between economies and cultures all over the world

_____ 3. Promotes international trade by removing trade barriers between nations

_____ 4. Global system of computer networks

_____ 5. Enables people to access information from computers around the world

_____ 6. Rapid increase in the use of computers and the Internet to access and share information

_____ 7. Scientific undertaking that identified more than 30,000 genes in human DNA

_____ 8. Disease that shuts down the body's immune system

_____ 9. Thin layer of gas in the upper atmosphere that blocks harmful solar rays

_____ 10. Term used to describe climate change

a. AIDS

b. economists

c. globalization

d. global warming

e. Human Genome Project

f. industry

g. Information Revolution

h. Internet

i. ozone layer

j. service economy

k. tuberculosis

l. World Trade Organization

m. World Wide Web

Progress Assessment

**America Looks to the Future**                    Chapter Test

                                                   **Form A**

**MULTIPLE CHOICE** For each of the following, write the letter of the best choice in the space provided.

_____ **1.** Which of the following statements best describes globalization?
   **a.** rising hostilities between wealthy nations and poor nations
   **b.** growing connections between the economies and cultures of the world
   **c.** decreasing importance of individual nations
   **d.** people identifying as global citizens

_____ **2.** What has led to the decline in importance of manufacturing to the U.S. economy?
   **a.** Laborers have found higher pay in the service economy.
   **b.** High-tech companies have forced manufacturers out of business.
   **c.** Manufacturers have moved operations to places where labor is less expensive.
   **d.** The U.S. government has focused its resources on globalization projects.

_____ **3.** In their 1994 Contract with America congressional Republicans promised to
   **a.** lower taxes and ensure less government.
   **b.** sustain Republican majorities in the House and Senate.
   **c.** repeal the North American Free Trade Agreement.
   **d.** turn the federal deficit into a surplus.

_____ **4.** In 2000 the Census Bureau began allowing people to indicate on official surveys that they
   **a.** had two primary wage-earners in their families.
   **b.** belonged to more than one race.
   **c.** preferred a language other than English.
   **d.** wanted to keep their telephone numbers private.

_____ **5.** A healthy ozone layer protects human beings by
   **a.** filtering carbon monoxide from polluted air.
   **b.** blocking harmful solar rays.
   **c.** trapping heat from the sun in Earth's atmosphere.
   **d.** stabilizing sea levels.

Progress Assessment

_____  **6.** What was the significance of Vice President Dick Cheney's role during George W. Bush's first term?

    **a.** Cheney often served as the tie-breaker on votes in the evenly divided Senate.

    **b.** Many members of Congress vied for power because of Cheney's failing health.

    **c.** Cheney's liberal politics contrasted with the president's, creating tension in the White House.

    **d.** President Bush put Cheney in charge of investigations against suspected terrorists.

_____  **7.** What did a French newspaper mean by the headline "We are all Americans" after September 11, 2001?

    **a.** Americans could come to France to escape terrorism.

    **b.** The French sympathized with the United States.

    **c.** Terrorist attacks had spread to France.

    **d.** Al Qaeda would likely attack France next.

_____  **8.** What led to a rising federal deficit in the first decade of the 21st century?

    **a.** slow economic growth, the cost of the war in Iraq, and tax cuts

    **b.** increased domestic spending, anti-terrorism programs, and unemployment

    **c.** the tech stock collapse, national debt, and the war in Afghanistan

    **d.** the housing bubble, higher taxes, and increased consumer spending

_____  **9.** What did Saddam Hussein agree to do after the Persian Gulf War ended in 1991?

    **a.** draft a constitution

    **b.** give up Iraq's weapons of mass destruction

    **c.** negotiate a peace agreement with Iran

    **d.** bring any al Qaeda fugitives to justice

_____  **10.** German reunification was a triumph for which form of government?

    **a.** Communist

    **b.** Socialist

    **c.** Democratic

    **d.** Capitalist

**PRACTICING SOCIAL STUDIES SKILLS** Read the quotation below and answer the question that follows.

> "We are watching something historic happening, and it will affect the world . . . the same way the scientific method, the invention of printing, and the arrival of the Industrial Age did."
>
> —Bill Gates, quoted in *Newsweek*

_____ **11.** In the quotation above, Bill Gates is referring to the
   **a.** shift to a service economy in the United States.
   **b.** effects of global warming.
   **c.** spread of AIDS.
   **d.** emergence of the Information Revolution.

**TRUE/FALSE** Indicate whether each statement below is true or false by writing **T** or **F** in the space provided.

_____ **12.** Although the House of Representatives voted to impeach President Bill Clinton in 1998, the Senate acquitted him of all charges in 1999.

_____ **13.** Originally, the Internet did not include the World Wide Web, which was developed by programmers in the 1990s.

_____ **14.** Beginning in 2004, doctors began using the information gained by the Human Genome Project to treat genetically transmitted diseases.

_____ **15.** President George W. Bush signed an education reform plan called No Child Left Behind to create a national set of standards for every school and student.

America Looks to the Future, *continued*                Chapter Test Form A

---

**MATCHING**  In the space provided, write the letter of the term, place, or person that matches each description. Some answers will not be used.

_____ **16.** destroyed much of the Gulf Coast region, leaving many residents without resources

_____ **17.** President Reagan's vice president

_____ **18.** leader of al Qaeda

_____ **19.** promotes international trade

_____ **20.** where 52 percent of foreign-born U.S. residents were born

_____ **21.** led the U.S. air offensive during the Persian Gulf War

_____ **22.** ruled the country that sheltered and supported al Qaeda

_____ **23.** where 25 percent of foreign-born U.S. residents were born

_____ **24.** independent candidate in the 1992 presidential election

_____ **25.** Democratic candidate in the 2000 presidential election

**a.** World Trade Organizaton

**b.** Norman Schwarzkopf

**c.** John Kerry

**d.** Latin America

**e.** Osama bin Laden

**f.** Ross Perot

**g.** Taliban

**h.** Hurricane Katrina

**i.** Saddam Hussein

**j.** Asia

**k.** Al Gore

**l.** George H. W. Bush

Progress Assessment

**America Looks to the Future**

Chapter Test

**Form B**

**SHORT ANSWER** On a separate sheet of paper, answer each of the following questions in complete sentences.

1. What chain of events led to the breakup of the Soviet Union?

2. What events made terrorism a major issue for the United States?

3. What made the 2000 presidential election so controversial?

4. What long-term factors from 1990–2002 led to war in Iraq?

5. How did the U.S. move to a service economy, and what are some examples of service economy industries?

6. What is globalization? Give some examples of this trend.

**PRACTICING SOCIAL STUDIES SKILLS** Study the information below and, on a separate sheet of paper, answer the question that follows.

**The Freedom Tower**

Skidmore, Owings and Merrill Ltd.

7. The proposed tower in the photo will stand where the World Trade Center towers once stood. Why do people want this very tall skyscraper to replace the World Trade Center towers, and what are the pros and cons of this? Explain.

# Modern America

**MULTIPLE CHOICE** For each of the following, write the letter of the best choice in the space provided.

_____ **1.** In *United States* v. *Nixon*, the Supreme Court had to decide on the right of the
  **a.** Committee to Re-elect the President to enter the Watergate Hotel.
  **b.** president to refuse to give prosecutors his Oval Office tapes.
  **c.** Senate to force a president's public resignation.
  **d.** press to keep the names of their sources secret.

_____ **2.** After succeeding Nixon as president, Gerald Ford
  **a.** appointed Nixon to his cabinet.
  **b.** granted Nixon a full pardon.
  **c.** had Nixon arrested.
  **d.** delivered a speech against Nixon.

_____ **3.** The Census Bureau predicts that by 2050, nonwhite citizens of America will be
  **a.** as numerous as white citizens.
  **b.** twice as wealthy as white citizens.
  **c.** more spread out geographically.
  **d.** better represented in Congress.

_____ **4.** Congress believed that President Carter's national energy plan
  **a.** solved the energy crisis.
  **b.** made unfair requests of the American people.
  **c.** was too complex and required changes.
  **d.** presented a financial disaster and would not work.

_____ **5.** What was the extent of U.S. involvement in Nicaragua after the overthrow of Nicaragua's pro-American dictator?
  **a.** funding patrols of the Nicaraguan border
  **b.** supporting pro-government officials
  **c.** helping rebel forces known as Contras
  **d.** planning to assassinate the Sandinista president

_____ **6.** What was the main criticism of the war in Iraq?
  **a.** Saddam Hussein was not a dictator.
  **b.** Al Qaeda no longer posed a threat.
  **c.** Foreign armies could have been more forceful.
  **d.** No weapons of mass destruction were discovered in Iraq.

_____ **7.** Why did the Bush administration respond to the events of September 11, 2001 by invading Afghanistan?

**a.** Osama bin Laden, who organized the September 11 attacks, was based in Afghanistan.

**b.** The Taliban, Afghanistan's extremist Islamic government, had threatened to attack.

**c.** Afghanistan, a U.S. security threat, was concealing weapons of mass destruction.

**d.** Al Qaeda, a fundamentalist Islamic army, was leading a rebellion against the Taliban.

_____ **8.** President Ford argued that the main cause of the country's economic troubles was

**a.** stagflation.

**b.** the trade deficit.

**c.** inflation.

**d.** high oil prices.

_____ **9.** American fast-food restaurants in Russia is an example of

**a.** globalization.

**b.** the Information Revolution.

**c.** a service economy.

**d.** stagflation.

_____ **10.** From which source did Woodward and Bernstein get some of their information about the Watergate scandal?

**a.** a hidden camera

**b.** the Pentagon Papers

**c.** a government official

**d.** Oval Office tapes

_____ **11.** Which of the following best describes the Information Revolution?

**a.** growth of the stock market in the 1990s, fueled by high-tech companies

**b.** growth of service-industry jobs focused on buying and selling information

**c.** fast-growing availability of computers and the Internet

**d.** development of advanced electronic storage technology

_____ **12.** What event sparked the Persian Gulf War in 1990?

**a.** Iraqi leader Saddam Hussein sent troops into neighboring Kuwait.

**b.** The UN sent investigators into Iraq to search for biological weapons.

**c.** Kuwait permitted U.S. forces to land aircraft on its Iraqi border.

**d.** Iran attacked UN troops stationed in Kuwait to protect Saddam Hussein.

_____ **13.** President Reagan wanted to reduce government regulations of key industries because he

  **a.** thought fewer rules would encourage expansion of those industries, improving the economy.

  **b.** wanted to reduce the chance of the government being involved in a scandal if an industry was revealed to be corrupt.

  **c.** wanted the industries to come up with their own voluntary codes of ethics.

  **d.** felt that too much government regulation was a step toward socialism.

_____ **14.** What happened at Three Mile Island in March 1979?

  **a.** A reactor exploded and injured many workers.

  **b.** A reactor core overheated and the plant released a small amount of radioactive gas.

  **c.** Repair efforts failed and the power plant was forced to close.

  **d.** Repair work caused a small amount of radioactive waste to taint the local water supply.

_____ **15.** Why did the result of the 2000 presidential election depend on the outcome in Florida?

  **a.** Florida's polls opened later than other states' polls, so all other votes were in by the time Florida's votes were being counted.

  **b.** Because the popular vote was tied, Florida's electoral votes would be given to the candidate who had the most electoral votes nationwide.

  **c.** Voting in Florida was so close that a winner could not be declared, and Florida had enough electoral votes to sway the election.

  **d.** Florida had a large enough voting population that whoever won the election in Florida would win the national popular vote.

_____ **16.** What best defines the major domestic challenge posed by Hurricane Katrina?

  **a.** restricted troop movements in Iraq

  **b.** a nationwide power outage

  **c.** delayed Supreme Court nominations

  **d.** slow government response to the destruction of New Orleans

**PRACTICING SOCIAL STUDIES SKILLS** Study the quotation below and answer the question that follows.

> "If we keep shifting our manufacturing jobs across the border [to Mexico] and around the world and deindustrializing our country, we will not be able to defend this great country, and that is a risk we will never take."
>
> —H. Ross Perot

_____ **17.** What did Perot mean by "deindustrializing"?
  **a.** reducing or destroying a nation's industrial capacity
  **b.** threatening or abusing natural resources such as oil
  **c.** preventing unions from bargaining collectively
  **d.** putting laborers out of work against their will

**FILL IN THE BLANK** Read each sentence and fill in the blank with the word in the word pair that best completes the sentence.

**18.** President George H. W. Bush lost the 1992 presidential election because of concerns about _____. **(the economy/terrorism)**

**19.** Shortly after two planes flew into the World Trade Center in New York City, a third plane crashed into the _____ in Washington, D.C. **(Pentagon/Capitol Building)**

**20.** As the percentage of Americans working in manufacturing has fallen, the economy has shifted to a _____. **(global economy/service economy)**

**21.** Scientists warn that rising levels of carbon dioxide are trapping heat in Earth's atmosphere and worsening the climate change known as _____. **(global warming/ozone erosion)**

**22.** American control of _____ stood as a symbol of American power in Latin America. **(the Panama Canal/anti-Communist forces)**

**23.** People concerned about _____ worry that it will cause Americans to lose jobs. **(globalization/the Information Revolution)**

**24.** The candidates in the presidential election of 1988 were George H. W. Bush and

_____. **(Michael Dukakis/John Kerry)**

**25.** The Internet was first developed in 1969 by scientists at the U.S. Department of

_____. **(Education/Defense)**

**26.** _____ encouraged Russian protesters to stand strong in support of Gorbachev when Gorbachev was kidnapped by hard-line Communists trying to hold onto power. **(Vladimir Putin/Boris Yeltsin)**

**27.** _____ eliminated trade barriers between the United States, Canada, and Mexico. **(NAFTA/WTO)**

**TRUE/FALSE** Indicate whether each statement below is true or false by writing **T** or **F** in the space provided.

_____ **28.** U.S. embassy workers in Tehran were taken hostage by Iranian students.

_____ **29.** The Supreme Court stopped the manual vote recount in Florida, ruling that a continuing delay in naming the next president was a threat to national security.

_____ **30.** George W. Bush was the first president in more than 100 years to win the electoral vote while receiving fewer popular votes than his opponent.

_____ **31.** Colin Powell was the first African American man to become secretary of state.

_____ **32.** After the accident at Three Mile Island, President Carter agreed to compromise with Congress on a revision of his complex energy plan, which Congress quickly enacted.

_____ **33.** To balance the budget under "Reaganomics," Congress cut spending on social programs such as school lunches, and low-income housing.

_____ **34.** In 2005 the Census Bureau reported that Hispanics made up 14 percent of the U.S. population, making them the country's largest minority group.

_____ **35.** More than 35,000 American women served in the Persian Gulf War, but federal law prevented them from serving in combat.

**MATCHING** In the space provided, write the letter of the term that matches each description. Some answers will not be used.

_____ **36.** political leader who began a process of reform called *perestroika*

_____ **37.** agreement that opened a period of détente between the United States and the Soviet Union

_____ **38.** leader who represented Israel in the Camp David Accords

_____ **39.** practice of giving special consideration to some minority groups to compensate for previous discrimination

_____ **40.** group of mostly Arab countries that regulated oil in the 1970s

_____ **41.** theory that tax cuts for businesses will increase tax revenues in the long run

_____ **42.** slow economic growth matched by high inflation

_____ **43.** brought national attention to the dangers of environmental pollution

_____ **44.** strategy of approaching foreign policy decisions based on practical national interests

_____ **45.** policy of racial segregation adopted by the Republic of South Africa

**a.** stagflation

**b.** supply-side economics

**c.** Rachel Carson

**d.** Mikhail Gorbachev

**e.** SALT

**f.** Menachem Begin

**g.** affirmative action

**h.** OPEC

**i.** inflation

**j.** realpolitik

**k.** Golda Meir

**l.** apartheid

## America Looks to the Future

**SHORT ANSWER** On a separate sheet of paper, answer each of the following questions in complete sentences.

**1.** What was SALT and what happened as a result of it?

**2.** Explain what Title IX did and how it affected women.

**3.** What led up to Americans being taken hostage in Iran, and how long were they held hostage?

**4.** What happened in the Balkans in the 1990s, and how was the U.S. involved?

**5.** How would you describe global warming and its effects on Earth?

**6.** Why did the fourth hijacked plane crash in a Pennsylvania field on September 11, 2001?

**PRACTICING SOCIAL STUDIES SKILLS** Study the map below and, on a separate sheet of paper, answer the question that follows.

### The Persian Gulf War, 1990–1991

**7.** Locate where most scud missile attacks and UN air attacks took place. Why were those locations chosen? What key city received no attacks? Explain.

## End-of-Year Test

**MULTIPLE CHOICE** For each of the following, write the letter of the best choice in the space provided.

_____ **1.** The earliest known civilization in North America is the
  **a.** Aztec.
  **b.** Inca.
  **c.** Maya.
  **d.** Olmec.

_____ **2.** What does *Renaissance* mean?
  **a.** awakening
  **b.** enlightenment
  **c.** knowledge
  **d.** rebirth

_____ **3.** Finding a sea route to Asia was significant because it
  **a.** gave Europeans the opportunity to hold political positions in foreign lands.
  **b.** allowed Europeans to bypass merchants who monopolized trade.
  **c.** introduced Europeans to new investors who would support exploration.
  **d.** showed Europeans that interactions with Asians were nothing new.

_____ **4.** Searches for a Northwest Passage were significant because they
  **a.** caused France and Italy to claim land in North America.
  **b.** raised European interest in North America.
  **c.** led French and Italian sailors to sail for other nations.
  **d.** resulted in the peaceful division of North America among European powers.

_____ **5.** What was the Great Awakening?
  **a.** a movement of thinkers who believed in the idea that reason and logic could improve social and political life
  **b.** the migration of thousands of English people to the New England colonies and the Caribbean islands
  **c.** the series of witchcraft trials in which groups of young girls accused church ministers of casting spells
  **d.** a religious movement that swept through the colonies and changed colonial religion, society, and politics

Progress Assessment

_____ **6.** The Boston Tea Party was significant because it showed how

    **a.** unhappy colonists were with new British laws.

    **b.** important tea was to colonists in relation to other imports.

    **c.** easily colonists could tell cheap tea from expensive tea.

    **d.** angry colonists were even before the Boston Massacre.

_____ **7.** Why was the phrase "taxation without representation" so important to the revolutionary cause?

    **a.** Colonists did not wish to support a government in which they had no voice.

    **b.** Great Britain would have ended taxation if colonists had kept the peace.

    **c.** Colonists believed that Great Britain should only tax certain items.

    **d.** Great Britain only taxed the colonists to force them into war.

_____ **8.** According to the Constitution, what is the role of the judicial branch?

    **a.** giving legal advice

    **b.** interpreting the law

    **c.** writing new laws

    **d.** setting legal precedents

_____ **9.** The framers of the Constitution created a system of checks and balances to

    **a.** outline the powers held by each branch of government.

    **b.** keep any one branch of government from becoming too powerful.

    **c.** give the people an opportunity to control the government.

    **d.** strengthen the powers held by each branch of government.

_____ **10.** The Bill of Rights was added to the Constitution to

    **a.** protect citizens' rights.

    **b.** limit the powers of state governments.

    **c.** outline the rights of the federal government.

    **d.** state the ways in which citizens can participate in government.

_____ **11.** The new federal government in America took actions that would set an example for the future. In George Washington's words, these exemplary actions "will serve to establish a

    **a.** procedure."

    **b.** precursor."

    **c.** policy."

    **d.** precedent."

_____ **12.** What is required for a person to become a naturalized citizen?

   **a.** obtaining legal-immigrant status and serving five years in the armed forces

   **b.** moving to the United States permanently and applying for citizenship

   **c.** surrendering any foreign passports and renouncing foreign citizenship

   **d.** reciting the pledge of allegiance once before a judge and daily thereafter

_____ **13.** The national debt can best be defined as the amount of money owed

   **a.** to the nation by the nation's citizens and by foreign countries.

   **b.** by the nation to foreign countries and the nation's citizens.

   **c.** to the federal government by individual states.

   **d.** by the federal government to domestic debtors.

_____ **14.** What happened to California's population as a result of the Gold Rush?

   **a.** The population grew, but not as much as it had during the Spanish and Mexican periods of settlement.

   **b.** The population boomed during "gold fever," but declined just as quickly because of inflation.

   **c.** Immigrants and Americans flocked to California to "get rich quick" and stayed to build a stable frontier society.

   **d.** Californios and Native Americans still outnumbered immigrants after the Gold Rush.

_____ **15.** Which of the following statements about the War of 1812 is true?

   **a.** It worsened the conflict between the North and the South.

   **b.** It intensified American Indian resistance to Americans.

   **c.** It severely damaged American manufacturing.

   **d.** It strengthened patriotism among Americans.

Progress Assessment

_____ **16.** What was a consequence of the Missouri Compromise?
   **a.** Missouri entered the Union as an independent territory.
   **b.** The practice of slavery was pronounced unconstitutional.
   **c.** Free states won a majority in the House of Representatives.
   **d.** An equal balance between free and slave states was maintained.

_____ **17.** The Oregon Trail
   **a.** ran through the Sierra Nevada.
   **b.** required protection by U.S. troops.
   **c.** was a popular route for merchants.
   **d.** took six months to travel.

_____ **18.** The nullification crisis was a dispute over the
   **a.** states' power to secede from the Union.
   **b.** states' power to reject federal laws they deemed unconstitutional.
   **c.** federal government's power to end tariffs.
   **d.** federal government's power to favor one region over another.

_____ **19.** Which of the following best describes the Trail of Tears?
   **a.** streams of blood that flowed from the Sauk Indians in the Black Hawk War
   **b.** forced 800-mile march Cherokee Indians made in their removal from Georgia
   **c.** line connecting Seminole Indian settlements up and down Florida's east coast
   **d.** unpublished works on the Cherokee population written by Sequoya

_____ **20.** The Industrial Revolution can best be described as a
   **a.** period of rapid growth during which machines became essential to manufacturing.
   **b.** series of explosive encounters between workers and wealthy factory owners.
   **c.** time of great excitement about mechanical approaches to controlling Nature.
   **d.** period of turmoil and upheaval within the U.S. government.

_____ 21. Which of the following best describes a trade union?
- **a.** organization of workers who tried to improve pay and working conditions for members
- **b.** collection of workers who appealed to the courts for assistance against employers
- **c.** group of workers who arrived from poor countries and were willing to work for low pay
- **d.** alliance of workers who wanted to prevent their employers from competing with other manufacturers

_____ 22. In the first half of the 1800s, what portion of white southern families had slaves?
- **a.** one-third
- **b.** one-half
- **c.** two-thirds
- **d.** three-quarters

_____ 23. What did most cities rely on to fight crime in the mid-1800s?
- **a.** police forces
- **b.** volunteer night watches
- **c.** state troopers
- **d.** salaried war veterans

_____ 24. In late 18th century America, the Second Great Awakening was a period of
- **a.** rebirth that led to the development of a culture centered on education.
- **b.** Christian renewal that began in the northeastern United States.
- **c.** reform that focused on improving the quality of life of the poor.
- **d.** American revival that brought back pre-Revolutionary War traditions.

_____ 25. Which statement expresses the reason why the southern states decided to secede from the Union after the election of 1860?
- **a.** The southern economy and way of life would be destroyed.
- **b.** Slaves would begin an uprising if the states did not secede.
- **c.** Seceding from the Union would end the possibility of war.
- **d.** Secession would end the conflicts between northern states over slavery.

Progress Assessment

_____ **26.** Life for African Americans in the South changed after the Civil War because many African Americans

    **a.** were now free because of the Emancipation Proclamation.

    **b.** received equal rights and opportunities under the law.

    **c.** had gained the respect of the white population of the South.

    **d.** won citizenship as a result of the Union victory in the war.

_____ **27.** The Reconstruction Acts, passed by Congress in March 1867, affected the makeup of the southern states by

    **a.** creating new governments and appointing Republican governors to each state in the South.

    **b.** dividing the South into new states controlled by leaders who had not been supporters of the Confederacy.

    **c.** dividing the South into five military districts controlled by a military commander.

    **d.** creating a new boundary that separated Northern states that had seceded from the Union.

_____ **28.** Which of these events marked the beginning of the Civil War?

    **a.** the election of Abraham Lincoln to the presidency

    **b.** the abolition of slavery in the South

    **c.** the declaration of war by President Lincoln

    **d.** the firing of Confederate guns on Fort Sumter

_____ **29.** What was the transcontinental railroad meant to connect?

    **a.** the southern United States to the North

    **b.** the eastern United States to the West

    **c.** Canada to the southern United States

    **d.** Canada to Mexico and Central America

_____ **30.** Which of the following is true about stockholders?

    **a.** They must pay the corporation's debts.

    **b.** They can sell their stock shares at any time.

    **c.** They are responsible for the corporation's policies.

    **d.** They vote directly for the corporation's president.

Progress Assessment

_____ **31.** The reason for the decline in working conditions in American industries in the late 1800s was the
  **a.** drive to regulate monopolies.
  **b.** weakening of labor unions.
  **c.** emphasis on high profits and efficiency.
  **d.** elimination of health benefits.

_____ **32.** When did the "new immigrants" pour into the United States?
  **a.** from 1800 to 1860
  **b.** from 1850 to 1870
  **c.** during the 1880s
  **d.** during the 1900s

_____ **33.** What does the term mass transit refer to?
  **a.** the problem of traffic in big cities in the late 1800s
  **b.** a system of public transportation created to move a large number of passengers
  **c.** migration of middle-class families from the suburbs into big cities
  **d.** construction of electric trolleys in the major American cities of the late 1800s

_____ **34.** Politics during the Gilded Age can best be characterized as
  **a.** corrupt.
  **b.** useless.
  **c.** honest.
  **d.** helpful.

_____ **35.** What is one of the fundamental differences between capitalism and socialism?
  **a.** Under socialism, the government owns the factories and raw materials.
  **b.** Under socialism, unions are organized by industry rather than skill level.
  **c.** Under capitalism, the government can interfere in the marketplace and set prices.
  **d.** Under capitalism, unions use collective bargaining rather than aggressive tactics.

_____ **36.** Imperialism can best be described as
  **a.** a system in which there is no private property.
  **b.** a government run by the people.
  **c.** an empire built by founding colonies or conquering other nations.
  **d.** a method of ruling similar to communism.

Progress Assessment

_____ **37.** What happens in the situation known as a "stalemate"?
   **a.** Two countries are forced to break their alliance.
   **b.** Neither side can win a decisive victory.
   **c.** A victor is declared.
   **d.** Neither side is allowed to launch an attack.

_____ **38.** What hardships did American soldiers face in World War I?
   **a.** insufficiently trained for battle against the Central Powers
   **b.** forced to live amongst rats, lice, and the bodies of dead soldiers
   **c.** malnourished and often contracted Lyme disease
   **d.** forced to fight alongside French troops, who often mistreated them

_____ **39.** "Buying on margin" means buying stocks
   **a.** during a bull market at an inflated price.
   **b.** during a bear market in hopes of selling at a higher price.
   **c.** with borrowed money.
   **d.** directly at the stock market, instead of through a stockbroker.

_____ **40.** The decade after World War I was characterized by a clash between the ideals and values of
   **a.** rich and poor Americans.
   **b.** native-born Americans and immigrants.
   **c.** traditional rural and modern urban Americans.
   **d.** American women and men.

_____ **41.** What did the most popular art forms of the Depression era do?
   **a.** offered an escape from reality
   **b.** focused on the sadness of the time
   **c.** reminded people of their folk roots
   **d.** portrayed ordinary people

_____ **42.** The policy of avoiding war with an aggressive nation by giving into its demands is called
   **a.** blitzkrieg.
   **b.** brinksmanship.
   **c.** Luftwaffe.
   **d.** appeasement.

_____ **43.** *Sputnik* was the world's first
  **a.** artificial satellite.
  **b.** computer.
  **c.** hydrogen bomb.
  **d.** spaceship.

_____ **44.** How did the Vietnam War highlight race and class differences in the United States?
  **a.** College students, most of whom were white and from wealthier families, were able to get deferments releasing them from the draft.
  **b.** Minority Americans protested the killing of Vietnamese civilians, while most white Americans ignored the situation overseas.
  **c.** Americans with skilled jobs, mostly white workers who received higher-than-average salaries, were not drafted.
  **d.** The government cracked-down most violently on antiwar protests led by minorities in poor neighborhoods.

_____ **45.** A sit-in is a
  **a.** protest in which striking workers leave the work site.
  **b.** demonstration in which protesters sit down and refuse to leave.
  **c.** voter registration drive coordinated to alter the outcome of an election.
  **d.** meeting held by rights activists to plan their next course of action.

_____ **46.** What does the War Powers Act state?
  **a.** The public must be granted access to any information about the country's progress in war.
  **b.** The president can stop aggressors by any means necessary.
  **c.** The president must get congressional approval before committing troops to an armed struggle.
  **d.** Military officials can decide whether the country enters a war.

_____ **47.** Which act banned segregation in public places and outlawed discrimination in the workplace?
 **a.** Civil Rights Act of 1964
 **b.** Freedom Summer Act
 **c.** Voting Rights Act of 1969
 **d.** Montgomery Bus Act

_____ **48.** What is stagflation?
 **a.** rising employment without a change in prices
 **b.** fixed prices with rising unemployment
 **c.** falling prices with rising unemployment
 **d.** rising prices without economic growth

_____ **49.** In a service economy many people
 **a.** work for the government.
 **b.** serve in the military.
 **c.** provide services rather than produce goods.
 **d.** have jobs requiring little training.

_____ **50.** The term "global warming" refers to the
 **a.** policy that bans chemicals that damage the ozone layer.
 **b.** warming of the earth's surface due to holes in the ozone layer.
 **c.** rise in air temperature caused by carbon dioxide in the atmosphere.
 **d.** rise in ocean temperatures due to a lack of carbon dioxide in the atmosphere.

Progress Assessment

## Diagnostic Test

| | |
|---|---|
| **1.** d | **26.** a |
| **2.** d | **27.** c |
| **3.** b | **28.** d |
| **4.** b | **29.** b |
| **5.** d | **30.** b |
| **6.** a | **31.** c |
| **7.** a | **32.** c |
| **8.** b | **33.** b |
| **9.** b | **34.** a |
| **10.** a | **35.** a |
| **11.** d | **36.** c |
| **12.** b | **37.** b |
| **13.** b | **38.** b |
| **14.** c | **39.** c |
| **15.** d | **40.** c |
| **16.** d | **41.** a |
| **17.** d | **42.** d |
| **18.** b | **43.** a |
| **19.** b | **44.** a |
| **20.** a | **45.** b |
| **21.** a | **46.** c |
| **22.** a | **47.** a |
| **23.** b | **48.** d |
| **24.** b | **49.** c |
| **25.** a | **50.** c |

## The World before the Opening of the Atlantic

### SECTION QUIZ
### Section 1

1. Ice Age
2. glaciers
3. Bering Land Bridge
4. Paleo-Indians
5. migration
6. hunter-gatherers
7. Mesoamerica
8. Olmec
9. Aztec
10. Inca

### Section 2

1. T
2. F; Pueblos were aboveground adobe houses.
3. F; It declined by AD 700.
4. T
5. F; It helped the Iroquois.

### Section 3

| | |
|---|---|
| **1.** Berbers | **6.** Muslims |
| **2.** Ghana | **7.** Mansa Musa |
| **3.** Soninke | **8.** Africans |
| **4.** salt | **9.** Timbuktu |
| **5.** Islam | **10.** slaves |

### Section 4

1. l, Socrates
2. j, Plato
3. a, Aristotle
4. c, democracy
5. f, knights
6. i, plague
7. k, Renaissance
8. d, Johannes Gutenberg
9. g, mercantilism
10. e, joint-stock companies

### CHAPTER TEST FORM A

| | |
|---|---|
| **1.** b | **7.** b |
| **2.** d | **8.** d |
| **3.** c | **9.** b |
| **4.** a | **10.** d |
| **5.** c | **11.** b |
| **6.** b | **12.** b |

13. b

14. Paleo-Indians
15. culture
16. Mansa Musa
17. Johannes Gutenberg
18. knights

| | |
|---|---|
| **19.** F | **23.** F |
| **20.** T | **24.** T |
| **21.** T | **25.** T |
| **22.** F | |

### CHAPTER TEST FORM B

1. The sea level dropped and people crossed the Bering Land Bridge from northeastern Asia to present-day Alaska.
2. In a joint-stock company, people invest together. This way, they share the profits and losses. In a joint-stock company, if the

investment doesn't pay off, a single investor loses less than he or she would as the sole owner of a company. It lets investors take fewer risks.

3. The printing press allowed for the mass production of printed materials, such as books and pamphlets. These printed materials allowed for the spread of information to the masses.

4. Arab Muslims and then Europeans became slave traders. Before, only Black Africans were involved in the slave trade.

5. They belonged to the Iroquois League, whose goal was to create a strong force to fight against invasion.

6. Roman law and American law are both written and the laws are known to the public. Citizens are equal before the law. Citizens are innocent until proven guilty. All of these features of the law protect the rights of citizens.

7. Possible answer: The lines and arrows represent trade routes and trade goods. They indicate that trade was important in Mali and Songhai.

# New Empires in the Americas

## SECTION QUIZ
### Section 1
1. T
2. T
3. F; Prince Henry the Navigator never set sail himself.
4. F; An astrolabe helped navigators.
5. T

### Section 2
1. Christopher Columbus
2. Ferdinand, Isabella
3. Line of Demarcation
4. Amerigo Vespucci
5. Ferdinand Magellan
6. circumnavigate
7. Columbian Exchange
8. Treaty of Tordesillas
9. diseases
10. Africans

### Section 3
1. b, conquistadors
2. e, Hernán Cortés
3. h, Moctezuma II
4. m, Tenochtitlán
5. g, Malintzin
6. k, presidios
7. j, Ponce de León
8. c, encomienda
9. i, plantations
10. a, Bartolomé de Las Casas

### Section 4
1. Martin Luther
2. Protestant Reformation
3. printing press
4. Huguenots
5. sea dogs
6. Spanish Armada
7. Northwest Passage
8. Jacques Cartier
9. charter
10. Florida

### Section 5
1. c, European diseases killed many Native Americans.
2. b, Bartolomé de Las Casas
3. a, voyage of Africans across Atlantic to be sold as slaves
4. b, about 12 million
5. d, property

## CHAPTER TEST FORM A
1. d
2. b
3. b
4. a
5. c
6. d
7. b
8. b
9. b
10. b
11. a
12. b
13. c
14. Hernán Cortés
15. Native Americans
16. astrolabe
17. Vasco da Gama

18. e          22. d
19. k          23. i
20. g          24. b
21. f          25. h

## CHAPTER TEST FORM B

1. The Vikings were the first Europeans to reach North America.

2. Protestants believed people should read and think about the Bible on their own, rather than relying on the teachings of a priest, so they used the press to print Bibles. They also used it to print short essays explaining their ideas, which helped spread the ideas of the Reformation throughout Europe.

3. Generally, they increased European interest in North America. Specifically, French sailors Jacques Cartier and Samuel de Champlain made significant explorations into North America, including Canada and the Great Lakes. Englishman Henry Hudson, hired by the Dutch, was the first to sail to present-day New York.

4. The *encomienda* system gave settlers the right to tax local Native Americans or make them work. In return, settlers had to protect local Native Americans and convert them to Christianity. It was established by the Spanish Crown to reward settlers for bringing the Crown so much wealth.

5. The Inca fell second. Francisco Pizzaro led the conquest.

6. King Philip II of Spain gathered a huge fleet of warships to attack Queen Elizabeth I of England and bring down the Anglican Church. The Armada outnumbered the English fleet, but was defeated in battle in 1588. The loss greatly weakened the Spanish Empire.

7. Christopher Columbus spent about nine years on his four voyages.

# The English Colonies

## SECTION QUIZ
## Section 1

1. g, Jamestown
2. f, John Smith
3. j, Powhatan Confederacy
4. c, headright system
5. d, indentured servants
6. l, Toleration Act of 1649
7. h, James Oglethorpe
8. b, cash crops
9. k, slaves
10. i, Olaudah Equiano

## Section 2

1. F; The Pilgrims drew up the Mayflower Compact to create fair laws.
2. T
3. T
4. F; The New England economy was based on trade, fishing, shipping, and skilled crafts.
5. F; Education was important in New England because parents wanted their children to be able to read the Bible and to make sure there would be educated ministers in the future.

## Section 3

1. d          4. a
2. a          5. b
3. c

## Section 4

1. b, colonial courts
2. a, assemblies
3. c, English Bill of Rights
4. l, town meetings
5. j, Middle Passage
6. h, Great Awakening
7. d, Enlightenment
8. f, French
9. g, French and Indian War
10. k, Pontiac's Rebellion

## Section 5

1. a standing army
2. Sugar Act
3. consent or permission
4. Samuel Adams
5. boycott
6. Stamp Act
7. Sons of Liberty
8. Boston Massacre
9. Boston Tea Party
10. Intolerable Acts

## CHAPTER TEST FORM A

| | | | |
|---|---|---|---|
| **1.** a | | **5.** a | |
| **2.** a | | **6.** d | |
| **3.** a | | **7.** c | |
| **4.** b | | **8.** c | |

| | |
|---|---|
| **9.** F | **13.** T |
| **10.** T | **14.** F |
| **11.** T | **15.** T |
| **12.** F | |

**16.** c

| | |
|---|---|
| **17.** c | **22.** d |
| **18.** g | **23.** b |
| **19.** j | **24.** e |
| **20.** a | **25.** i |
| **21.** f | |

## CHAPTER TEST FORM B

**1.** The colonists were not prepared for life in Jamestown. Many were adventurers who lacked useful experience and skills such as farming and carpentry. For this reason, they did not have enough food or decent housing. They also got sick from disease-carrying mosquitoes that filled the marshes surrounding the settlement.

**2.** Anne Hutchinson believed that people could have a relationship with God without the help of ministers. This belief posed a threat to the authority of the Church in the community. If people didn't need ministers, they didn't need the Church.

**3.** Britain wanted to restore order in the colony. Parliament passed the Coercive Acts, which colonists called the Intolerable Acts, to punish Massachusetts. Boston Harbor was closed until the ruined tea was paid for. The colony's charter was canceled and the governor had to approve any meetings of the legislature. Royal officials accused of crimes in the colony were sent home to Britain, where they faced trial by a friendlier judge and jury. And the Crown appointed the colony's new governor.

**4.** Pontiac opposed British settlement west of the Appalachians.

**5.** William Penn started a colony west of New Jersey to provide a safe home for Quakers.

**6.** A British soldier hit a colonist during an argument.

**7.** The population of slaves in the colonies grew to be about seven or eight times larger in 1750 than in 1700.

# The American Revolution

## SECTION QUIZ
### Section 1
1. Continental Congress
2. Patriots
3. Declaration of Rights
4. Minutemen
5. Samuel Prescott
6. Redcoats
7. Continental Army
8. George Washington
9. Olive Branch
10. Battle of Bunker Hill

### Section 2
1. d, Thomas Paine
2. b, Declaration of Independence
3. a, Loyalists
4. b, Abigail Adams
5. c, New England colonies

### Section 3
1. f, George Washington
2. k, Nathan Hale
3. i, mercenaries
4. m, Thomas Paine
5. c, Deborah Sampson
6. b, Battle of Trenton
7. h, Marquis de Lafayette
8. g, John Paul Jones
9. a, American Indians
10. e, George Rogers Clark

### Section 4
1. F; The British agreed to free slaves that fought for them.
2. T
3. T
4. F; Charles Cornwallis led British troops.
5. T

## CHAPTER TEST FORM A

| | |
|---|---|
| **1.** a | **6.** b |
| **2.** b | **7.** a |
| **3.** d | **8.** d |
| **4.** c | **9.** b |
| **5.** c | |

**10.** a

**11.** George Washington
**12.** Saratoga
**13.** Valley Forge
**14.** Charles Cornwallis
**15.** Redcoats
**16.** Thomas Paine
**17.** British

| | |
|---|---|
| **18.** F | **22.** T |
| **19.** F | **23.** F |
| **20.** F | **24.** F |
| **21.** T | **25.** T |

## CHAPTER TEST FORM B

1. Francis Marion was given this name because of his stealth and lightning speed in carrying out guerrilla warfare in the South.

2. The Patriots' fleet was tiny compared to Britain's huge navy. They did not have enough ships to fight large battles against the British, so they fought small battles. They attacked hundreds of individual ships. Sailors such as John Paul Jones overcame challenges through their courage.

3. He was the Spanish governor of Louisiana. He joined the Patriots in fighting against the British. He put together a small army of Spanish soldiers, French Americans, colonists, and American Indians who took British posts from Louisiana to Florida.

4. They created the Continental Army to fight the British.

5. Paine argued that citizens, not monarchs, should make laws. At the time, much of the world was ruled by monarchs so people were probably surprised by his ideas. But Paine convinced many people not to accept tyranny or economic dependence. The document announced that the colonies had the right to break free from the British Crown. It convinced many colonial leaders that the colonies should be free. His ideas influenced Thomas Jefferson, the main author of the Declaration of Independence.

6. Thomas Jefferson was the main author of the Declaration of Independence.

7. Answers may vary. It was not wise for the British to retreat to Yorktown because the French and American soldiers were able to surround them on land.

# Our Colonial Heritage

## UNIT TEST FORM A

| | |
|---|---|
| **1.** b | **9.** b |
| **2.** b | **10.** a |
| **3.** a | **11.** d |
| **4.** a | **12.** b |
| **5.** a | **13.** a |
| **6.** d | **14.** b |
| **7.** a | **15.** a |
| **8.** c | |

| | |
|---|---|
| **16.** F | **22.** T |
| **17.** T | **23.** F |
| **18.** T | **24.** T |
| **19.** F | **25.** T |
| **20.** T | **26.** F |
| **21.** F | |

**27.** a

**28.** Christopher Columbus
**29.** Concord
**30.** town meeting
**31.** Plato
**32.** Cuzco
**33.** Earth
**34.** John Winthrop
**35.** Mayflower Compact
**36.** Squanto
**37.** Loyalist
**38.** Bacon's Rebellion

| | |
|---|---|
| **39.** f | **45.** h |
| **40.** k | **46.** i |
| **41.** b | **47.** e |
| **42.** c | **48.** l |
| **43.** a | **49.** d |
| **44.** j | **50.** n |

Progress Assessment

## UNIT TEST FORM B

1. The Black Death killed 25 million people during the Middle Ages.
2. The surviving members of Magellan's crew were the first to sail completely around, or circumnavigate, the world.
3. John Smith took over and improved conditions in Jamestown by creating rules that rewarded workers with food. These rules forced people to work harder and build better housing. He also made an agreement with the Powhatan Confederacy. They brought food to the colonists and taught them to grow corn.
4. Religious tension in England remained high after the Protestant Reformation. Tension arose between Pilgrims and the Church of England because Pilgrims thought bishops and priests had too much power over church members. Pilgrims were Separatists, people who wanted to separate from the Anglican Church. Anglican leaders punished Separatists. To escape punishment, Pilgrims immigrated to the Netherlands. When they began to fear that their children were losing their heritage to Dutch culture and language, they got a charter from England to start a colony in America.
5. The practice of slavery went against the message of liberty and the notion that all men are created equal.
6. Options are George Washington, Comte de Rochambeau, the Marquis de Lafayette, and Charles Cornwallis.
7. The South had the highest percentage of African Americans in 2000. During colonial times, 600,000 slaves were shipped to Britain's colonies in North America. They were brought to work on plantations, which were located in the South.

# Forming a Government

## SECTION QUIZ
### Section 1

1. Magna Carta
2. Parliament
3. court system
4. Land Ordinance of 1785

5. Mayflower Compact
6. Religious Freedom
7. suffrage
8. Articles of Confederation
9. slavery
10. constitutions

### Section 2

1. c, Britain restricted trade with the United States
2. a, high taxes
3. a, people who loan money
4. c, a weak central government
5. d, Great Britain

### Section 3

1. b, Constitutional Convention
2. l, Virginia Plan
3. f, James Madison
4. m, William Paterson
5. e, Great Compromise
6. d, federalism
7. g, legislative branch
8. j, popular sovereignty
9. k, Three-fifths Compromise
10. a, checks and balances

### Section 4

1. F; They did want the Constitution to have a bill of rights.
2. F; Federalists did support the Constitution.
3. T
4. T
5. F; Amendments are official changes to the Constitution.

## CHAPTER TEST FORM A

| | |
|---|---|
| 1. d | 6. c |
| 2. a | 7. b |
| 3. a | 8. b |
| 4. d | 9. d |
| 5. b | |
| 10. c | |
| 11. T | 14. F |
| 12. T | 15. F |
| 13. F | |

**16.** d     **21.** j
**17.** g     **22.** b
**18.** f     **23.** h
**19.** c     **24.** a
**20.** j     **25.** e

## CHAPTER TEST FORM B

**1.** Americans modeled their government after Magna Carta and the English Bill of Rights.

**2.** In order to pay its war debt, Massachusetts decided to issue a tax on land. As land-owners, farmers had to pay the tax but they also had debts that they had trouble paying. The courts began forcing them to sell their land or risk being sent to debtors' prison. Upset by this practice, Daniel Shays and other Massachusetts farmers began a revolt. Its purpose was to shut down the courts so that no more property could be taken.

**3.** The Great Compromise resolved the dispute between delegates to the Constitutional Convention over how states would be represented in the federal government. It created a bicameral or two-house legislature.

**4.** The Three-Fifths Compromise declared that a slave would count as three-fifths of a person when determining a state's representation in Congress.

**5.** The *Federalist Papers* were a series of essays by Alexander Hamilton, James Madison, and John Jay. The *Federalist Papers* strongly supported the Constitution. Its authors believed that the Constitution provided a good balance of power among the branches of government. The *Papers* reassured Americans that the new federal government would not try to overpower the states. They also argued that America's diversity would prevent any one group from dominating the government.

**6.** Popular sovereignty is the idea that political authority belongs to the people.

**7.** The Land Ordinance of 1785 divided western land into townships. Townships were made up of 36 one square mile plots of land that were divided into 36 lots of 640 acres each.

# Citizenship and the Constitution

## SECTION QUIZ
### Section 1
**1.** g, legislative
**2.** c, elastic clause
**3.** l, Twenty-second Amendment
**4.** e, House of Representatives
**5.** b, concurrent powers
**6.** f, impeach
**7.** m, veto
**8.** k, Thurgood Marshall
**9.** a, appeals courts
**10.** h, president

### Section 2
**1.** T
**2.** T
**3.** F; They protect the rights of the accused.
**4.** F; It allows jury trials for civil cases.
**5.** F; The Tenth Amendment states that powers not granted to the federal government or prohibited to states belong to the states and the people.

### Section 3
**1.** naturalization
**2.** immigrants
**3.** one
**4.** laws
**5.** taxes
**6.** Selective Service
**7.** volunteer
**8.** political action committees
**9.** voting
**10.** U.S. history

## CHAPTER TEST FORM A
**1.** b     **6.** a
**2.** c     **7.** b
**3.** a     **8.** c
**4.** a     **9.** d
**5.** a

**10.** separation of powers
**11.** majority rule
**12.** naturalized citizens
**13.** impeach
**14.** Congress

**15.** c

**16.** c          **21.** i
**17.** a          **22.** l
**18.** k          **23.** g
**19.** d          **24.** j
**20.** h          **25.** e

## CHAPTER TEST FORM B

1. Separation of powers divides the powers of government so that no one branch can pose a threat to the rights of the people.
2. Unlike native-born Americans, naturalized citizens cannot run for president or vice president and they can lose their citizenship.
3. The main purpose of the Bill of Rights was to define clearly the rights and freedoms of individual citizens. In addition, people were afraid that a strong central government might take away the rights that states had granted to individuals.
4. The congressman could sue the newspaper for libel because intentional false statements that hurt another person are not protected by freedom of speech.
5. Eminent domain allows the government the power to take personal property to benefit the public.
6. De Tocqueville believes that political groups in America do a tremendous amount of valuable work. For that reason de Tocqueville seems to be suggesting that citizens interested in political action would be wise to join political groups.

# Launching the Nation

## SECTION QUIZ
### Section 1

1. George Washington
2. departments
3. Martha Washington
4. countryside
5. precedent
6. Judiciary Act of 1789
7. protect
8. New York City
9. Philadelphia
10. Thomas Jefferson

### Section 2

1. T
2. F; Alexander Hamilton believed in a strong federal government.
3. T
4. F; Hamilton supported a national bank and mint, but Jefferson did not.
5. F; Thomas Jefferson believed in strict construction, Hamilton in loose construction.

### Section 3

1. whiskey
2. Neutrality Proclamation
3. John Jay
4. privateers
5. debt
6. Pinckney's Treaty
7. Little Turtle
8. French Revolution
9. Treaty of Greenville
10. Whiskey Rebellion

### Section 4

1. a, Alexander Hamilton
2. d, Federalist Party
3. i, political parties
4. b, Alien and Sedition Acts
5. c, Democratic-Republican Party
6. g, John Adams
7. l, Thomas Jefferson
8. j, South
9. m, XYZ affair
10. e, France

## CHAPTER TEST FORM A

**1.** a          **6.** b
**2.** a          **7.** d
**3.** a          **8.** a
**4.** b          **9.** c
**5.** c

**10.** c

**11.** F          **15.** F
**12.** T          **16.** T
**13.** T          **17.** T
**14.** T          **18.** F

**19.** electoral college
**20.** precedent
**21.** Kentucky and Virginia Resolutions
**22.** Little Turtle

23. protective tariff
24. national bank
25. national debt

## CHAPTER TEST FORM B

1. Jay's Treaty angered southerners.
2. Congress passed a tax on American-made whiskey. Answers may add that farmers could not afford the tax on whiskey and didn't understand why they should have to pay taxes on something they made themselves.
3. Hamilton suggested limiting the charter of the national bank to 20 years. (Congress could decide whether or not to extend it beyond that time.) He also asked each state to start its own bank. He did these things because he did not want to upset supporters of states' rights, and he did not want to allow the national bank to have a monopoly.
4. Madison thought President George Washington had gone beyond his authority when he made the proclamation. He did not think Washington had the right to issue the proclamation without the approval of Congress.
5. A citizen might have complained about the electoral college.
6. Hamilton wanted to add a tariff to foreign goods, called a protective tariff. He knew higher taxes on foreign goods would make those goods more expensive. He thought higher prices would make Americans buy more U.S. goods. Hamilton's intention was to protect American manufacturers from foreign competition.
7. The U.S. southern boundary was defined by 31° N latitude.

## A New Nation

### UNIT TEST FORM A

| | |
|---|---|
| 1. d | 10. c |
| 2. a | 11. b |
| 3. b | 12. a |
| 4. a | 13. d |
| 5. b | 14. d |
| 6. c | 15. c |
| 7. c | 16. a |
| 8. d | 17. a |
| 9. c | 18. a |

19. b
20. Magna Carta
21. tariffs
22. Daniel Shays
23. *Federalist Papers*
24. representation
25. ratification
26. depression
27. New Jersey
28. Antifederalists
29. Northwest Ordinance of 1787

| | |
|---|---|
| 30. F | 36. T |
| 31. F | 37. F |
| 32. F | 38. T |
| 33. F | 39. T |
| 34. F | 40. T |
| 35. T | |

| | |
|---|---|
| 41. e | 46. c |
| 42. b | 47. i |
| 43. d | 48. j |
| 44. h | 49. a |
| 45. f | 50. g |

## UNIT TEST FORM B

1. Antifederalists opposed the Constitution because they thought it gave the central government too much power. They also thought the document should include a section that guaranteed individual rights.
2. The Virginia Statute for Religious Freedom stated that no person could be required to attend or be forced to pay taxes for a specific church.
3. The president can veto, or reject, laws that Congress passes.
4. Majority rule is the idea that the greatest number of people in a society make policy for everyone. This principle can interfere with the individual rights of people in minority groups. Examples can include: If most people are Protestant, they might vote to restrict or ban the practice of other religions. If most people are white, they might vote to limit the rights of another racial or ethnic group.

**5.** Loose construction is a way of interpreting the Constitution. Loose constructionists argue that the federal government can take reasonable actions that the Constitution does not specifically forbid. Hamilton argued that the Constitution did not specifically forbid creating a national bank, which meant that one could legally be created.

**6.** President George Washington issued the Neutrality Proclamation. It stated that the United States would not take sides with any European countries that were at war.

**7.** In 1790 five out of every 100 Americans lived in urban areas.

# The Jefferson Era

## SECTION QUIZ
### Section 1
**1.** Aaron Burr
**2.** House of Representatives
**3.** government
**4.** political party
**5.** Alien and Sedition Acts
**6.** Bank of the United States
**7.** John Marshall
**8.** *Marbury* v. *Madison*
**9.** judicial review
**10.** limited

### Section 2
**1.** F; It doubled the size of the United States.
**2.** F; Napoleon Bonaparte sold Louisiana to the United States for money to fund his war.
**3.** T
**4.** F; Meriwether Lewis and William Clark were sent to explore the West.
**5.** T

### Section 3
**1.** d, Great Britain
**2.** e, impressment
**3.** f, James Madison
**4.** a, Embargo Act
**5.** i, Tecumseh
**6.** m, William Henry Harrison
**7.** l, War Hawks
**8.** k, USS *Constitution*

**9.** b, France
**10.** g, Non-Intercourse Act

### Section 4
**1.** Great Britain
**2.** manufacturing
**3.** Oliver Hazard Perry
**4.** New Orleans
**5.** Andrew Jackson
**6.** Washington, D.C.
**7.** navy
**8.** Hartford Convention
**9.** Treaty of Ghent
**10.** patriotism

## CHAPTER TEST FORM A

| | |
|---|---|
| **1.** d | **7.** c |
| **2.** a | **8.** c |
| **3.** a | **9.** c |
| **4.** c | **10.** b |
| **5.** b | **11.** d |
| **6.** c | |

| | |
|---|---|
| **12.** c | **17.** k |
| **13.** a | **18.** l |
| **14.** l | **19.** e |
| **15.** b | **20.** i |
| **16.** j | |

| | |
|---|---|
| **21.** John Adams | **23.** Impressment |
| **22.** War Hawks | **24.** Federalist |

**25.** b

## CHAPTER TEST FORM B

**1.** *Marbury* v. *Madison* helped establish the power of the Supreme Court to check the power of the other branches of government. It also established the power of judicial review, which is the Supreme Court's power to declare acts of Congress unconstitutional. This power was used to make the judiciary equal in strength to the other branches of the federal government.

**2.** The United States was shipping goods and war supplies to both countries. This caused each side to stop American merchant ships and take goods meant for the enemy.

**3.** American merchants hated the Embargo Act because it banned foreign trade and caused American merchants to lose large amounts of money. It also had little effect on Britain and France, the countries it was intended to hurt.

4. The Lousiana Purchase roughly doubled the size of the country. Also, as Napoléon suggested, the purchase strengthened America in relation to Britain. The purchase also paved the way for westward expansion and exploration (by Lewis and Clark and Zebulon Pike).

5. The Battle of Tippecanoe destroyed Tecumseh's dream.

6. People in New England had been hurt by impressment and trade restrictions. They wanted to renew friendly business ties with Britain, not fight another war.

7. They traveled along the Missouri River.

## A New National Identity

### SECTION QUIZ
### Section 1

1. F; The Convention of 1818 established the border.
2. T
3. F; The war began because U.S. troops invaded Florida to capture Seminole raiders.
4. F; Most Americans did support them.
5. F; The Monroe Doctrine warned European nations not to interfere in the Americas.

### Section 2

1. j, Missouri
2. g, Henry Clay
3. h, John Quincy Adams
4. k, Missouri Compromise
5. d, Era of Good Feelings
6. e, Erie Canal
7. m, sectionalism
8. c, Cumberland Road
9. a, American System
10. b, Andrew Jackson

### Section 3

1. b, Washington Irving
2. d, historical fiction
3. c, spirituals

4. c, Hudson River school
5. a, state-funded schools

## CHAPTER TEST FORM A

| | |
|---|---|
| **1.** d | **6.** b |
| **2.** b | **7.** b |
| **3.** b | **8.** c |
| **4.** d | **9.** b |
| **5.** b | |

**10.** c

**11.** Washington Irving
**12.** Rush-Bagot Agreement
**13.** Hudson River school
**14.** Monroe Doctrine
**15.** John Quincy Adams
**16.** Era of Good Feelings
**17.** Erie Canal
**18.** James Monroe

| | |
|---|---|
| **19.** F | **23.** F |
| **20.** T | **24.** F |
| **21.** F | **25.** T |
| **22.** T | |

## CHAPTER TEST FORM B

1. The Monroe Doctrine warned European countries not to interfere with the Americas. It stated that the United States would recognize colonies that already existed in North and South America, and not interfere in the affairs of European nations. It declared the Western Hemisphere off-limits to future colonization by foreign powers. It also stated that the U.S. government would consider any European power's attempt to colonize or interfere with any nation in the Western Hemisphere to be a hostile act.

2. Henry Clay developed the American System.

3. This balance ensured that neither the North nor the South would have an unfair advantage in the representation of states in the federal government.

4. The spiritual developed from calling out text from the Bible.

5. Washington Irving's focus on American settings and characters, led painters in the United States to begin painting landscapes

that showed the history of America and the beauty of the land.

6. During the early and mid-1800s Americans were experiencing a period of religious revivalism. People held meetings for the purpose of strengthening and reawakening their religious faith.

7. Oregon Country and northern Maine were disputed by the United States and Great Britain.

# The Age of Jackson

## SECTION QUIZ
### Section 1
1. women
2. officeholders
3. Jacksonian Democracy
4. kitchen cabinet
5. Democrat
6. war hero
7. Martin Van Buren
8. Andrew Jackson
9. John Quincy Adams
10. democracy

### Section 2
1. c, Martin Van Buren
2. d, North
3. j, states' rights
4. a, Daniel Webster
5. g, Second Bank of the United States
6. i, south
7. e, Nullification Crisis
8. k, Tariff of Abominations
9. m, William Henry Harrison
10. h, regional

### Section 3
1. a, to open more land up for settlement by American farmers
2. d, those living east of the Mississippi River
3. d, by adopting American culture
4. c, Cherokee
5. a, He ignored it.

## CHAPTER TEST FORM A

| | |
|---|---|
| 1. c | 6. d |
| 2. c | 7. c |
| 3. c | 8. c |
| 4. d | 9. c |
| 5. b | |
| 10. d | |

| | |
|---|---|
| 11. F | 14. F |
| 12. T | 15. F |
| 13. F | 16. T |

| | |
|---|---|
| 17. a | 22. h |
| 18. k | 23. l |
| 19. i | 24. d |
| 20. b | 25. j |
| 21. f | |

## CHAPTER TEST FORM B

1. Jacksonian Democracy is the term for the period of expanding democracy during the 1820s and 1830s. Jacksonian Democracy included such reforms as public nominating conventions and changes in the qualifications needed to vote.

2. Ill feelings between northerners and southerners grew because of the tariff. The North wanted the tariff while the South did not. In fact, angry southerners named the tariff on woolen goods the "Tariff of Abominations," to show how much they hated it.

3. The court ruled that the state of Georgia had no legal power over the Cherokee, which was a distinct community. It also said that only the federal government, not the states, had authority over American Indians.

4. It authorized moving American Indians living east of the Mississippi River to lands in the West.

5. Manufacturing was an important part of the North's economy. Northerners supported tariffs because tariffs helped them compete with British factories.

6. Calhoun was from the South and joined southerners in protesting against the Tariff of Abominations. He said that the tariff went against the states' rights doctrine. He also said the federal govern-

Progress Assessment

ment should not favor one region over another. Most importantly, he said states had the right to reject, or "nullify," any federal law they thought was unfair. The issue was called the "nullification crisis."

**7.** The battle of Fort Lauderdale occurred last.

# Expanding West

## SECTION QUIZ
### Section 1

1. f, mountain men
2. e, Mormon Trail
3. c, John Jacob Astor
4. g, Oregon Country
5. h, Oregon Trail
6. k, Santa Fe Trail
7. d, Mormons
8. b, fur
9. a, Astoria
10. j, Salt Lake City

### Section 2

1. F; They were defeated by Mexican forces.
2. T
3. T
4. F; They had to become Mexican citizens, obey Mexican laws, and practice Roman Catholicism.
5. F; Mexico banned further American settlement or the importation of slaves.

### Section 3

1. Mexican Cession
2. James K. Polk
3. Rio Grande
4. Guadalupe Hidalgo
5. Mexico City
6. slave
7. Oregon
8. Californios
9. manifest destiny
10. Bear Flag Revolt

### Section 4

1. T
2. F; She was a freed slave.
3. F; Those who supplied the miners profited as well.

4. F; Gold was discovered at Sutter's Mill.
5. F; It attracted settlers from around the world.

## CHAPTER TEST FORM A

| | |
|---|---|
| **1.** d | **6.** a |
| **2.** c | **7.** b |
| **3.** c | **8.** a |
| **4.** a | **9.** c |
| **5.** b | |
| **10.** a | |
| **11.** F | **14.** F |
| **12.** F | **15.** T |
| **13.** T | |
| **16.** a | **21.** c |
| **17.** h | **22.** d |
| **18.** k | **23.** e |
| **19.** g | **24.** i |
| **20.** b | **25.** j |

## CHAPTER TEST FORM B

1. "Manifest destiny" was an idea that inspired many Americans to move west all the way to the Pacific Ocean in order to spread democracy. The slavery issue came up because there were debates about whether slavery should be allowed in the new territories.
2. The population boomed during The Gold Rush. Immigrants and Americans flocked to California to get rich quick and stayed to build a stable frontier society.
3. President Jackson did not want to annex Texas as a state because Texas would have entered the union as a slave state. He did not want to upset the balance between free and slave states. He also did not want to go to war with Mexico over Texas.
4. Under the treaty, Mexico turned over much of its northern territory to the United States. This land was called the Mexican Cession. It totaled more than 500,000 square miles and increased the size of the United States by almost 25 percent.
5. The U.S. government paid Mexico $10 million for the southern parts of what are now Arizona and New Mexico.
6. Stephen F. Austin started a colony on the Colorado River.

**7.** The California and Oregon Trails were the same length and took the same amount of time to travel.

# The New Republic

## UNIT TEST FORM A

| | |
|---|---|
| **1.** d | **11.** b |
| **2.** c | **12.** a |
| **3.** a | **13.** b |
| **4.** d | **14.** a |
| **5.** a | **15.** a |
| **6.** d | **16.** c |
| **7.** a | **17.** a |
| **8.** c | **18.** a |
| **9.** c | **19.** c |
| **10.** d | **20.** b |

**21.** b

| | |
|---|---|
| **22.** F | **27.** F |
| **23.** T | **28.** T |
| **24.** T | **29.** F |
| **25.** F | **30.** T |
| **26.** F | **31.** F |

**32.** Louisiana Purchase
**33.** Choctaw
**34.** Mormons
**35.** nominating conventions
**36.** USS *Constitution*
**37.** tariffs
**38.** mountain men
**39.** Second Bank of the United States
**40.** their northern territory

| | |
|---|---|
| **41.** f | **46.** e |
| **42.** h | **47.** a |
| **43.** i | **48.** d |
| **44.** g | **49.** c |
| **45.** k | **50.** l |

## UNIT TEST FORM B

**1.** Impressment is the practice of forcing people to serve in the army or navy. The British practiced impressments on sailors who had run away from the British navy. Trouble started when the British began searching American merchant ships and navy ships for runaway sailors, sometimes capturing U.S. citizens by mistake. Impressment violated U.S. neutrality, which led to the Embargo Act, and eventually led to the War of 1812.

**2.** They were founded on the same democratic and republican ideals as the new nation.

**3.** The American System was a plan introduced by Henry Clay that would make the United States more economically independent through internal improvements.

**4.** The Supreme Court ruled that the national bank was constitutional.

**5.** Many states changed voting qualifications, lowering or even eliminating property ownership requirements. Political parties began holding nominating conventions, which allowed party members, rather than just party leaders, to choose a party's candidates.

**6.** The Gadsden Purchase made the boundary with Mexico permanent. It gave the United States the southern parts of what are now Arizona and New Mexico. It guaranteed that any southern railroad to California would be built completely on American soil.

**7.** The legend would be completed by adding the term "Louisiana Purchase".

# The North

## SECTION QUIZ
### Section 1

**1.** h, Northeast
**2.** k, textile
**3.** f, mass production
**4.** c, Industrial Revolution
**5.** d, interchangeable
**6.** b, Great Britain
**7.** m, War of 1812
**8.** a, Eli Whitney
**9.** j, Samuel Slater
**10.** g, mills

### Section 2

**1.** F; Workers created trade unions.
**2.** T
**3.** T
**4.** F; It hired young, unmarried women from local farms.
**5.** F; Sarah Bagley founded this reform group.

Progress Assessment

## Section 3

1. m, Transportation Revolution
2. j, Robert Fulton
3. b, Chicago
4. e, *Gibbons* v. *Ogden*
5. i, railroad
6. c, coal
7. k, steamboat
8. h, Peter Cooper
9. l, steel
10. d, deforestation

## Section 4

1. d, Cyrus McCormick
2. b, they lowered
3. a, Morse code
4. a, sewing machine
5. b, telegraph

## CHAPTER TEST FORM A

| | |
|---|---|
| 1. c | 6. d |
| 2. c | 7. b |
| 3. d | 8. d |
| 4. a | 9. b |
| 5. b | 10. c |

11. b

| | |
|---|---|
| 12. F | 15. T |
| 13. T | 16. T |
| 14. T | |

| | |
|---|---|
| 17. g | 22. a |
| 18. h | 23. f |
| 19. j | 24. c |
| 20. i | 25. e |
| 21. b | |

## CHAPTER TEST FORM B

1. The Transportation Revolution made travel faster and more convenient. It reduced the time and cost of shipping. It led to the expansion of roads and canals. It also led to changes in the type of fuel used, from wood to coal. As it caused cities to grow, it increased the need for wood and led to an expansion of the lumber industry.
2. Samuel F. B. Morse perfected the telegraph.
3. It does not run on steam.
4. The Lowell system was developed by Francis Cabot Lowell. The system included a loom

that could both spin thread and weave cloth. It depended on the labor of young, unmarried women hired from local farms.

5. The Court ruled that federal law overruled state law. This ruling reinforced the federal government's authority over the states. In other words, the federal government had authority to regulate interstate commerce.
6. Samuel Slater defied Parliament.
7. any three of the following states: Maine, New York, Pennsylvania, Virginia, Kentucky, Missouri, Indiana, Michigan, Wisconsin

# The South

## SECTION QUIZ
## Section 1

1. fell
2. cotton
3. Eli Whitney
4. South
5. planters
6. slave trade
7. scientific agriculture
8. sugar cane
9. tobacco
10. Tredegar Iron Works

## Section 2

1. T
2. F, In the early 1800s only about one third of Southern families had slaves.
3. F, Yeomen were owners of small farms. They commonly owned few slaves or none at all.
4. T
5. T

## Section 3

1. slave
2. fields
3. drivers
4. home
5. plantations
6. property
7. auctions
8. family
9. heritage
10. Nat Turner's Rebellion

## CHAPTER TEST FORM A

**1.** a    **6.** c
**2.** b    **7.** b
**3.** c    **8.** b
**4.** b    **9.** c
**5.** c    **10.** d

**11.** T    **15.** T
**12.** F    **16.** F
**13.** T    **17.** F
**14.** T

**18.** spirituals    **22.** auctions
**19.** short-staple    **23.** tobacco
**20.** factors    **24.** religion
**21.** Yeoman

**25.** b

## CHAPTER TEST FORM B

**1.** Crop rotation involves changing the type of plant grown on a given plot of land each year. Part of scientific agriculture, crop rotation is meant to ensure healthy harvests by protecting the soil. It was introduced because farmers were focusing on growing cash crops and some scientists thought it was unhealthy to grow a single crop in the same spot year after year.
**2.** White southerners feared former slaves would try to encourage slave rebellions.
**3.** The quality of the roads made shipping by land very difficult.
**4.** Turner believed he was on a mission from God to free the slaves.
**5.** A yeoman was a white owner of a small farm who usually did not own slaves. Yeomen represented the largest portion, about 80 percent, of all southern farmers by 1860.
**6.** Drivers supervised the work of slaves. They made sure slaves followed orders and, if they did not, they carried out punishments. Answers may add that some slaves served as drivers.
**7.** 3, the brushes on the second roller

# New Movements in America

## SECTION QUIZ
### Section 1
**1.** b, Europe    **4.** c, middle class
**2.** a, the Northeast    **5.** a, tenements
**3.** d, nativists

### Section 2
**1.** k, transcendentalism
**2.** i, Ralph Waldo Emerson
**3.** f, Margaret Fuller
**4.** l, utopian communities
**5.** h, Nathaniel Hawthorne
**6.** g, *Moby-Dick*
**7.** b, Edgar Allan Poe
**8.** c, Emily Dickinson
**9.** d, Henry Wadsworth Longfellow
**10.** m, Walt Whitman

### Section 3
**1.** Second Great Awakening
**2.** Charles Grandison Finney
**3.** Lyman Beecher
**4.** temperance movement
**5.** Dorothea Dix
**6.** houses of correction
**7.** common-school
**8.** Samuel Gridley Howe
**9.** Catharine Beecher
**10.** Oberlin College

### Section 4
**1.** T
**2.** F, Antislavery reformers varied widely in their opinions regarding how much equality African American should have.
**3.** T
**4.** T
**5.** F, While the North was the center of abolitionist movement, there were many northerners who were not, for various reasons, abolitionists.

## Section 5
1. c, Sarah Grimké
2. d, Sojourner Truth
3. b, Seneca Falls Convention
4. a, Lucy Stone
5. b, Susan B. Anthony

## CHAPTER TEST FORM A
1. a
2. b
3. b
4. b
5. b
6. b
7. d
8. a
9. a

10. middle class
11. Second Great Awakening
12. Declaration of Sentiments
13. Dorothea Dix
14. American Anti-Slavery Society

15. a

16. h
17. i
18. e
19. f
20. c
21. g
22. j
23. a
24. d
25. b

## CHAPTER TEST FORM B
1. In the mid-1840s, Ireland experienced a potato blight, which caused the potato crop in the country to rot. This left many families with little or no food. As a result, many Irish people fled to the United States to escape starvation.
2. Answers may vary. Transcendentalist writers include Ralph Waldo Emerson, Margaret Fuller, and Henry David Thoreau.
3. The Seneca Falls Convention was the first public meeting about women's rights held in the United States. It brought the women's rights movement to the attention of many groups in the United States.
4. After visiting prisons in Massachusetts, Dorothea Dix brought the poor conditions of prisons to the attention of the Massachusetts government. As a result, the government made changes to the prison system.
5. The federal government prevented members of Congress from discussing any petition that promoted antislavery. This prevented emotional debates from occurring in Congress, but violated the First Amendment rights of the petitioners.
6. Garrison published a newspaper called the *Liberator* that spread the abolitionist message to a wide range of people. He also founded the American Anti-Slavery Society, which called for the immediate emancipation of slaves.
7. The various routes of the Underground Railroad all went in the same direction—north.

# A Divided Nation

## SECTION QUIZ
### Section 1
1. Missouri Compromise
2. Wilmot Proviso
3. sectionalism
4. Compromise of 1850
5. John C. Calhoun
6. Daniel Webster
7. Anthony Burns
8. Fugitive Slave Act
9. *Uncle Tom's Cabin*
10. Harriet Beecher Stowe

### Section 2
1. c, Franklin Pierce
2. b, Democrats
3. j, Stephen Douglas
4. f, Kansas-Nebraska Act
5. e, Kansas
6. d, John Brown
7. a, Charles Sumner
8. h, Preston Brooks
9. i, slavery
10. k, The Sack of Lawrence

### Section 3
1. j, Republican Party
2. e, James Buchanan
3. c, Dred Scott
4. k, Roger B. Taney
5. a, Abraham Lincoln
6. d, Freeport Doctrine
7. i, Lincoln-Douglas

**8.** g, John C. Frémont
**9.** m, Supreme Court
**10.** l, slavery

## Section 4
**1.** F, John Brown led the raid.
**2.** F, African Americans did not come, fearing punishment.
**3.** T
**4.** T
**5.** T

## CHAPTER TEST FORM A

| | |
|---|---|
| **1.** d | **6.** d |
| **2.** b | **7.** d |
| **3.** a | **8.** a |
| **4.** a | **9.** a |
| **5.** d | |

**10.** c

**11.** Confederate
**12.** Compromise of 1850
**13.** Dred Scott
**14.** Kansas-Nebraska Act
**15.** Republican

| | |
|---|---|
| **16.** e | **21.** a |
| **17.** k | **22.** b |
| **18.** g | **23.** h |
| **19.** d | **24.** j |
| **20.** c | **25.** f |

## CHAPTER TEST FORM B
**1.** John Brown led the Pottawatomie Massacre.
**2.** In his inaugural address President Lincoln told Americans that he believed in the power of citizens to change the government through majority rule. He stated that the federal government would maintain control of property in the South and that the Union would not begin a war with the South.
**3.** In the election of 1860, the Democrats could not agree upon a single candidate, so the party divided into southern and northern Democrats. This act split the Democratic vote between two candidates. The Republicans united to support Lincoln and he won both the popular vote and the electoral college vote.

**4.** The Freeport Doctrine placed the question of slavery back into the hands of American voters and helped Douglas win the Senate race.
**5.** Dred Scott was a slave who sued for his freedom in federal court after living in free territory.
**6.** The Missouri Compromise of 1820 had created a border between slave and free states. President Polk wanted to extend the border and divide the Mexican Cession into two parts, slave and free. Other leaders proposed that the issue of slavery in the territory should be determined by popular sovereignty. In other words, the people who lived in the territory should vote on the question of slavery themselves.
**7.** Answers may vary. The cartoon shows that the issue of slavery caused heated debate on both sides of the issue. The abolitionist movement caused violent opposition on both sides of the issue.

# The Nation Expands

## UNIT TEST FORM A

| | |
|---|---|
| **1.** b | **9.** c |
| **2.** b | **10.** c |
| **3.** d | **11.** b |
| **4.** b | **12.** a |
| **5.** d | **13.** a |
| **6.** c | **14.** a |
| **7.** a | **15.** c |
| **8.** d | |

| | |
|---|---|
| **16.** T | **23.** F |
| **17.** T | **24.** F |
| **18.** F | **25.** T |
| **19.** T | **26.** F |
| **20.** T | **27.** T |
| **21.** F | **28.** T |
| **22.** F | **29.** T |

**30.** d

**31.** Industrial Revolution
**32.** water frame
**33.** textiles
**34.** trade union
**35.** *Gibbons* v. *Ogden*
**36.** *Clermont*
**37.** telegraph

**38.** *Tom Thumb*
**39.** sectionalism
**40.** Harriet Beecher Stowe

| | |
|---|---|
| **41.** f | **46.** l |
| **42.** j | **47.** a |
| **43.** g | **48.** h |
| **44.** e | **49.** k |
| **45.** b | **50.** c |

## UNIT TEST FORM B

**1.** Sarah Bagley fought to ensure that employees of private businesses got the same 10-hour working day that public employees already had.

**2.** Nat Turner's Rebellion prompted many states to strengthen their slave codes.

**3.** John Brown wanted to promote his anti-slavery ideas by starting an uprising at Harpers Ferry in Virginia. His goal was to seize weapons from the federal reserve there.

**4.** Cotton was cheap to market. It was light, which made it cheaper to transport over long distances than heavier crops. Unlike food crops, harvested cotton could be stored for a longer time.

**5.** Senator Stephen Douglas proposed the Kansas-Nebraska Act. He wanted a U.S. railroad to be built that ran from Chicago to the Pacific Ocean.

**6.** Answers may vary but should include two of the following: A) The supply of factory labor was lower in America than in Britain because land was more available and less expensive. Americans preferred to buy farms rather than work in factories. B) British workers were willing to work for lower wages than American workers, so American factory owners had higher costs. C) British workers were more skilled than American workers, so they could produce large amounts of goods for less. As a result, the British could charge less money for their products, making it difficult for American manufacturers to compete. All of these factors discouraged American investment in new factories.

**7.** Answers may vary. Romantic painters focused on the beauty and simplicity of nature, which provided a contrast to the huge cities that were rising up across the country. The painting illustrates human beings living in harmony with nature, an ideal that Romantic artists believed in.

## The Civil War

### SECTION QUIZ
### Section 1
**1.** T
**2.** F; He promised not to end slavery.
**3.** T
**4.** T
**5.** F; It was the idea that Great Britain would support the Confederacy because it needed the South's cotton.

### Section 2
**1.** Thomas "Stonewall" Jackson
**2.** First Battle of Bull Run
**3.** George B. McClellan
**4.** Robert E. Lee
**5.** Seven Days' Battles
**6.** Battle of Antietam
**7.** navy
**8.** Ironclads
**9.** John Ericsson
**10.** *Virginia*

### Section 3
**1.** b, Mississippi River
**2.** a, Ulysses S. Grant
**3.** b, Battle of Shiloh
**4.** d, Vicksburg
**5.** c, Cherokee

### Section 4
**1.** f, emancipation
**2.** a, Abraham Lincoln
**3.** g, Emancipation Proclamation
**4.** c, contrabands
**5.** m, 54th Massachusetts Infantry
**6.** l, Sally Louisa Tompkins
**7.** i, habeas corpus
**8.** e, draft
**9.** b, Clara Barton
**10.** d, Copperheads

Progress Assessment

## Section 5

1. j, Stonewall Jackson
2. c, Battle of Gettysburg
3. f, Gettysburg Address
4. l, Wilderness Campaign
5. m, William Tecumseh Sherman
6. k, total war
7. g, Jefferson Davis
8. a, Atlanta
9. b, Appomattox Courthouse
10. d, four years

## CHAPTER TEST FORM A

1. a
2. b
3. d
4. b
5. d

6. d
7. b
8. d
9. a

10. a

11. F
12. T
13. T

14. T
15. T

16. g
17. j
18. d
19. b
20. a

21. i
22. h
23. e
24. f
25. c

## CHAPTER TEST FORM B

1. Many civilians were able to contribute to the war effort by working in factories and on farms. Women provided medical services to wounded soldiers and often performed the chores previously done by the men who were now away at war. Clara Barton, who founded the Red Cross, organized supplies and medicines which were brought to soldiers on the battlefield. She also worked at field hospitals.
2. The Union went into the Civil War with the idea that it would be easy to defeat the South. The First Battle of Bull Run was a hard-fought battle that showed the North that the Civil War would not be won quickly or easily.
3. The Battle of Antietam stopped the Confederacy's northward advance.
4. The goal of the Union's western campaign

was to gain control of the Mississippi River. The Union victory in the Siege of Vicksburg helped the Union accomplish this goal.
5. He referred to liberty, equality, and democracy because he wanted to remind people of the reasons for fighting the Civil War.
6. Control of the border states gave the Union an advantage. Specifically, Kentucky and Missouri controlled parts of important rivers and Maryland separated the Union's capital from the North.
7. This cartoon shows Scott's plan to destroy the South's economy with a naval blockade of southern ports. The giant snake, which represents the Union, shows the North's power and ability to crush the South economically.

# Reconstruction

## SECTION QUIZ
## Section 1

1. F, Soldiers returned home to find most everything destroyed.
2. T
3. F, The Freedmen's Bureau provided relief to freed people and certain poor people in the South.
4. F, The Thirteenth Amendment made slavery illegal in the United States, thereby legitimizing the Emancipation Proclamation.
5. T
6. F, The Ten Percent plan was President Lincoln's plan for readmitting the southern states to the union.

## Section 2

1. b, Black Codes
2. h, Radical Republicans
3. i, Reconstruction Acts
4. j, Thaddeus Stevens
5. f, impeachment
6. e, Fifteenth Amendment
7. a, Andrew Johnson
8. k, Thirteenth Amendment
9. l, Ulysses S. Grant
10. c, Congress

## Section 3

1. Republican
2. Hiram Revels
3. African Americans
4. Ku Klux Klan
5. Redeemers
6. segregation
7. Jim Crow
8. poll tax
9. sharecroppers
10. Civil Rights Act

## CHAPTER TEST FORM A

| | |
|---|---|
| 1. d | 6. b |
| 2. d | 7. a |
| 3. b | 8. a |
| 4. c | 9. c |
| 5. c | 10. a |

11. c

12. Fourteenth
13. impeach
14. voting
15. Compromise of 1877
16. Ten Percent Plan
17. Radical Republicans
18. Jim Crow laws

| | |
|---|---|
| 19. T | 23. F |
| 20. F | 24. T |
| 21. T | 25. T |
| 22. F | |

## CHAPTER TEST FORM B

1. The Civil War damaged the South's economy. Confederate currency was worthless and many banks failed and merchants went bankrupt. After the war there was a southern crop failure, which drove up the price of food. As a result, many southerners faced starvation.
2. The Thirteenth Amendment to the Constitution made slavery illegal throughout the United States.
3. The Compromise of 1877 called for the removal of all federal troops from the South, officially ending Reconstruction in the United States.
4. Under Reconstruction governments many African Americans began to be elected to public office and gain power. In addition, federal troops were stationed in southern states to restore order to the Union. This angered many southern Democrats, some of whom formed the Ku Klux Klan in response. The organization terrorized African Americans and fought against Reconstruction governments.
5. The Fifteenth Amendment granted African American men the right to vote. Congressional Republicans believed that African American voters would strengthen their support in Congress.
6. Black Codes were laws passed by southern states that limited the freedom of African Americans.
7. South Carolina had the highest concentration of African American state legislators in 1870.

# The Nation Breaks Apart

## UNIT TEST FORM A

| | |
|---|---|
| 1. a | 9. a |
| 2. c | 10. d |
| 3. a | 11. c |
| 4. c | 12. b |
| 5. d | 13. c |
| 6. a | 14. d |
| 7. a | 15. c |
| 8. d | |

| | |
|---|---|
| 16. T | 20. F |
| 17. T | 21. F |
| 18. T | 22. F |
| 19. T | |

23. William Tecumseh Sherman
24. Fort Sumter
25. North
26. Seven Days' Battles
27. habeas corpus
28. Clara Barton
29. Reconstruction
30. Ku Klux Klan
31. Thirteenth
32. First Battle of Bull Run
33. Battle of Gettysburg
34. Gettysburg Address

35. d

Progress Assessment

**36.** j

**37.** i

**38.** d

**39.** a

**40.** b

**41.** e

**42.** c

**43.** f

**44.** l

**45.** g

## UNIT TEST FORM B

1. The Civil War began when Confederate troops fired on Fort Sumter.

2. The Union blockade severely damaged the southern economy. It prevented the South from selling or receiving goods, and the loss of trade meant a loss of revenue for the Confederacy.

3. President Lincoln suspended habeas corpus in order to silence those who were opposed to the Civil War. As a result, citizens could no longer benefit from the constitutional protection against unlawful imprisonment. Many of the Union's enemies were jailed.

4. President Johnson's Reconstruction plan allowed former leaders of the Confederacy to hold positions of power in southern states. Congress disliked the idea of giving Confederate leaders power and therefore refused to support President Johnson's Reconstruction plan.

5. The Redeemers established the poll tax, which was a special tax people had to pay before they could vote. African Americans often could not afford this tax. The Redeemers also introduced Jim Crow laws that enforced the legal segregation of African Americans.

6. At harvest time, sharecroppers had to give most of their crop to the landowner. They were able to sell the remaining crop in the hope of saving enough money to buy their own farms. However, most sharecroppers had to buy goods on credit from the landowner. When they sold their crops, they hoped to pay off this debt, but often could not. As a result, they were unable to save money and remained in a cycle of debt.

7. According to the map, slavery was abolished in Texas, most of Louisiana, Arkansas, Mississippi, Alabama, Florida, Georgia, South Carolina, North Carolina, West Virginia, and Virginia by the Emancipation Proclamation.

## Americans Move West

### SECTION QUIZ
### Section 1

1. f, frontier
2. d, Comstock Lode
3. a, boomtowns
4. h, open range
5. m, vaqueros
6. b, cattle drive
7. c, Chisholm Trail
8. j, Pony Express
9. l, transcontinental railroad
10. i, Pacific Railway Acts

### Section 2

1. buffalo
2. Treaty of Fort Laramie
3. reservations
4. Crazy Horse
5. Sitting Bull
6. Battle of Little Big Horn
7. Long Walk
8. Nez Percé
9. Geronimo
10. Massacre at Wounded Knee

### Section 3

1. f, Homestead Act
2. h, Morill Act
3. e, Exodusters
4. l, sodbusters
5. d, dry farming
6. c, deflation
7. a, Annie Bidwell
8. i, National Grange
9. m, William Jennings Bryan
10. j, Populist Party

### CHAPTER TEST FORM A

| | |
|---|---|
| **1.** a | **6.** d |
| **2.** d | **7.** c |
| **3.** a | **8.** a |
| **4.** c | **9.** b |
| **5.** b | **10.** b |
| **11.** T | **13.** F |
| **12.** T | **14.** T |
| **15.** d | |

| | |
|---|---|
| **16.** e | **21.** j |
| **17.** d | **22.** c |
| **18.** f | **23.** h |
| **19.** b | **24.** g |
| **20.** i | **25.** a |

## CHAPTER TEST FORM B

1. The winters were extremely harsh, adding to a ranching situation that was already bad because the huge cattle herds had eaten most of the prairie grass. Thousands of cattle died and many ranchers did not survive financially.
2. The federal government passed the Pacific Railway Acts, granting railroad companies loans and land grants to help pay for construction.
3. It was the first major treaty between the U.S. government and the Plains Indians.
4. The Homestead Act was federal legislation that granted government land to small farmers. The promise of land led people from New England and similar regions to move because farmland there was becoming scarce or expensive.
5. The Dawes General Allotment Act tried to reduce traditional influences on Native American society by making land ownership private. This demonstrated the belief of some reformers that Native Americans should adopt the ways of white people. Traditionally, ownership of land was shared among Native Americans. The Act ultimately took about two-thirds of Native American land.
6. Sitting Bull was a leader of the Lakota Sioux. He argued against selling the Black Hills to the U.S. government, which wanted the land because gold had been found there. Along with Crazy Horse, Sitting Bull led Sioux forces in the Battle of Little Bighorn, also known as "Custer's Last Stand." The Sioux won, but Sitting Bull was killed years later, in 1890, by reservation police.
7. They are closely linked, but it's not clear whether higher prices caused an increase in wheat production, or overproduction of wheat caused prices to drop.

# The Industrial Age

## SECTION QUIZ
### Section 1
1. Second Industrial Revolution
2. Steel
3. Bessemer process
4. Thomas Edison
5. patent
6. Alexander Graham Bell
7. Orville and Wilbur Wright
8. Henry Ford
9. Edwin L. Drake
10. gasoline

### Section 2
1. T
2. T
3. F, They were both very successful.
4. T
5. F, As the new law was difficult to enforce, corporations continued to grow in size at the end of the 19th century.

### Section 3
1. m, specialization
2. c, Frederick W. Taylor
3. b, collective bargaining
4. h, Mary Harris Jones
5. d, Haymarket Riot
6. a, American Federation of Labor
7. f, Knights of Labor
8. l, Samuel Gompers
9. e, Homestead Strike
10. k, Pullman Strike

## CHAPTER TEST FORM A

| | |
|---|---|
| **1.** b | **6.** a |
| **2.** d | **7.** a |
| **3.** d | **8.** d |
| **4.** a | **9.** c |
| **5.** c | |

10. c

11. Alexander Graham Bell
12. Stockholders
13. Knights of Labor
14. gas
15. Haymarket Square

**16.** g          **21.** f
**17.** d          **22.** l
**18.** h          **23.** c
**19.** e          **24.** j
**20.** i          **25.** b

## CHAPTER TEST FORM B

1. The Homestead strike occurred because a plan to buy new machinery and cut jobs upset workers. Refusing to negotiate with the union, company leaders locked workers out of the plant. Workers then seized control of the plant. The company brought in detectives to retake control of the plant. A battle between the workers and the detectives left sixteen people dead.

2. The railroad industry grew because the reduced price of steel made it cheaper to build railroads. Railroad companies used steel to build thousands of miles of track. Service improved with the design of elegant passenger and sleeping cars. The growth of the industry led to its employment of more workers.

3. The Knights of Labor invited both skilled and unskilled laborers to become members. The American Federation of Labor limited its membership to skilled workers.

4. Stockholders are, through the money they invest through the purchase of stock shares, the owners of a corporation. Although stockholders actually own the corporation, they do not run its day-to-day business. Instead, they elect a board of directors that chooses the corporation's main leaders.

5. Specialization is when workers repeat a single step again and again, as in an assembly line. Specialization led to increased production and brought costs down. However, it also made workers tired, bored, and more likely to be injured.

6. The Wright brothers invented the first lightweight airplane, which was powered by a small, gas-powered engine. The airplane later revolutionized the way Americans travel.

7. 1890

# Immigrants and Urban Life

## SECTION QUIZ
### Section 1

1. j, old immigrants
2. i, new immigrants
3. l, steerage
4. f, Ellis Island
5. b, Angel Island
6. a, Amadeo Giannini
7. c, benevolent societies
8. m, sweatshops
9. h, nativists
10. d, Chinese Exclusion Act

### Section 2

1. immigrants
2. railroad
3. slaughterhouses
4. skyscrapers
5. Mass transit
6. subways
7. suburbs
8. Joseph Pulitzer
9. department stores
10. Central Park

### Section 3

1. c, Jacob Riis
2. d, air pollution
3. b, New York State Tenement House Act
4. a, education, recreation, and social activities
5. c, Florence Kelley

## CHAPTER TEST FORM A

1. c          **6.** a
2. b          **7.** a
3. b          **8.** a
4. c          **9.** b
5. c

10. d

11. new
12. New York State Tenement House Act
13. benevolent societies
14. mass transit
15. mass culture
16. suburbs

**17.** steerage
**18.** nativists

| | |
|---|---|
| **19.** T | **23.** T |
| **20.** T | **24.** F |
| **21.** F | **25.** F |
| **22.** T | |

## CHAPTER TEST FORM B

**1.** Skyscrapers were built to use ground space more efficiently. Mass transit systems were created to move people cheaply and quickly to and from work. Many people began moving to suburbs outside of downtown areas.

**2.** Newspaper publishing boomed in the cities. Shopping opportunities grew with the creation of department stores. The St. Louis World's Fair produced many new ideas. Public entertainment became more widely available.

**3.** Unsanitary conditions led to the spread of deadly diseases such as cholera, tuberculosis, typhoid, and influenza. This caused particularly high death rates among children. People in tenements were also exposed to great risk from fire and crime.

**4.** Immigrants were attracted by the possibility of jobs, land, religious freedom, and the chance to start new lives.

**5.** Many European immigrants settled in Chicago, as did many African Americans fleeing discrimination in the South. Major railroad lines ran through Chicago, which put the city at the heart of trade in lumber, grain, and meat. This trade provided lots of work for Chicago's growing number of new residents.

**6.** Only Chinese people whose fathers were U.S. citizens were allowed to immigrate to the United States.

**7.** The population of Chicago increased by over one million people from 1880 to 1900.

# A Growing America

## UNIT TEST FORM A

| | |
|---|---|
| **1.** b | **11.** c |
| **2.** b | **12.** b |
| **3.** d | **13.** c |
| **4.** d | **14.** b |
| **5.** d | **15.** a |
| **6.** c | **16.** a |
| **7.** a | **17.** c |
| **8.** b | **18.** d |
| **9.** d | **19.** d |
| **10.** d | **20.** b |

**21.** telegrams
**22.** Nez Percé
**23.** social Darwinism
**24.** open range
**25.** moving assembly line
**26.** horizontal integration
**27.** Homestead Strike
**28.** Long Walk
**29.** Homestead Act

**30.** d

| | |
|---|---|
| **31.** f | **36.** a |
| **32.** c | **37.** b |
| **33.** j | **38.** d |
| **34.** e | **39.** g |
| **35.** k | **40.** h |
| **41.** F | **46.** F |
| **42.** F | **47.** T |
| **43.** F | **48.** F |
| **44.** F | **49.** T |
| **45.** F | **50.** T |

## UNIT TEST FORM B

**1.** In the Homestead Strike, the governor of Pennsylvania used the state militia to restore order. In the Pullman Strike, President Grover Cleveland ordered federal troops to end the strike.

**2.** Exodusters were the 20,000 to 40,000 African Americans who moved to Kansas from the South in 1879. The name shows their similarity to the Hebrew slaves who fled from Egypt in the Bible's book of Exodus. Exodusters felt they had escaped from a land of chains to a promised land.

**3.** These immigrants had left Mexico.

**4.** The discovery of gold in Colorado brought thousands of miners to the West. This in turn caused clashes between the new settlers and Plains Indians. The U.S. government negotiated treaties with the Native Americans in 1861, confining them to reservations. This made it nearly impossible for the Native Americans to continue buffalo hunting for food and hides.

**5.** Answers may vary in detail. Refineries were built in which crude, unprocessed oil was turned into other products, such as gasoline and kerosene. Gasoline was (and still is) used for cars and planes. Kerosene was the fuel commonly used for cooking, heating, and lighting.

**6.** Some nativists were violent toward immigrants, and others advocated laws that would stop or limit immigration.

**7.** The cartoon shows Rockefeller's power by making him appear large in size and by putting the White House in the palm of his hand.

# Progressive Spirit of Reform

## SECTION QUIZ
### Section 1
1. Political machines
2. Progressives
3. muckrakers
4. settlement
5. Seventeenth Amendment
6. recall
7. initiative
8. referendum
9. William Marcy Tweed (Boss Tweed)
10. Robert M. La Follette

### Section 2
1. F; Adult wages were low, so children often worked as well.
2. F; Massachusetts passed the first minimum wage law in 1912.
3. T
4. T

5. F; This economic system is called capitalism.

### Section 3
1. d, Eighteenth Amendment
2. a, Alice Paul
3. i, Nineteenth Amendment
4. b, Booker T. Washington
5. g, Ida B. Wells
6. f, grandfather clauses
7. l, Wyoming
8. k, W. E. B. Du Bois
9. j, Smith College
10. c, Chinese

### Section 4
1. c
2. a
3. b
4. d
5. a

## CHAPTER TEST FORM A
1. a
2. a
3. c
4. a
5. b
6. c
7. b
8. c
9. b
10. a
11. d
12. c
13. National Association for the Advancement of Colored People (NAACP)
14. spoils system
15. Alice Paul
16. William Howard Taft
17. capitalism
18. Seventeenth
19. F
20. T
21. F
22. T
23. T
24. F
25. T

## CHAPTER TEST FORM B
1. Capitalism is an economic system in which most industries are run by private businesses, and competition determines how much goods costs. Socialism is a system under which the government owns industries and sets prices.
2. Stanton and Anthony founded the National American Woman Suffrage

Association (NAWSA). Paul founded the National Woman's Party (NWP). The NAWSA devoted itself to getting women the vote. They organized volunteers and argued that women should have a say in creating the laws that affected them. The second group was more controversial. The NWP called attention to the issue of women's suffrage through public demonstrations and parades.

3. The Woman's Christian Temperance Union (WCTU) pushed for the Eighteenth Amendment, which banned the production, sale, and transport of alcoholic beverages.

4. Possible answer: Despite refusing to welcome immigrants, women, and African Americans into its ranks, the AFL likely outlasted the IWW because it did not seek to undermine the American system of capitalism.

5. The NAACP used the courts to fight discrimination. For example, in 1915 it won the case of *Guinn* v. *United States*, which made grandfather clauses illegal.

6. Under the spoils system, winners of elections rewarded their political backers with jobs, even if they were unqualified. The Pendleton Service Act set up a merit system for assigning some government jobs. It required that more than 10 percent of applicants for civil service jobs pass an exam before they could be hired.

7. The Sixteenth Amendment took longest to ratify. It made it possible for the government to tax the income of individual citizens.

# America as a World Power

## SECTION QUIZ
### Section 1
1. imperialism
2. isolationism
3. William H. Seward
4. Hawaii
5. Matthew Perry
6. Open Door Policy
7. spheres of influence

8. Boxer Rebellion
9. Beijing
10. United States

## Section 2
| | |
|---|---|
| 1. d | 4. a |
| 2. b | 5. c |
| 3. b | |

## Section 3
| | |
|---|---|
| 1. g | 6. m |
| 2. j | 7. k |
| 3. l | 8. d |
| 4. b | 9. c |
| 5. e | 10. h |

## CHAPTER TEST FORM A
| | |
|---|---|
| 1. d | 6. a |
| 2. a | 7. c |
| 3. a | 8. b |
| 4. c | 9. b |
| 5. b | 10. a |

11. b

12. Queen Liliuokalani
13. Commodore Matthew Perry
14. spheres of influence
15. the Isthmus of Panama

| | |
|---|---|
| 16. e | 21. c |
| 17. j | 22. g |
| 18. a | 23. i |
| 19. f | 24. l |
| 20. h | 25. d |

## CHAPTER TEST FORM B
1. In the late 1800s and early 1900s the United States expanded its influence in the Pacific and Latin America.
2. Cuba was fighting for its independence from Spain; the United States sent the battleship *Maine* to Havana Harbor to protect American economic interests; the *Maine* exploded and Spain was blamed; Congress passed a resolution stating that Cuba was independent; Spain declared war on America; McKinley asked Congress to pass a declaration of war on Spain.
3. The United States wanted to be the most dominant power in the Western Hemisphere. To do this, the United States

had to intervene in European nations' disputes in Latin America—and hopefully end up with control over Latin America. The United States also wanted to expand its economy with overseas trading bases, U.S.-owned overseas industry, and by controlling or profiting from others' trade economies.

4. Aguinaldo helped the United States take control of Manila from Spain in the 1898 war. Spain surrendered the Philippines to the United States, which then decided to annex it rather than grant its freedom. This action prompted Aguinaldo to lead a guerrilla war against U.S. forces in the Philippines until 1902.

5. about 7,800 miles

6. Under Washington, there was to be <u>no involvement</u> in other nations of the Western Hemisphere. Then, under the Monroe Doctrine, the mission was to <u>defend U.S. interests from European powers</u> by keeping them out of the area. Under the Roosevelt Corollary, the goal was to <u>police wrongdoing by Western Hemisphere nations</u>—mostly Latin American ones. Then, under Taft's Dollar Diplomacy, the goal was to <u>promote U.S. economic interests in Latin America</u> specifically. Finally, under Wilson, the mission of the United States was to <u>promote and protect democracy in the Western Hemisphere</u>—again, mostly in Latin America.

# World War I

## SECTION QUIZ
### Section 1

1. Nationalism
2. militarism
3. Archduke Francis Ferdinand
4. Central Powers
5. western front
6. Trench warfare
7. machine guns
8. stalemate
9. blockaded
10. U-boats

### Section 2

1. f, *Lusitania*
2. m, Zimmerman Note
3. l, Woodrow Wilson
4. i, Selective Service Act
5. a, Committee on Public Information
6. b, Espionage Act of 1917
7. e, Liberty bonds
8. k, War Industries Board
9. d, Jeannette Rankin
10. g, National War Labor Board

### Section 3

1. T
2. T
3. F; group of Russians known as the Bolsheviks
4. T
5. F; It was the 11th hour, 11th day, and the 11th month.

### Section 4

1. b, League of Nations
2. d, reparations
3. b, Treaty of Versailles
4. a, Henry Cabot Lodge
5. c, Kansas

## CHAPTER TEST FORM A

| | |
|---|---|
| 1. b | 7. b |
| 2. d | 8. c |
| 3. c | 9. b |
| 4. c | 10. d |
| 5. c | 11. d |
| 6. a | |

12. c

13. stalemate
14. women
15. Archduke Francis Ferdinand
16. Fourteen Points
17. Nationalism

| | |
|---|---|
| 18. e | 22. b |
| 19. j | 23. h |
| 20. a | 24. d |
| 21. g | 25. c |

## CHAPTER TEST FORM B

1. In November 1917, Russia's government was overthrown by Communists. Russian

soldiers were deserting, and the Russian people were starving. So Russia signed a peace treaty with the Central Powers in March 1918.

**2.** American Expeditionary Force

**3.** In June 1914 the Archduke of Austria-Hungary and his wife were killed by a Serbian nationalist while visiting Sarajevo. Austria-Hungary declared war on Serbia. Russia was committed to protecting Serbia, so Russia declared war on Austria-Hungary. Germany declared war on Russia and France and marched into Belgium. Britain, which had pledged to support Belgium, declared war on Germany.

**4.** 8.5 million

**5.** The Germans probably would have captured Paris and forced the French to surrender.

**6.** President Wilson stated that: "The world must be made safe for democracy." The Allied Powers; possible answer: Many young men in both the Central Powers and the Allied Powers died during World War I. As a result, this huge loss of life caused a labor shortage in these countries. A decrease in production no doubt affected the economics of both the Central and Allied Powers.

# The Beginning of Modern America

## UNIT TEST FORM A

| | |
|---|---|
| **1.** c | **10.** d |
| **2.** b | **11.** c |
| **3.** a | **12.** b |
| **4.** b | **13.** d |
| **5.** b | **14.** d |
| **6.** a | **15.** a |
| **7.** c | **16.** a |
| **8.** d | **17.** b |
| **9.** c | |

**18.** c

**19.** imperialism
**20.** *Lusitania*
**21.** trench
**22.** referendum
**23.** arbitration

**24.** Nineteenth
**25.** dollar diplomacy
**26.** yellow journalism
**27.** influenza epidemic
**28.** Marne
**29.** nationalism

| | |
|---|---|
| **30.** T | **36.** F |
| **31.** F | **37.** T |
| **32.** T | **38.** T |
| **33.** F | **39.** F |
| **34.** T | **40.** T |
| **35.** T | |

| | |
|---|---|
| **41.** l | **46.** h |
| **42.** f | **47.** d |
| **43.** e | **48.** g |
| **44.** c | **49.** j |
| **45.** a | **50.** k |

## UNIT TEST FORM B

**1.** The recall allowed voters to force a corrupt politician out of office before the next election. The initiative allowed voters to propose new laws by collecting signatures on a petition. The referendum permitted voters to approve or reject laws that had already been proposed or passed by the government.

**2.** For many families to make enough money, all of their members had to be working.

**3.** Mexico, Cuba, the Philippines, China, Japan

**4.** Because the Philippines and Hawaii were considered U.S. territories, U.S. actions in these areas were not thought of as a violation of the country's isolationism.

**5.** Answers will vary but may include the following: Pershing didn't want American soldiers to be scattered among British and French soldiers, where they would have no identity as Americans. He didn't want them to be led by French officers who might not speak English, or by British officers who might not inspire them like a fellow American would. He didn't want American soldiers who had become friends in training camp to be split up. He

# Answer Key

wanted Americans fighting for and with each other.

6. Tanks could not be stopped by machine gun fire and could roll over enemy trenches and fire on them.

7. Answers will vary but may include the following: *Schenck* v. *United States* is important because it said the U.S. government could limit free speech in a time of war. This reflected the change in U.S. policy from isolationism to imperialism. Going to war was now seen as important to the United States, in order to gain territories. Protesting war was therefore harmful to the United States and could not be protected by the First Amendment's right to freedom of speech. Before 1919, the Supreme Court had never had a case where it had to interpret the limits of the First Amendment. In *Schenck* it decided that the right of American citizens to free speech was not more important than the successful conduct of war. If protest hurt America's ability to win a war, then protest could not be allowed. During this period, the United States intervened militarily and economically in Mexico, Panama, Cuba, the Philippines, Hawaii, Puerto Rico, Japan, and China.

# The Roaring Twenties

## SECTION QUIZ
### Section 1
1. m, Warren G. Harding
2. c, Calvin Coolidge
3. l, trickle-down theory
4. k, Teapot Dome Scandal
5. h, Kellogg-Briand Pact
6. e, Henry Ford
7. i, Model T
8. b, moving assembly line
9. g, installment plan
10. f, Herbert Hoover

### Section 2
1. flappers
2. Red Scare
3. American Civil Liberties

4. Anarchists
5. Emergency Quota
6. Twenty-first Amendment
7. fundamentalism
8. Great Migration
9. Ku Klux Klan
10. Marcus Garvey

### Section 3
1. national radio networks
2. talkie
3. Jazz Age
4. Louis Armstrong
5. Harlem Renaissance
6. Langston Hughes
7. Lost Generation
8. expatriates
9. F. Scott Fitzgerald
10. Nobel Prize

## CHAPTER TEST FORM A
1. b    6. b
2. b    7. d
3. c    8. b
4. b    9. a
5. c

10. c

11. T    14. F
12. F    15. T
13. T

16. f    21. b
17. e    22. c
18. i    23. a
19. j    24. k
20. g    25. d

## CHAPTER TEST FORM B
1. President Harding's "trickle-down" incentive plan first set the economic boom in motion. It helped business bounce back from the postwar recession, creating new jobs with better pay.

2. The pros were that workers got $5 a day (instead of the usual $2 or $3), the workday was reduced to 8 hours, and Ford hired African Americans and disabled people, whom other employers refused to hire. The cons were that the work was very

fast-paced and repetitive, leaving workers exhausted.

**3.** There had never been a Catholic president before, and some Americans were afraid that Smith would be controlled by the pope or by other Catholic Church officials, risking U.S. independence.

**4.** Flappers were controversial because they openly challenged ideas about how women were supposed to behave and what they were allowed to do.

**5.** Answers will vary but may include the following: Sacco and Vanzetti were Italian immigrants arrested in 1920 for the robbery and murder of a factory paymaster and his guard. Sacco and Vanzetti were anarchists—they didn't believe in organized government. This made them fit the popular idea of the dangerous, radical immigrant out to destroy America that so many Americans were afraid of at the time. The two men were found guilty even though there was very little evidence to prove they committed the crime. Both were executed in 1927.

**6.** Garvey encouraged black people around the world to express pride in their culture. Black nationalism was the idea that black people should establish economic independence from white society by starting their own businesses and communities.

**7.** Possible answers: Bryan said people were using science to attack religious faith. They called evolution science when it really wasn't, and they were using science to support atheism (the belief that there is no God). Science is supposed to be objective, and to focus on the machines that support society. When it's used to promote atheism, then it's not really science, it's opinion dressed up as science (what he referred to as "so-called science"); Darrow said banning the teaching of evolution in public schools at the time would just pave the way for more censorship of ideas by the government. It could even lead to a war between different religions, as each

tries to make it illegal to teach any idea that it doesn't approve of.

# The Great Depression

## SECTION QUIZ
### Section 1
1. bull market
2. buying on margin
3. bear market
4. Black Tuesday
5. business cycle
6. President Hoover
7. Bonus Army
8. Douglas MacArthur
9. Franklin D. Roosevelt
10. Emergency Relief

### Section 2
| | |
|---|---|
| 1. h | 6. b |
| 2. d | 7. j |
| 3. k | 8. a |
| 4. e | 9. i |
| 5. c | 10. f |

### Section 3
1. F; The Great Plains were destroyed because of severe drought.
2. T
3. T
4. T
5. F; Critics believe it did not end the Great Depression.

### CHAPTER TEST FORM A
| | |
|---|---|
| 1. b | 6. b |
| 2. a | 7. c |
| 3. d | 8. d |
| 4. a | 9. c |
| 5. c | |

10. c

11. buying on margin
12. John Steinbeck
13. Herbert Hoover
14. soil erosion
15. overproduction of
16. Mary McLeod Bethune
17. Congress of Industrial Organizations
18. Works Progress Administration

Progress Assessment

**19.** T   **23.** T
**20.** T   **24.** F
**21.** F   **25.** T
**22.** T

## CHAPTER TEST FORM B

1. Buying on margin meant borrowing money to buy stocks. It was popular in the 1920s because stock values in that decade were rising sharply. People who didn't have enough money to buy stocks borrowed money, certain they could later sell the stocks at a higher price, making more than enough money to pay back the loans.

2. Hoover did not want to provide direct federal relief to unemployed individuals, and he used force to remove the Bonus Army camp outside the White House.

3. Each Sunday President Roosevelt gave a radio address to the nation. These talks were known as the fireside chats. He talked directly to Americans about their problems, and, importantly, what he was doing to try to solve them.

4. The NIRA allowed collective bargaining. When it was struck down, the NLRA allowed workers to join unions and take part in collective bargaining. The National Labor Relations Board was established to oversee union activities. The CIO was founded in 1935 to include workers who were not welcome in the existing unions. Major strikes by workers tested the new laws, and the workers won. Organized labor unions grew and became a powerful political force.

5. She encouraged the president to include African Americans in his recovery programs. In 1939, when the DAR refused to rent its auditorium to Marian Anderson, Roosevelt resigned her membership in the DAR and helped arrange a concert at the foot of the Lincoln Memorial.

6. They listened to the radio and went to the movies.

7. It could be used to prove that Roosevelt's programs stopped the Depression because the unemployment rate dropped in 1933, when he took office, and kept falling overall until 1941, when the Depression was officially over. It could be used to prove the opposite because, while unemployment dropped when he took office in 1933, it rose in 1939 and only dropped again because World War II started and American businesses had to produce war materials.

# World War II

## SECTION QUIZ
### Section 1
1. e, Benito Mussolini
2. g, fascism
3. a, Adolf Hitler
4. h, Joseph Stalin
5. d, Axis Powers
6. c, appeasement
7. m, Winston Churchill
8. b, Allied Powers
9. i, Lend-Lease Act
10. l, Pearl Harbor

### Section 2
1. Factories
2. American
3. War Production Board
4. women
5. A. Philip Randolph
6. African American
7. zoot-suit riots
8. internment
9. draft
10. taxes

### Section 3
1. F; The Allies were in trouble
2. T
3. T
4. F; D-Day stood for designated day
5. T

### Section 4
1. f, Douglas MacArthur
2. a, Bataan Death March
3. e, Chester Nimitz
4. b, Battle of the Coral Sea
5. d, Battle of Midway
6. h, island-hopping
7. c, Battle of Leyte Gulf

**8.** i, Iwo Jima
**9.** l, Okinawa
**10.** j, kamikaze

## Section 5
**1.** b
**2.** d
**3.** a
**4.** a
**5.** c

## CHAPTER TEST FORM A
**1.** c
**2.** b
**3.** b
**4.** a
**5.** b
**6.** a
**7.** c
**8.** b
**9.** b
**10.** d

**11.** d

**12.** China
**13.** Leyte Gulf
**14.** Warsaw Ghetto
**15.** internment

**16.** g
**17.** e
**18.** h
**19.** a
**20.** c
**21.** k
**22.** d
**23.** j
**24.** i
**25.** b

## CHAPTER TEST FORM B
**1.** Hitler began to rebuild the German military, in violation of the Treaty of Versailles. In 1936, German troops invaded the Rhineland, a former German territory lost during World War I. That year, Hitler also signed an alliance with Mussolini, forming the Axis Powers. In 1938, Hitler forced Austria to unite with Germany and then demanded control of the Sudetenland, a region of Czechoslovakia where many Germans lived. When the Czechs refused, Hitler threatened war.

**2.** In 1940, after the fall of France, Great Britain was the only nation left to fight the Axis. To prepare for what seemed like an inevitable invasion of Britain, the Nazis began attacking British fighter planes and airfields, trying to knock out Britain's air defenses so German equipment and troops could land safely on the British coast. The British Royal Air Force fought air battles over England against the German Luftwaffe. The Luftwaffe began bombing British cities, including London, in the hope of crushing British morale. These attacks by the Luftwaffe became known as the Battle of Britain. But the British people remained undaunted, and by using radar, the RAF was able to detect and destroy more than 2,000 Luftwaffe planes. The British won the Battle of Britain, and the Axis invasion was called off.

**3.** War bonds were essentially loans that average Americans made to the U.S. government. People who bought war bonds gave the government money it needed to keep up production of war materials. People who bought war bonds could cash them in 10 years later and get their money back with interest.

**4.** Dorie Miller was on board the USS *West Virginia* at Pearl Harbor when the Japanese attacked. He left his post in the kitchen to man a machine gun on the deck of the ship. He stayed at the gun, shooting at Japanese planes, until he was ordered to abandon the ship because it was sinking. At the time, African Americans were not allowed to participate in combat.

**5.** The Allied nations knew they had to work together to beat the Axis. If even one nation dropped out of the alliance, the chances of winning the war diminished. The Allies also knew they had to be able to trust each other—if one nation was suspected of having second thoughts about fighting, the others would not be able to work with that nation. So, to strengthen their alliance, the Allies agreed that no country would accept a separate peace with the Axis.

**6.** While the U.S. recovered from Pearl Harbor, Japan conquered large areas of Asia and the Pacific, including Thailand, Burma, the British colonies of Hong Kong and Singapore, and the U.S. territories of Guam and Wake Island. Japan next attacked the American-controlled Philippines.

**7.** Causes: The Great Depression was a global economic problem, and the high cost of WWI reparations and rebuilding were local European economic problems; Japan, Germany, and Italy had totalitarian governments; Germany seized Austria, the Sudetenland, and the Rhineland; Japan attacked China, French Indochina, and the United States.

Effects: Six million Jewish people died in the Holocaust, and millions of Soviet soldiers and civilians died on the Eastern Front; German cities were firebombed, destroying them, and Axis industry was destroyed by bombing; six million Jewish people died, and hundreds of thousands of other people also died in camps; the U.S. was the only country that hadn't had its industries and cities bombed, so it was the only major provider of goods to the world after the war.

Answers will vary on which cause and effect students feel were most important.

# Boom Times and Challenges

## UNIT TEST FORM A

| | |
|---|---|
| 1. b | 10. c |
| 2. d | 11. b |
| 3. b | 12. a |
| 4. a | 13. a |
| 5. a | 14. a |
| 6. d | 15. c |
| 7. b | 16. b |
| 8. b | 17. d |
| 9. b | |

18. c

19. Warren G. Harding
20. immigrants
21. Georgia O'Keeffe
22. Midway
23. Installment plans
24. recession
25. Kellogg-Briand Pact
26. Emergency Banking Relief Act
27. female
28. ACLU
29. nonstop solo flight

| | |
|---|---|
| 30. T | 36. T |
| 31. F | 37. F |
| 32. T | 38. T |
| 33. F | 39. F |
| 34. F | 40. T |
| 35. T | 41. F |

| | |
|---|---|
| 42. e | 47. j |
| 43. k | 48. c |
| 44. h | 49. g |
| 45. i | 50. a |
| 46. d | |

## UNIT TEST FORM B

1. The rise of the automobile industry meant that millions of Americans found work making steel for car bodies, rubber for tires, and glass for windows. The government spent millions of dollars building new roads and paving old ones. Roadside businesses sprang up, like gas stations, restaurants, and motels. Car repair shops and car insurance businesses were also started. Other manufacturers began using assembly lines and allowing people to pay for their products on installment plans, like Ford did.

2. After a recession, the economy bounces back. Consumers purchase surplus goods, and companies increase production to meet the increased demand. Soon, more workers are hired, and unemployment drops. This up-and-down pattern is called the business cycle.

3. American farmers experienced hard times well before the start of the Depression because despite the widespread prosperity of the 1920s, prices for farm products remained low. The Depression worsened this already bad situation.

4. Radios were cheap, and they offered a range of programs, from upbeat music to westerns and dramas, to help people escape their troubles.

5. The policy of appeasement was an approach that the leaders of France and Britain hoped would avoid armed conflict with Germany. They thought that giving in to German demands for control of the Sudetenland would satisfy Hitler. This policy failed disastrously; Hitler

simply marched into Czechoslovakia and Poland and shortly afterward seized other European countries.

6. By the summer of 1940 German forces had conquered many European nations, including France, Britain's main ally. The U.S. had not yet entered the war, so only Great Britain was left to fight the might of the Axis powers in Europe. Meanwhile, the Japanese were conquering nation after nation in East Asia and the Pacific.

7. Answers may vary in level of detail. Women's roles changed during World War II because many men had gone off to fight in the war, so women were needed to fill their jobs. Many of these jobs were once considered "unladylike," such as working in factories and serving in the military.

# Early Years of the Cold War

## SECTION QUIZ
### Section 1
1. m, Yalta Conference
2. h, Nuremberg trials
3. k, United Nations
4. a, Cold War
5. b, containment
6. f, Marshall Plan
7. g, North Atlantic Treaty Organization
8. e, GI Bill of Rights
9. j, Truman Doctrine
10. c, Fair Deal

### Section 2
1. Mao Zedong
2. 38th Parallel
3. North Korea and China
4. Red Scare
5. Joseph McCarthy
6. hydrogen bomb
7. arms race
8. *Sputnik*
9. brinkmanship
10. communism

### Section 3
1. T
2. T

3. F; Not everyone was satisfied with society
4. F; There were not a lot of job options for women
5. T

## CHAPTER TEST FORM A
1. b
2. b
3. b
4. c
5. d
6. b
7. a
8. c
9. b
10. b

11. c

12. United Nations
13. Red Scare
14. Sun Belt
15. *Invisible Man*
16. Suez Canal
17. consumer culture
18. containment

19. F
20. F
21. F
22. F
23. T
24. T
25. T

## CHAPTER TEST FORM B
1. When France, Britain, and the United States decided to merge their occupation zones of Germany, it sparked a panic in the Soviet Union, which feared the creation of a strong West German state. On June 24, the Soviet Union suddenly blocked all rail, highway, and water traffic between western Germany and the city of Berlin. West Berlin's 2 million residents were trapped behind the Iron Curtain. To respond to this crisis without using military force, U.S. and British planes began airlifting supplies into West Berlin. In May 1949, the Soviet Union finally lifted the blockade.

2. The Dixiecrats were southern Democrats who didn't like Truman's support for civil rights laws. They joined the States' Rights Party, which favored racial segregation and ran South Carolina governor Strom Thurmond for president against Truman in 1948.

3. In 1956, Egypt's president Gamal Adbel Nasser decided to nationalize, or take control of, the Suez Canal, a vital waterway connecting the Mediterranean and Red Seas. Britain, France, and Israel, which

Progress Assessment

# Answer Key

relied on the canal for trade, invaded the area around the canal. The Soviet Union, an ally of Egypt, threatened to "crush" the invaders. This forced the U.S. to defend its allies. Finally, the Americans and the Soviet Union agreed to condemn the invasion, and the crisis was over.

4. Americans at first accepted Joseph McCarthy and his anti-Communist campaign because a new "Red Scare" was sweeping the nation after World War II. The Soviet Union controlled half of Europe. Atomic weapons made another war seem even more dangerous. Government officials fed these fears by making sweeping claims that "Communists are everywhere in America." When people called to testify at HUAC hearings refused to name names, it made Americans think they had something to hide—it made the claims of "Communists everywhere" seem real. The spy case of the Rosenbergs also seemed to confirm the fears. McCarthy claimed to have State Department documents verifying that Communists were active in the U.S. government. And finally, McCarthy bullied people who challenged him, claiming they were trying to help the Communists. All this created a climate of panic that allowed McCarthy to pursue his activities for years.

5. Suburban homes usually had driveways, large lawns, and labor-saving appliances. Suburban children could participate in a wide variety of sports and other activities. Suburban homes, mass-produced, were simple and affordable. And with new highways, it was easy to move to the suburbs and commute to jobs in cities.

6. They began shopping in malls that were basically the same no matter where in the country they were located. They ate at fast-food restaurants that were also always the same. They watched the same TV news, comedy, and sports programs.

7. Answers will vary. Sample response: More people had more disposable income, so this allowed them to buy homes for the first time. Since homes had two or three bedrooms, there was room to start a family. And since families had more money, they were able to have more children. More children meant having to move to a bigger home at some point, which meant more houses were built, driving up new home construction even further.

# The Civil Rights Movement

## SECTION QUIZ
## Section 1

1. segregation
2. Thurgood Marshall
3. *Brown* v. *Board of Education*
4. Little Rock Nine
5. Rosa Parks
6. Montgomery bus
7. Martin Luther King Jr.
8. sit-in
9. nonviolent
10. Student Nonviolent Coordinating Committee

## Section 2

1. h, John F. Kennedy
2. f, Freedom Rides
3. k, March on Washington
4. i, Lyndon B. Johnson
5. b, Civil Rights Act of 1964
6. m, Voting Rights Act of 1965
7. g, Great Society
8. a, Black Power
9. j, Malcolm X
10. d, Department of Housing and Urban Development

## Section 3

1. Hispanic
2. Cesar Chavez
3. United Farm Workers
4. Betty Friedan
5. National Organization for Women
6. Equal Rights Amendment
7. Phyllis Schlafly
8. American Indian Movement
9. Disabled in Action
10. Education of Handicapped Children

Progress Assessment

## CHAPTER TEST FORM A

| | |
|---|---|
| **1.** d | **6.** c |
| **2.** d | **7.** d |
| **3.** c | **8.** d |
| **4.** b | **9.** a |
| **5.** c | |

**10.** a

| | |
|---|---|
| **11.** T | **14.** T |
| **12.** F | **15.** F |
| **13.** T | |

| | |
|---|---|
| **16.** f | **21.** i |
| **17.** g | **22.** j |
| **18.** k | **23.** d |
| **19.** h | **24.** a |
| **20.** b | **25.** e |

## CHAPTER TEST FORM B

1. After Rosa Parks was arrested for refusing to give up her seat to a white rider, African American citizens of Montgomery organized a bus boycott. They formed the MIA, or Montgomery Improvement Association, led by Martin Luther King Jr. MIA leaders created a carpool system to get African Americans around without buses; MIA members paid for gas and other items to keep the carpool going for 381 days. White activists responded by threatening King, sending hate mail and harassing phone calls, and even bombing his home. White police offices harassed and arrested carpool drivers. In November 1956, the Supreme Court ruled that segregation on public transportation was illegal. The boycott ended, and African American riders were back on the buses.

2. The sit-ins were staged by students who wanted to challenge the segregation of private businesses. In February 1960 the student protesters sat down at the "whites only" lunch counter at a Woolworth in Greensboro, NC, and stayed there until the store closed. The next day they did the same, with dozens more students. The sit-in spread to other stores and cities. The students were non-violent. They formed the Student Nonviolent Coordinating Committee in the spring of 1960. Because of their actions, many businesses were integrated.

3. The New Frontier was a set of proposals that included a higher minimum wage and tax cuts to help stimulate economic growth. It also called for new spending on the military and the space program, and new programs to help poor and unemployed Americans. President Kennedy also proposed greater financial help for public schools.

4. The Civil Rights Act of 1964 banned segregation in public places and outlawed discrimination in the workplace on the basis of color, gender, religion, or national origin.

5. In 1962, Chavez formed a union that would later become the United Farm Workers. The union was committed to the goal of better pay and working conditions for migrant workers. Chavez led the UFW in a five-year strike and boycott against California grape growers. The workers finally won better wages and benefits in 1970. Chavez was dedicated to non-violent change, and helped inspire young leaders of the Chicano movement.

6. The ERA would have outlawed all discrimination based on sex. It was approved by Congress in 1972, but failed to be ratified by the necessary number of states. Conservative opponents, including Phyllis Schlafly, founded a group called STOP ERA to prevent its ratification. They argued that the ERA would hurt families by encouraging women to focus on careers rather than motherhood.

7. Answers will vary. Sample response: Civil rights activism changed over time. First, protests became larger—originally, protests were more individual. One person, like Rosa Parks, made a stand and paid the price. But as the civil rights movement gained momentum, more people got involved. The sit-ins started with just four African American students; quickly, they grew to dozens of African American—and white—students. Second, white citizens got involved. Third, it also got more dan-

gerous to be an activist—four little girls were killed when an African American church was bombed, and riots and other large-scale unrest took place.

# The Vietnam War Years

## SECTION QUIZ
### Section 1
1. h, John F. Kennedy
2. l, Peace Corps
3. e, Fidel Castro
4. a, Berlin Wall
5. c, Cuban Missile Crisis
6. i, Limited Nuclear Test Ban Treaty
7. j, Neil Armstrong
8. g, Ho Chi Minh
9. d, domino theory
10. m, Vietcong

### Section 2
1. F; President Johnson made the commitment to victory
2. T
3. T
4. T
5. F; They searched the jungles and small villages for hidden enemy camps

### Section 3
1. Americans
2. Students for a Democratic Society
3. Hippies
4. Richard M. Nixon
5. Henry Kissinger
6. Vietnamization
7. Twenty-sixth Amendment
8. cease-fire
9. War Powers Act
10. Vietnam Veterans

## CHAPTER TEST FORM A
1. c
2. b
3. b
4. d
5. c
6. d
7. b
8. a
9. b
10. b

11. c

12. Peace Corps
13. Tet Offensive

14. Pentagon Papers
15. Cuban missile crisis

16. f
17. j
18. d
19. i
20. k
21. a
22. l
23. b
24. c
25. h

## CHAPTER TEST FORM B
1. West Berlin was a model of prosperity and freedom in the heart of Soviet East Germany. About 2.5 million East Germans fled to West Berlin between 1949 and 1961. Calling this open border a "handy escape route," Soviet premier Khrushchev demanded the border be closed and threatened to take over West Berlin. Kennedy vowed to defend the city. In the middle of the night in August 1961, the East German government began building the Berlin Wall, a barrier of concrete and barbed wire between East and West Berlin.
2. The Cuban missile crisis began in October 1962, when American spy planes discovered that the Soviets were installing nuclear missiles in Cuba. If launched, these missiles could have reached American cities within minutes. Kennedy demanded that the Soviets remove the missiles, and a U.S. Navy blockade around Cuba was created to stop Soviet ships from bringing in more weapons. Approaching Soviet ships turned back, but the nation and the world were terrified that nuclear war would break out. After tense weeks, Khrushchev agreed to remove the missiles from Cuba, and in return Kennedy promised not to invade Cuba and to remove some missiles in Italy and Turkey.
3. The Vietcong and NVA used guerrilla warfare tactics. Moving secretly, they set deadly traps and landmines. They also had the advantage of knowing the local geography, which allowed them to make quick surprise assaults on small groups of U.S. soldiers. They were able to keep sending new troops into combat, and they also received supplies and weapons from Communist China and the Soviet Union.

**4.** In March 1968 a company of U.S. soldiers entered the South Vietnamese village of My Lai, expecting to find Vietcong forces there. This search-and-destroy mission turned into a massacre when American soldiers opened fire, killing hundreds of unarmed villagers, including women and children. At first news of this attack was covered up. But when the public found out, many Americans questioned U.S. involvement in Vietnam.

**5.** Humphrey, the Democratic candidate, was damaged by the riots that broke out at the Democratic National Convention, which were broadcast live to the nation. Second, Nixon identified Democrats with the riots, promising to restore order to American society and to bring "peace with honor" to Vietnam.

**6.** When fighting broke out between North and South Vietnam in 1974, the U.S. refused to send troops back to South Vietnam. In 1975 North Vietnam invaded the South. Thousands of American embassy workers and South Vietnamese scrambled to evacuate Saigon. The city was captured by the North Vietnamese, who then created the Socialist Republic of Vietnam, with Hanoi as capital. Life remained difficult for the people, whose land and cities had been destroyed. Millions of people had been killed, and 1.5 million fled the country.

**7.** Answers will vary. Sample response: The passage reveals that neither side was ready for nuclear war, but, alarmingly, neither knew exactly how to avoid such a war.

# Postwar America

## UNIT TEST FORM A

**1.** c
**2.** b
**3.** a
**4.** a
**5.** c
**6.** d
**7.** a
**8.** d
**9.** b
**10.** c
**11.** a
**12.** d
**13.** b
**14.** b
**15.** a
**16.** b
**17.** c

**18.** Cesar Chavez
**19.** Montgomery
**20.** Phyllis Schlafly
**21.** sit-in
**22.** interstate bus stations
**23.** Hubert Humphrey
**24.** Twenty-sixth
**25.** *Brown* v. *Board of Education*
**26.** Civil Rights Act
**27.** Black Power
**28.** Vietnamization
**29.** Martin Luther King Jr.

**30.** T
**31.** T
**32.** F
**33.** F
**34.** T
**35.** F
**36.** F
**37.** F
**38.** T
**39.** F
**40.** b
**41.** b
**42.** i
**43.** g
**44.** h
**45.** a
**46.** c
**47.** j
**48.** e
**49.** f
**50.** d

## UNIT TEST FORM B

**1.** New highways made it easier for people to move to suburbs and commute to jobs in cities. The rising demand for homes in the suburbs encouraged builders to build preplanned neighborhoods of low-priced, mass-produced homes that were simple and affordable. Suburbs were comfortable and convenient; homes had large lawns and labor-saving appliances.

**2.** Japan had controlled Korea from 1910 to the end of WWII. After the war, the Allies divided Korea at the 38th parallel. The Soviet Union controlled the northern part of Korea, and the United States occupied the South. In 1950, North Korea invaded the South, and the U.S. and UN both sent troops to South Korea. Just as the U.S. was headed for a quick victory, Communist China sent its forces to join the North Koreans.

Progress Assessment

3. The 1896 Supreme Court case *Plessy* v. *Ferguson* established the "separate-but-equal" doctrine. This stated that federal, state, and local governments could allow segregation as long as separate facilities were equally good. But in fact, schools for African American children typically received far less funding.

4. In the summer of 1964 civil rights activists began to push for equal voting rights for African Americans in the south. Threats and unfair election rules often kept them from going to the polls to vote. Hundreds of volunteers came to Mississippi to help African Americans register to vote. These volunteers were threatened and attacked. Two white students from the North and an African American man from Mississippi were killed. Martin Luther King Jr., organized a voting rights march from Selma, Alabama, to Montgomery. Many marchers were beaten and jailed.

5. Both the United States and the Soviet Union believed that whichever country won the space race and put a man on the moon first would be perceived as the more powerful nation. If the Soviets won, it would seem like Communism was better than democracy, and vice-versa. Each side also worried that if the other got to the moon first it meant that side had better missiles—missiles that could be used to launch nuclear weapons.

6. A U.S. ship had exchanged gunfire with North Vietnamese torpedo boats in the Gulf. Two days later, during a night of thunderstorms, U.S. ships reported a second attack, but the captain of the ship whose men reported being hit was not sure an attack actually took place. He thought it might just have been turbulence from the storms. Another ship insisted it had picked up high-speed attack vessels on its radar, and this convinced President Johnson an attack had actually taken place.

7. The photo shows that one side felt it was a patriotic duty to support American soldiers who were fighting for freedom and democracy. The other side felt American forces were not actually promoting or representing democracy, but were using extreme force that harmed both soldiers and civilians.

# Searching for Order

## SECTION QUIZ
### Section 1
1. i, Silent Majority
2. e, New Federalism
3. j, stagflation
4. f, Organization of Petroleum Exporting Countries
5. h, realpolitik
6. k, Strategic Arms Limitations Talks
7. a, détente
8. l, Watergate
9. d, Gerald Ford
10. g, pardon

### Section 2
1. Title IX
2. Affirmative action
3. Jimmy Carter
4. human rights
5. Apartheid
6. sanctions
7. Soviet Union
8. Summer Olympics
9. Camp David Accords
10. Iran hostage

### Section 3
1. F; He was very conservative
2. T
3. T
4. F; There was no evidence of illegal activity by President Reagan
5. F; It was Mikhail Gorbachev

## CHAPTER TEST FORM A
| | |
|---|---|
| 1. a | 7. b |
| 2. a | 8. b |
| 3. c | 9. c |
| 4. d | 10. d |
| 5. c | 11. b |
| 6. b | |
| 12. b | |

13. Silent Majority 17. Contras
14. nuclear 18. China
15. sanctions 19. Sandra Day O'Connor
16. Supply-side

20. F 23. F
21. F 24. T
22. F 25. T

## CHAPTER TEST FORM B

1. By the early 1970s, the U.S. was importing almost one-third of its oil. Much of this oil was purchased from Middle Eastern nations that were members of the Organization of Petroleum Exporting Countries, or OPEC. OPEC worked to control the production and sale of oil to keep prices high. Most OPEC countries were Arab states opposed to the creation of the state of Israel. In October 1973 Egypt and Syria attacked Israel, and the U.S. sent military supplies to help Israel. OPEC members responded angrily to this by declaring an embargo, or ban, on oil sales to the U.S.

2. The Committee to Re-elect the President tried to sabotage the Democratic presidential campaign. They spread false rumors about Democratic candidates, and they broke into Democratic party campaign headquarters in June 1972 to plant secret recording devices and cameras to learn about Democratic strategy and other information. They could use the information to stay one step ahead of the Democrats and foil any Democratic plans to win the election.

3. Affirmative action gives special consideration to minorities and women to make up for past discrimination. Supporters of affirmative action argued that it was needed to improve educational and job opportunities for minorities and women. Opponents insisted that any race- or gender-based preferences were unfair.

4. the Camp David Accords

5. "Reaganomics" was based on "supply-side economics," a theory calling for large tax cuts to leave people and businesses with more money to invest. This investment would lead to economic growth and the creation of new jobs. Over time, the expanding economic activity would produce more tax money for the government. To balance the budget after cutting tax revenue, "Reaganomics" called for government spending cuts.

6. When rebels called Contras began fighting the Sandinista government in Nicaragua, the U.S. supported the Contras with arms and aid. This led to fears in Congress that the U.S. would be drawn into a civil war in Nicaragua. In 1984 Congress passed a ban on further U.S. military aid to the Contras. But a group of U.S. government officials continued to fund the Contras. Oliver North helped arrange the sale of U.S. missiles to Iran; in exchange, Iran released the U.S. hostages in Teheran, and profits from the sale of weapons to Iran were sent to the Contras. This Iran-Contra affair was exposed in 1986, but Congressional hearings found no evidence that President Reagan was involved in it. Several White House officials, however, were convicted of crimes.

7. Answers will vary. Sample response: The ruling in *United States* v. *Nixon* was so important because it established that the president is not above the law. A president can't use executive privilege to avoid answering to the law. Executive privilege is the principle that presidents can't be forced to make their private communications public if doing so would endanger national security. The Supreme Court ruling in 1974 basically said the president has to *prove* that making private communications public would endanger national security—he can't just *say* that it will. Like any other citizen, the president has to obey requests made by a court of law. This was important in 1974 because it helped the truth come out about Watergate. It has been important since then because it keeps any president from trying to function above the law. For example, Reagan had to testify before Congress at the Iran-Contra hearings.

Progress Assessment

# America Looks to the Future

## SECTION QUIZ
### Section 1
1. George H.W. Bush
2. Berlin Wall
3. Saddam Hussein
4. Operation Desert Storm
5. Colin Powell
6. Bill Clinton
7. North American Free Trade
8. impeached
9. Madeleine Albright
10. terrorism

### Section 2
1. b
2. d
3. a
4. b
5. c

### Section 3
1. j, service economy
2. c, globalization
3. l, World Trade Organization
4. h, Internet
5. m, World Wide Web
6. g, Information Revolution
7. e, Human Genome Project
8. a, AIDS
9. i, ozone layer
10. d, global warming

## CHAPTER TEST FORM A
1. b
2. c
3. a
4. b
5. b
6. a
7. b
8. a
9. b
10. c

11. d

12. T
13. T
14. F
15. T

16. h
17. l
18. e
19. a
20. d
21. b
22. g
23. j
24. f
25. k

## CHAPTER TEST FORM B
1. Pro-democracy movements arose in Eastern European nations under Soviet control after Soviet premier Gorbachev began his program of reform. In October 1989, massive protests in East Germany led to the resignation of Communist leader Erich Honecker. The new government agreed to open the East German borders, including the border in Berlin—the Berlin Wall. After the wall was torn down, other Soviet republics declared independence. When hard-line Communists took Gorbachev hostage and tried to seize control of the Soviet government, thousands of Soviet citizens took to the streets to protest. Many soldiers sent to stop them joined them. The Soviet Union soon broke apart.

2. In April 1995, American terrorists bombed the Murrah Federal Building in Oklahoma City, killing 168 people. The U.S. also faced increasingly deadly attacks by extremist Islamic groups. Hundreds were killed in bomb attacks on U.S. embassies in Africa in 1998. On September 11, 2001 fundamentalist Islamic terrorists took control of four commercial airliners. Using them as weapons, they destroyed the two towers of the World Trade Center and heavily damaged the Pentagon. The fourth plane was crashed into a field in Pennsylvania.

3. On election night, the voting in some states was so close that no winner was declared. It became clear that Florida's 25 electoral votes would determine the outcome of the election. A machine recount gave Florida to Bush, but Gore supporters wanted the votes in four counties recounted by hand to make sure all votes were counted. The Bush campaign challenged this manual recount, and eventually the Supreme Court ruled that manual recounts could not ensure all votes would be counted the same way. The court stopped the recount, and Florida's electoral votes went to Bush. Bush became president although Gore actually won the popular vote—the first time this had happened in over 100 years.

Progress Assessment

# Answer Key

4. In the 1990s, Iraqi president Saddam Hussein refused to allow UN weapons inspectors to come into the country to make sure Iraq was not producing weapons of mass destruction. Although Hussein allowed inspectors back in 2002, his interference made the U.S. suspect he did have these weapons. At the UN, many countries said inspectors should be given more time to find out for sure. But the U.S. and other nations felt inspections would not work. The U.S. and its allies decided to attack Iraq.

5. As high-tech industries grew, textile and other traditional manufacturing industries declined, moving their factories to countries where labor is less expensive. As fewer manufacturing jobs became available, workers moved into service economy jobs—providing services rather than producing goods. Top service economy industries are health care, computer engineering, and education.

6. Globalization is the growing connections between economies and cultures all over the world. Multinational corporations—companies doing business in more than one country—play a large part in globalization. American fast food restaurants are in Russia, and Japanese car factories are in the U.S.

7. Answers will vary. Sample response: People want to build a very tall skyscraper to serve as a memorial of the WTC buildings that were destroyed, and to show that America is not afraid of another terrorist attack. The pro is the building will memorialize the WTC, but the con is that the building may be targeted by terrorists.

## Modern America

### UNIT TEST FORM A

| | |
|---|---|
| 1. b | 9. a |
| 2. b | 10. c |
| 3. a | 11. c |
| 4. c | 12. a |
| 5. c | 13. a |
| 6. d | 14. b |
| 7. a | 15. c |
| 8. c | 16. d |

17. a
18. the economy
19. the Pentagon
20. service economy
21. global warming
22. the Panama Canal
23. globalization
24. Michael Dukakis
25. Department of Defense
26. Boris Yeltsin
27. NAFTA

| | |
|---|---|
| 28. T | 32. F |
| 29. F | 33. T |
| 30. T | 34. T |
| 31. T | 35. T |
| 36. d | 41. b |
| 37. e | 42. a |
| 38. f | 43. c |
| 39. g | 44. j |
| 40. h | 45. l |

### UNIT TEST FORM B

1. SALT refers to the Strategic Arms Limitation Talks held in Moscow in 1972 between Soviet premier Leonid Brezhnev and President Richard Nixon. These talks led to a treaty limiting each country's nuclear weapons. The SALT agreement opened a period of détente, or less hostile relations, between the U.S. and Soviet Union.

2. It bans discrimination on the basis of sex in educational programs that receive federal funds. The number of women admitted to medical and law schools climbed quickly. Title IX also opened the door for many more women to participate in college sports and earn athletic scholarships.

3. In 1979 rebels overthrew the pro-American shah of Iran. On November 4, 1979 a group of Iranian students attacked the U.S. embassy in Teheran, the capital of Iran, seizing about 90 American hostages. The Iran hostage crisis lasted for over a year.

Progress Assessment

**4.** In the 1990s in the Balkan region of Europe, the former nation of Yugoslavia broke apart. Different ethnic and religious groups fought for control of territory. U.S. diplomats helped negotiate an end to this war, and President Clinton sent 20,000 U.S. soldiers to the region to help keep the peace.

**5.** Many scientists believe that global warming happens when fossil fuels such as gasoline and coal release carbon dioxide into Earth's atmosphere, causing a greenhouse effect—heat is trapped in Earth's atmosphere. This causes temperatures to rise, which has dangerous effects, including rising sea levels and more severe weather patterns.

**6.** The passengers on board the plane learned about the other attacks after making cell phone calls for help. They fought back against the terrorists, causing the crash and preventing the hijackers from crashing the plane into another large target.

**7.** Answers will vary. Sample response: Most scud and UN air attacks took place in Iraq and Israel. The Iraqis fired scud missiles into Israel because it was the one nation in the region that was not Muslim and was an ally of the United States. The UN fired missiles into Iraq because that's where the Iraqi army and government were located. Kuwait City was not hit, although it was occupied by the Iraqi army and had to be freed. This was because the UN did not want to harm any of the Kuwaitis it was trying to liberate.

| | | |
|---|---|---|
| 23. b | 37. b | |
| 24. b | 38. b | |
| 25. a | 39. c | |
| 26. a | 40. c | |
| 27. c | 41. a | |
| 28. d | 42. d | |
| 29. b | 43. a | |
| 30. b | 44. a | |
| 31. c | 45. b | |
| 32. c | 46. c | |
| 33. b | 47. a | |
| 34. a | 48. d | |
| 35. a | 49. c | |
| 36. c | 50. c | |

# End-of-Year Test

| | |
|---|---|
| 1. d | 12. b |
| 2. d | 13. b |
| 3. b | 14. c |
| 4. b | 15. d |
| 5. d | 16. d |
| 6. a | 17. d |
| 7. a | 18. b |
| 8. b | 19. b |
| 9. b | 20. a |
| 10. a | 21. a |
| 11. d | 22. a |